A Physical Education

Part of the Goldsmiths Press Unidentified Fictional Objects series

A Physical Education

On Bullying, Discipline & Other Lessons

Jonathan Taylor

Goldsmiths
Press

Copyright © 2024 Goldsmiths Press
First published in 2024 by Goldsmiths Press
Goldsmiths, University of London, New Cross
London SE14 6NW

Printed and bound by Short Run Press Limited, UK
Distribution by the MIT Press
Cambridge, Massachusetts, USA and London, England

Text copyright © 2024 Jonathan Taylor

The right of Jonathan Taylor to be identified as the author of this work has
been asserted by him in accordance with sections 77 and 78 in the Copyright,
Designs and Patents Act 1988.

Every effort has been made to trace copyright holders and to obtain their
permission for the use of copyright material. The publisher apologises for any
errors or omissions and would be grateful if notified of any corrections that
should be incorporated in future reprints or editions of this book.

All Rights Reserved. No part of this publication may be reproduced,
distributed or transmitted in any form or by any means whatsoever without
prior written permission of the publisher, except in the case of brief
quotations in critical articles and review and certain non-commercial uses
permitted by copyright law.

A CIP record for this book is available from the British Library

ISBN 978-1-915983-14-5 (pbk)
ISBN 978-1-915983-13-8 (ebk)

www.gold.ac.uk/goldsmiths-press

For Mrs De Wet

[T]he abuse of irresponsible power [is] ... of all earthly temptations
the most difficult to be resisted.

Charles Dickens, *American Notes for General Circulation*

Timetable

1

P.E.

It ought to be such an unselfish game. It merges the individual in the eleven.

Thomas Hughes, *Tom Brown's School Days*[1]

It's January 1985. I'm eleven. We're lined up on the school football pitch, ankle-deep in slushy brown snow. It's -2 degrees and raining ice, blowing across our faces in gusts like acid – which may be *literally* true, given the air pollution in 1980s Stoke. We're shivering in shorts, white t-shirts, itchy ribbed socks, and football boots with studs on. I've got plastic studs on my boots, but others like Danny Beaker – who, already at 5'11, is a good foot taller than me – have got metal spikes. There are a couple of punctures in the tops of my boots from previous games, when Danny stamped on them.

The wet is seeping into my socks through the holes, while the sleet slanting from the sky is somehow creeping *up* my shorts, in a cruel contradiction of Newtonian physics. Every other part of my body is already soaking, and gradually freezing over. I glance around. The other boys are the same, wet through, hands in armpits, stamping up and down in a vain effort to keep warm, their smoky breath mingling above their heads like a big speech bubble: *Get on with it, Sir*.

---

[1] Full references and acknowledgements for all texts cited are given in Chapter 9, 'Extra-Curricular: Thanks, Notes, Contexts'.

Sir gets on with it, inevitably choosing the giant Danny Beaker as captain of one team, a second Godzilla-like boy as captain of the other. They take turns to nominate who they want on their teams. I'm usually last, after 'Pi' the school Tory (one and only), who looks like his parents mistook a Stoke comprehensive school for Marlborough, and my friend Steed, who's overweight, and pretends to have asthma to get out of running – and who looks nothing like his namesake in *The Avengers* or, for that matter, a knight's thoroughbred. In team sports, the three of us are the crumbs at the bottom of a crisp packet, the broken bits of Rich Tea in a biscuit barrel. Broken bits that no doubt Steed would gobble.

Steed's on Danny Beaker's team, so Godzilla II gets the final crumb that is myself. He doesn't even bother to call my name, merely rolls his eyes, and turns away. He slouches over to the centre spot – or, rather, the hole in the slushy snow Sir has dug with his heels, to mark the centre spot – and waits for Sir to blow the whistle. Godzilla II's holding his balls, jiggling on the spot, his vaporous speech bubble presumably saying: *Get on with it, Sir, before these freeze off.*

Sir's rather allegorical name is Mr Yorwin. He's dressed in a brown sheepskin knee-length coat, woolly tracksuit bottoms, and is smoking a cigarette. The smouldering cigarette end is the one bit of colour in the whole landscape. 'Taylor', he grunts out of the side of his mouth, 'get your arse in gear.' The other boys snigger.

I jog over to him: 'Sir, please, can't we wear...?' But he cuts me off.

'Don't be a poof, Taylor. You don't need yer tracksuits. You'll warm up on the pitch if you play proper.'

'But, Sir...'

'Shurrup. Get over there. You're defence.'

'Some defence,' mutters Godzilla II from a distance.

Mr Yorwin blows his whistle. Danny Beaker is immediately thundering down the pitch towards me like a bull. I *umm* and *ahh*, shifting my weight from side to side. I don't have a matador's cape, and I know I won't tackle him – that would be suicide – but can't decide which way to jump, to get out of his way. In the end, indecision wins the day, and I stay put. He dribbles the ball round me, round half a dozen other half-hearted defenders, and scores the first of the afternoon's seventeen goals. Which is a pretty low tally for him, to be honest, but even he's pissed off with the Siberian conditions.

It doesn't stop him scoring the second from a centre kick. Godzilla II, our team captain, is now swearing at us – and his swearing intensifies as, a couple of minutes later, Danny B. dribbles past Steed and me, both of us using the same well-choreographed technique of falling over whenever he and his metal spikes come close. The churned-up mud of the football pitch is hardening, yet a painful bump on the bum and imprecations from the captain are infinitely preferable to being run over, flattened like cartoon characters – Wile E. Coyote, or Daffy Duck – under the oncoming juggernaut that is Danny Beaker.

Meanwhile, Mr Yorwin has turned his back on us, as if in disgust, and is vacating the field. He's striding towards his shed, where he'll sit smoking for the next half hour or so, wrapped up in his sheepskin coat, with the electric fire on. We watch his retreating back enviously, smoky speech bubbles mingling again: *Why the hell are we out here freezing our arses off? Sir's heading inside. The girls are all inside. The school hall's free. We could do football in the warm.*

But instead we're doing it out here, in football Siberia. The sleet is coming down (and up) faster now, turning to snow, and the game is drowning in mud and hardening sludge. Steed is face down in ice, where he's been tripped over by another player (nothing to do with tackling – the other boy just felt like it). The latter, who will become head boy in a few years, pins Steed down, and force-feeds him ice: 'You like that, don't you, little Steedykins? Come on, eat your din-dins. Mmm, yes – yum yum. Acid snow.'

There's no referee on the pitch, but, following a three-way scuffle between Danny Beaker, future head boy, and Godzilla II,

Steed's awarded a free kick. Despite a big run up, lots of huffing and puffing, the ball only travels a few inches, sucked down into snowy mud.

Danny Beaker intercepts it, kicks it in the opposite direction. But he's struggling to see through the diagonal sleet, and for once, misses the goal-mouth. No one except Danny has any idea what the score is, and everyone's half-heartedly pretending to play, half-heartedly freezing to death. The ball feels like lead, and when Pi tries to take a kick at it, he falls over. The ball doesn't budge.

Danny gets it again. He kicks it straight at me. I move too slowly, and it hits me between the legs. I fall over, clutching myself in pain. Ten yards away, Steed skids, and lands on his back, as though in sympathy. Everyone's falling over; there are no vertical shapes in sight. Cold like gravity is pulling us all downwards into frozen slime. Evolution in reverse.

After a couple of abortive attempts, I pull myself to my feet, and wipe the sleet from my eyes. Twenty yards away, a shape like Danny Beaker is charging at the white silhouette of a terrified goalie. All I can see are vague shapes of boys, outlines under erasure, fading into the whites and browns surrounding us. We're becoming mud, snow, falling ice.

Danny carries the ball back to the hole he thinks is the centre spot, although it's now disappearing under new-fallen snow. Someone kicks the ball to someone else who kicks it back to the first person, who stands there, frowning down at it – as if he doesn't quite know what it is, or why he's here. Godzilla II yells: 'Pass the bloody ball, y'wuss!' But the game's grinding to a halt, in a sludge of grumbling. Most of the boys are gathering round the centre spot, scattered players gradually coalescing into a group for warmth, like penguins. I move closer too, though I don't stand too close, in case someone decides to lash out at a softer target than the ball.

Steed is crying. Pi screws up his face and declares he'd very much like to stuff the snow down Mr Yorwin's woolly trousers – which is quite a thing for a Pi to say. The harder boys are swearing: 'Bastard, sending us out here while he's sunning himself in that shed of his.' 'Twat.' 'Wanker.' 'Probably wanking in there, while we're freezing out here.'

I've had enough. The cold has become pain, and I can't imagine being warm ever again. I want to be inside, in a book, anywhere that cold and football don't happen. 'Look,' I say. The harder boys turn round, surprised Taylor has made a noise – surprised Taylor *can* make a noise. 'I think we should say something when Yorwin comes out. Tell him what we think. Tell him we shouldn't be out in this weather. It's, like, erm, *bad* for us. Child cruelty. Human rights.'

All round me, boys nod in agreement, shocked by cold into an unusual alliance between hard boys and geeks, Godzillas and Godzukis: 'Yeah, if we tell him together, he'll have to listen.' 'We'll go on strike like the miners.' 'We'll stick that ball up his arse.' 'Let's mug the bastard when he gets out,' suggests one boy. 'Well,' I suggest tentatively, 'that's not quite what I meant...'

By the time Mr Yorwin finally emerges from his shed, and strides back to the pitch, his indistinct shape growing, darkening, until he's right in front of us, we're not even pretending to play – just hugging ourselves, hovering, waiting for him. Only Danny Beaker is away, down one end of the pitch, scoring goals by himself, on auto-pilot. He tackles himself, and then scores a goal for the opposite team, celebrating for them by waving his arms, doing a somersault. He's two teams, spectators and commentator all in one.

Meanwhile, near the centre spot, Mr Yorwin is standing, legs apart, scowling at us, puffing on his cigarette. He takes it out of his mouth for a moment. 'What?' he asks. 'Why aren't ye lazy gits playing? Gerron with it.'

Now he's here, in front of us, all too real, no one is saying anything, let alone mugging him or inserting a football into his rectum. Someone clears their throat, preparing to speak, but nothing comes out. The wind whistles round us.

'What?' Mr Yorwin asks, as if of the wind.

Neither wind nor anyone else answers.

So I step forward, shaking, stammering: 'Sir ... it's too c ... c ... cold, *Sir*. Honestly, Sir. We're ... we're *bloody* freezing here. Gonna get ill. I think ... we *all* think we should go in.'

He glowers at me over his cigarette: 'Taylor, did you just swear at me?'

I'm suddenly angry: 'Yes, Sir. But it is *bloody* freezing and we've had enough. You're wearing a coat. It's not fair. You're a bloody ... t ... *tyrant*, Sir.'

He takes a puff of his cigarette, and I think he's going to hit me. I flinch in anticipation. Instead, he glares over my head at the others: 'Is this just Taylor's opinion, or do you *all* wanna go inside?'

No one speaks. Without turning around, I can feel the opposition behind me melting away to slush. There are a few non-committal mumbles ('Shurrup, Taylor, you'll get us all done in'), shufflings of feet. One of the boys kicks my shins from behind. Others are backing away.

'*Well*?' booms Mr Yorwin.

There's a silence again, which is broken by Pi: 'No, Sir,' he chirps brightly between chattering teeth, 'we're all *terribly* enjoying ourselves here.' A few others, including Godzilla II, break off and chase up the field towards Danny Beaker.

Mr Yorwin turns back to me. 'So it's just you, Taylor?'

'No it isn't ... wasn't,' I say, exasperated. I glance around at my classmates: 'Tell him.' Some shake their heads, some turn their noses up at me. The smoke bubble above their heads would probably read. *How come the school wimp's trying to boss us around – who the hell does he think he is?*

Mr Yorwin flicks away the stub of his cigarette. 'Too cold, my arse. You've got no backbone, Taylor. Spineless, that's your problem.' He takes a step towards me. I step back and trip, falling on my bottom. 'There's cold for you,' he says. He blows on his whistle, waves Danny Beaker over: 'Gimme the ball.' Danny reluctantly picks it up, jogs over, and passes it to Mr Yorwin. Mr Yorwin throws it down at me. It hits me in the stomach. 'Your centre kick,' he says, and turns towards his shed. The boys take his place, close in on me: 'Haha,' they snigger, 'no backbone. Spineless. Taylor the Invertebrate.'

The names echo through the remainder of the game and into the changing rooms afterwards. In the communal showers, which never achieve anything but to make us more dirty, the other boys shove me around, calling me a beached jellyfish, a tape-worm, an amoeba, a pathetic eel – any species they can think of that seems contemptible, and doesn't have a backbone. I slip over, land flat on my back (which strangely hurts, despite my apparent spineless-ness), and Danny Beaker wees on me. He often wees on some-one in the showers, and today it's the turn of Jellyfish Taylor. 'Feel yourself honoured,' he declares. 'Loads of girls'd beg me to do that for them.'

'And piss, y'know, kills jellyfish, or cures stings, or summit,' says a Beaker sidekick, 'I saw it on the telly.'

'Yeah.'

When I stagger out of the shower, Mr Yorwin is there, star-ing at me as one might at a piss-covered jellyfish. 'Get yer clothes on, Taylor,' he snarls. 'You're too slow.' He pats Danny Beaker and some of the other lads on the back as they leave. Even Pi gets a 'Good effort today, lad.' I don't know how Mr Yorwin can judge what kind of effort Pi put into the game, given that he didn't actu-ally watch any of it. But I'm not about to point this out, and I scurry away, trying to merge with the walls. Jellyfish can be see-through, I think, and that's what I want for myself.

My attempt at invisibility is futile, though, and the inverte-brate names follow me around for the rest of the day, and – off and on – for the next few years.

Sticks and stones may break my bones, but names will never hurt me: everyone knows that old rhyme's a lie. Names echo, linger, persist. They attach themselves like limpets to your identity, your sense of self.

In my case, though, the names didn't hurt the high-school me so much as the very idea that *I* was the spineless one. In my confused, teenage way, I kept thinking, kept trying to explain to others: 'But look, *I'm* the one who stood up to Yorwin, who called him a bloody tyrant, while you Judases shrank away, went back on what you'd said. And yet, somehow, *I'm* the invertebrate.' It seemed so unfair.

I even tried pointing this out, in a far-future lesson near the end of high school, to Mr Yorwin himself: 'I'm *not* spineless, Sir. I stood up to you when everyone else backed off.' But he couldn't understand me any more than I could understand him. Our very notions of invertebracy were incommensurate, maybe diametrically opposed. For me, spinelessness was *not* standing up to 'bloody tyranny'; to him, spinelessness was whingeing about a little icy rain. And more: to me, spinelessness was submitting to collective cowardice; to him, spinelessness was not joining in, not playing as part of a team – and, above all, being crap at sport.

For all her faults, I've always been more drawn to Miss Jean Brodie's (admittedly suspect) philosophy than Mr Yorwin's. In Muriel Spark's 1961 novel, *The Prime of Miss Jean Brodie*, her teacher-heroine sees the 'team spirit' as the enemy and wages a war against it. 'Phrases like "the team spirit",' she remarks, 'are always employed to cut across individualism.' Ultimately, she manages to win 'the battle over the team spirit' for her favourites, the so-called 'Brodie set'. By the last year of school, their 'disregard' of the team spirit has 'become an institution, to be respected, ... their position enviable.' My disregard of it, by contrast, never achieved such an elevated status, and my position remained, in the eyes of Mr Yorwin and others, that of unenviable invertebrate.

I suppose, in the end, the question of whether or not Mr Yorwin was right boils down to a simple one: namely, do jellyfish enjoy competitive team sports, or do individual jellyfish sometimes rebel, and complain how cold the water is?

*

Thirteen or so years later, I'm half-drunk at a dinner party being held by my PhD supervisor. Everyone's rabbiting on about football. Away from his day job as poststructuralist critic and continental philosopher, my supervisor's also a Watford FC fan, and manager of a church football team (complete with sheepskin coat and shed). Somehow, these things go together – or at least they do for my supervisor; I find it hard to imagine my old P.E. teacher voluntarily reading Derrida or Wittgenstein. But maybe I'm being unfair to Mr Yorwin. Who knows how he whiled away the time in his shed, as boys turned to snowmen on the football pitch?

Anyway, the point is that, thirteen years later, my PhD supervisor lives in a state of constant disappointment that literary criticism, philosophy, church, sheds, and especially football don't go together for me. I'd thought that reading, writing, and a PhD in English Lit were the opposite of sport, the antidote to it. 'Of course,' he says, 'Jonathan'll be really bored now, with all this football talk.'

'Yesh,' I slur, 'talking about the weather's one up from it. I thought doing English'd get me away from kicking round pigs' bladders.'

'So, go on then, tell us,' he says, 'why you hate it so much.'

'I don't *hate* it,' I say. 'Sometimes, if it's on a screen, I can tolerate it.' I don't add: if balls are on a screen, on TV, or a computer game, they're safe, they can't come out of nowhere and hit me in the stomach. In real life, I still flinch whenever a ball sails through the air in my vicinity – still duck, involuntarily, if a ball passes within fifty yards of me. Which is unfortunate when you're doing your PhD at a university renowned for sporting prowess, and balls of various shapes and sizes are ubiquitous.

'Okay, so why do you dislike it then?'

'Balls to it,' I say, 'I'll tell you.' And I drunkenly recount the whole story of the ill-fated P.E. lesson, Mr Yorwin, and my invertebracy, beginning to end. I've not told the story to anyone before, and my supervisor's response is unexpected. Not only does he laugh, he also says to me: 'You know what that is? That's your PhD in a nutshell.'

'What do you mean?'

'I mean: that's what your PhD's about. You've just encapsulated your thesis, y'know, in one story. A kind of allegory.'

Even his wife, who doesn't work at a university, and who has the merit of being profoundly uninterested in most literary criticism, is intrigued, and asks him what he's talking about.

'Look,' he says, 'Jonathan's writing a PhD about the portrayal of slavery, servants, workers in Victorian literature. He's using the "Master-Slave Dialectic" by Hegel as a kind of philosophical frame to understand these things.'

'So?' his wife asks, already – and understandably – starting to lose interest.

'Well, one of the things he reckons is that Hegel's model only applies when master and slave work as individuals, isolated from everyone else. In reality, or in history or literature, the masters aren't usually separate. They band together as a class, while trying to keep the slaves, or whoever, atomised. You disempower your underlings by separating them – divide and conquer and all that.'[2]

His wife frowns, stifles a yawn. He continues regardless. 'It's obvious. Think about trades unions: that's why Victorian factory bosses hated them, because it meant the workers were uniting. Separate, they were powerless; united, they could stand up to the bosses, organise strikes, march on London. Think about a P.E. lesson where a teacher is faced by a rebellion. If it's all the boys together, he might be in trouble. They could mob him. It happens. But a rebellion of one vertically-challenged boy on his own isn't going to achieve much.' My supervisor turns to me: 'And when Mr Your-Winner, or whatever he was called, said you were spineless, and made the other boys laugh at you, well, that was his

---

[2]On Hegel's 'Master-Slave Dialectic', see 'Philosophy: An Interlude' in Chapter 4, 'Practical: The Cane and the Fist'.

masterstroke. He made *you* seem like the odd one out, the weak one, and got them on *his* side. Brilliant.'

'I'm not sure it's brilliant,' says my supervisor's wife, 'quite cruel really.'

'Whatever it is, it's the same kind of strategy you go on about in your PhD, Jonathan.'

I tell him I'd never thought about it that way, never connected the two things, which seem worlds apart from each other. 'Ah yes,' he says, almost triumphantly, 'but that's how the unconscious works. You never know what strange connections are going on up there.' He taps the side of his head. 'You're probably doing the PhD precisely because of that encounter on the football field years ago.'

'I don't think that's true...'

But he's too carried away with his own strange connections to listen to any objections: 'You wouldn't know if it's true or not – that's the point of the unconscious. Without being aware of it, you're not really writing about Victorian literature at all. You're actually writing about yourself.' He smiles, characteristically clinching his case with a quotation: 'It's what Wilde said somewhere: "All criticism is autobiography".'

I wonder if that famous Wilde (mis-)quotation is reversible: if most, if not all, autobiography is also a form of criticism. After all, autobiographies and memoirs are usually packed with quotations, allusions, references to other books. 'Criticism is as inevitable as breathing,' says T. S. Eliot – and a lot of autobiographical writing gives the impression that they are almost the same thing: to live, breathe, grow up in a literate world is to inhale texts, and exhale our mixed-up replays, revisions, and critiques of them.

This is especially the case with childhood and school, which have, of course, been written about *ad infinitum*. We can't escape these multitudinous texts. They surround us as we grow up, mirroring us as we mirror them, disciplining us, telling us what we should do, how we should behave, what we should feel; and we agree or disagree with them, recognise ourselves in them, answer them back ('You're a bloody tyrant, Sir'), tell them where to go.

That's what I want to do in this book: I want to explore the hall of mirrors that is criticism and autobiography. I want to connect up my own (no doubt relatively tame) experiences of discipline and bullying, with those depicted in literary texts. Such depictions also mirror, and sometimes distort, theoretical conceptions of education and power. I'll write about some of those ideas too; but in this book, the theory takes second place to the personal experiences – of myself and various literary characters – because I want to find out what discipline and bullying feel like from 'within', rather than from 'above'.[3] I want to explore the uses and abuses of educational power from a subjective, rather than pseudo-objective, perspective.

Above all, I want to explore *how* such experiences feel, *how* they work. There are lots of good books on the all-too-familiar, all-too-terrible 'whys' of abuses of power: racism, sexism, misogyny, homophobia, ableism, classism, physical difference, religious difference. This book, though, is less about the *whys*, more about the *hows* of educational power: its patterns, means, techniques, and weird incongruities – of which there are many – alongside the ecologies in which it flourishes, the discourses it assimilates, the ideology it weaponises. I want to understand *how* my own experiences in education connect with wider literary, social, and disciplinary contexts (and I mean 'disciplinary' in both senses of the word).

Still, it's often difficult, if not impossible, to talk about the *hows* without the *whys*. Sometimes, the *whys* and *hows* overlap, shade into each other; sometimes *whys* and *hows* are indistinguishable;

---

[3]I discuss theoretical contexts for the book at greater length in Chapter 9, 'Extra-Curricular: Thanks, Notes, Contexts'.

and sometimes, now and then, there are no separate *whys* – sometimes the exercise of power is sufficient cause in itself, all else mere pretext. Quite rightly, identity politics has taught us to detect conscious and unconscious prejudice in almost all human relations. But it shouldn't blind us to manifestations of power that transcend political categorisation – forms of sadism, for example, where (sexual, physical, ethnic, etc.) difference is only a pretext, and where the underlying driving force is the gleeful exercise of power for its own sake. As one theorist of bullying, Carsten Bagge Lausten, puts it, 'anyone can become a scapegoat. What people are ... bullied for is [often] quite arbitrary'. People might *seem* to be bullied for wearing 'ugly "supermarket clothes"', or 'the wrong brand of hair wax', or being 'religious', but these might just be arbitrary pretexts, to the extent that 'the right clothes one day can be completely wrong the next'.[4]

One pre-text – to use the term in a different sense – of my 1985 P.E. lesson is the famous football scene in Barry Hines's 1968 novel *Kestrel for a Knave*. My experience of school football partly mirrors that of Hines's main character, Billy Casper, albeit in a watered-down form. Unlike Billy, I certainly wasn't from a poverty-stricken broken home in Yorkshire; but, like myself, Billy is accused of having 'no backbone', and there are other points of connection too.

The scene is at once very sad and grotesquely funny. Hines's P.E. teacher, Mr Sugden, is a bully who singles out Billy Casper, and (in Billy's own words) 'picks' on him during the lesson because he's 't'littlest'. Being 'picked on' here consists of both threats of

---

[4]Mocol Ostow says something similar in her poem 'Twenty-Eight Things I've Been Made Fun of For'. These twenty-eight things include: 'Being half-Jewish / Being half-Puerto Rican / Not being Jewish enough / Not being Latina enough / ... Being taller than everyone else / Being shorter than everyone else / Being fat / Being thin', and so on.

violence and actual physical violence – Sugden hits Billy with the ball, and, at one point, traps Billy under freezing cold showers.

More than anything, though, being picked on is a matter of being singled out, differentiated from the other boys. Perhaps every P.E. teacher needs – or needed, back in the day – a scapegoat. So Mr Sugden singles out Billy ('Casper, you make me SICK'), and crucially tries to get the other boys on his side, through laughter. He mimics Billy's 'whipped-dog whining' voice; he dresses Billy in ludicrously large shorts; and he tells Billy he'll have to 'drip-dry' after the shower, seeing the latter has no towel: 'He thought this was funny. Billy didn't. So Sugden looked round for a more appreciative audience.' Bullying like Sugden's depends on an appreciative audience. In fact, bullying (almost) always needs an audience of some kind.

Throughout the scene, Sugden attempts to maintain an unspoken alliance with the other boys, through insults and laughter, which makes Billy feel victimised. As another teacher remarks, 'You always seem to cop it, don't you, Casper?', and Billy answers: 'I'm no worse than stacks o' kids, but they just seem to get away with it.... I seem to get into bother for nowt.... There's allus somebody after me.'

Towards the end of the lesson, Sugden's alliance with the other kids is starting to disintegrate, as they express increasing unease about Billy's shower-torture. 'He'll get pneumonia,' says one boy. 'There were signs of unrest and much muttering amongst the crowd: "He's had enough, Sir".... "Let him go".' The other boys are no longer entirely on Sir's side. Alliances like this are always fragile, depending as they do on pupils temporarily lending their support (through laughter) to a Mr Sugden – to, that is, the real enemy – in victimising an easy scapegoat, 't'littlest' one. No doubt, as my PhD supervisor might have said, there's a whole allegory of political power – of bullying, of fragile alliances, of scapegoating, as these things operate both within and outside school walls – all compacted into this one fictional P.E. lesson.

For now, I want to stay within school walls, and mention another reason why Mr Sugden's alliance with the other boys is fragile: because it depends on the assumption that the group is always stronger than the individual, that the scapegoat has next to no power. There's a lot to be said for this assumption. After all, I seem to have written a whole PhD about it. It is, more often than not, true, as can be seen from any number of infinitely more serious cases of scapegoating than Billy's or my own. But Billy-no-mates is also called by another teacher a 'lone wolf', a rather different image of individuality. Wolves are neither spineless nor powerless. A scapewolf, as opposed to a scapegoat, might bite back. For that matter, a scapejellyfish might sting, might stammer-shout: 'You're a bloody, tyrant, Sir!'

Having said (or stammer-shouted) all that, I'm not writing this memoir to sting or bite back Mr Yorwin, Danny Beaker, or my other long-time-ago classmates. I don't want this story to be an exercise in what Friedrich Nietzsche calls '*ressentiment*' – the revenge of the weak, the spineless, the jellyfish on the Danny Beakers or Mr Yorwins of the world. That's what social media – Friends Reunited and now Facebook – is for. No, I don't want this to be memoir-as-*ressentiment*. If all autobiography is criticism, it too readily becomes criticism of people, rather than texts, systems, organisations, which validate certain patterns of behaviour. I don't want to criticise Mr Yorwin – what's the point of that? He was merely part of a system, with its own set of assumptions (about competitiveness, stiff-upper-lipped masculinity, the weather, and so on); and compared to other members of that system, he was relatively mild, really. Nor do I want to criticise my classmates. I liked a lot of them, and some went on to become life-long friends.

There's no point criticising individuals when it's really the system that's at fault. Such criticism doesn't achieve anything, apart from a different kind of scapegoating. Instead, the starting-point should be to acknowledge that much of an individual's behaviour is determined by the system within which they work. The aim should be to modify the system, and the collective psychology that lies behind the system, rather than belatedly to wag fingers at particular people.

We were all part of that system, and hence all equally vulnerable to wagged fingers. 'I guess we are all guilty of everything', writes American author William Burroughs; and no doubt my ex-classmates might cite other lessons when I myself was on the opposite side, on the side of the wolf-pack, as alliances between pupils and teachers shifted and morphed: maybe in History, or English, for example – or a couple of years later, when Danny Beaker head-butted a Metalwork teacher, and we ganged up against him. It'd be hypocritical and absurd, after so many years, to bear anyone ill-will, because we can all be bullies, all be victims, and sometimes both at the same time.[5]

Notwithstanding popular wisdom, it's rare for bullying to be monolithic – one hard kid consistently abusing a softer kid without any let up. Rather, most bullying is complex, nuanced, full of incongruities and ambiguities. That's one reason why victims of domestic abuse, for instance, are usually conflicted: *But he's kind most of the time, and great with the kids. It's only now and then...* It's also why judging bullying and abuse, in court rooms, tribunals, etc., can be so challenging: *But look, my client did something nice and kind on this particular date, your honour...* Sometimes, this kind of inconsistency is deliberate (as in gaslighting), sometimes – perhaps most of the time – it's merely human. Abusers, bullies, disciplinarians get bored. They do something else. Their mood changes.[6]

---

[5]On the use of the term 'victim' in this book, see the short note in Chapter 9, 'Extra-Curricular: Thanks, Notes, Contexts'.

[6]For a particularly extreme example of bullying's incongruities, see Chapter 5, 'R.E.'. On 'non-linear' bullying, see Chapter 7, 'Politics'.

As for Mr Yorwin, he didn't hold onto his bad mood for long. He and I reached a sort of understanding by the end of high school, whereby I'd accept, even embrace, the appellation 'spineless', in return for his allowing me, Steed, and Pi to go off and play badminton or (believe it or not) crown green bowls, *sans* Danny Beaker or Godzilla II. Bowling balls, thank God, were too heavy to fly through the air and hit you in the stomach or between the legs. And, actually, instead of ill-will towards anyone in particular, the chief legacy of those long-ago P.E. lessons is a muscle memory, that fear of flying balls.

Which is why, in my mid-forties, after being repeatedly threatened by GPs with diabetes and high cholesterol, I decided on a ball-less form of exercise as a way of trying to get fit. That is, thirty years after a certain P.E. lesson – thirty years of desk-sitting and book-reading, where only my eyes received regular exercise – I took up running, as if by mistake.

This isn't, however, intended as a feel-good story about how I discovered the joys of physical exercise, years after being put off it. It's not a narrative of overcoming, any more than it is one of *ressentiment*. I'm not 'overcoming' my fear of balls by running, and nor am I 'overcoming' my ex-P.E. teacher. Quite the opposite: I'm doing exactly what he'd have wanted me to do. I'm belatedly (and probably posthumously) joining him, rather than beating him.

No, if I'm overcoming anything, if I'm sticking up two fingers to anything, it's actually myself, given that running represents the negation of everything I'd stood for (or, to be more precise, sat for) since 1985 – that is, books, PhDs, desks, doughnuts, and so on. Indeed, my mother was initially disappointed by my new hobby: 'This isn't *you*,' she declared. 'You might damage your knees. Or fall over. Or break something. There was a thing on *Woman's Hour* yesterday about how running isn't as good for you as eating cream cakes.'

Okay, I'm exaggerating a bit. And to be fair, my mum and *Woman's Hour* were right, insofar as running has caused me numerous injuries, and wasn't a magic bullet for my cholesterol levels. Nonetheless, both running *and* giving up cream cakes seem to have helped, to universal surprise, in the longer term.

Another ex-cream-cake-eater, my friend Steed, also took up running in his forties. Oddly enough, the two crappiest sportspeople in the school, the two broken bits at the bottom of the P.E. biscuit barrel, are now avid runners in middle age.

I can't speak for Steed, but I'm still crap. I'm still agonisingly slow, and manage to come last even though it's only me running – to the extent that Mr Yorwin would, quite probably, still not approve ('Get yer arse in gear, Taylor!'). If he weren't in jail, Danny Beaker would probably wee on me again, literally or metaphorically speaking.

But there is a value in persisting at something you're crap at, a value incomprehensible to an education system obsessed with competitiveness (a very English disease) and its uneasy (some might say contradictory) correlate, team playing. While running, I feel excused for a utopian moment from competitiveness and the 'team spirit' – as if my mum has written a retrospective note to Mr Yorwin:

Dear Mr Yorwin,

Jonathan will not be footballing today because he's rubbish at it. Instead, he will be running, which he's also rubbish at. Get that? Running. I ask you. I mean, I think he'd be better off eating cream cakes, but he seems to prefer this running business – even if it's -2 degrees and snowy outside. He says that running's a form of P.E. which actually encourages you to be a lone wolf, or a lone jellyfish. I've no idea what he's talking about: everyone knows that aquatic invertebrates don't run, and generally swim together in schools...

2

Playtime: Games of Soldiers

Decent little beggars individually, but as a mob, just pitiless and implacable.

James Hilton, *Goodbye, Mr Chips*

As well as running, there are other contexts, too, where being a lone wolf or jellyfish is not necessarily a sign of weakness – whatever P.E. teachers might think. It all depends on perspective: as I say, different people have different, and sometimes incommensurate, notions of spinelessness.

For example:

It's October 1983. I'm in the final year of primary school. Our class has crocodiled over to the music room to watch a big TV on legs. There's a video recorder beneath it. Our teacher, Mrs Dee, slots in a video cassette, presses play. There are crackles and hisses. Mrs Dee fiddles with the channels. She peers round the back of the TV and unplugs one wire, plugs another one in. She looks at the screen: it's purple snow. She hits the side of the TV, turns it off and on again at the mains.

Finally, something rolls into view: a view of Tower Bridge. Tower Bridge keeps sinking, while the Thames keeps swapping places with the sky. Mrs Dee hits the TV again. The image stabilises. A Schools Programme starts. It's called *Middle English*, and the title of the three interlinked episodes we're watching is *A Game of Soldiers*. I find out years later that it's a play by Jan Needle. At the time I think we're just watching a lesson.

The play's set during the Falklands War, which happened the previous year. I'd caught monochrome snippets of it on the kitchen TV at home: the naval task force setting off, the sinking of the *General Belgrano*, the Battle of Mount Tumbledown. My father hadn't said much about it – merely tutted and shook his head, even when the British had taken Port Stanley; my mother had switched it off, horrified by anything involving missiles, flags, Thatchers, or history: 'We don't want to watch that. Horrible. It'll ruin the soup.'

So my knowledge of the war, up till now, has been at best fragmentary, a melange of interrupted images, mixed up with Heinz Oxtail Soup. But here, now, in front of me is a joined-up story – one involving not Thatchers or Galtieris but everyday people, like me and my friends. In the play, three children on the Falkland Islands discover an injured Argentinian conscript, who isn't much older than them. Initially, the bloodthirsty older boy, Michael, wants to kill him, perhaps with a gun, perhaps with a rock; the girl, Sarah, wants to bring him food, clothes; the younger boy, Thomas, doesn't know what he wants, keeps changing his mind, all too easily swayed by whoever's bullying him at the time.

A Game of Soldiers is a problem play for children, asking them: which of these three positions do you associate with? What would you do in these circumstances? In her Introduction to the published playscript, Needle herself talks about how she 'wanted to allow each viewer to bring his or her mind to bear on the possibilities inherent [in the scenario]'. These possibilities often polarised viewers' reactions, as is apparent from a report compiled by the then-Education Officer for Central Independent Television. In one rural middle school, the Education Officer writes,

two teachers ... were horrified at the effect the Falklands story had on their class.... The boys in the class were all for shooting the soldier, he was an enemy, kill before you get killed, the Argentinians are the scum of the earth and he deserved it, etc., etc. There followed a very traumatic half hour as they let them talk it out. Desire for violence and revenge emerged and a stream of invective followed, which led also onto unemployment, and a line in politics far to the right of Margaret Thatcher. At first the teachers thought it was macho bravado but realised that they had lifted a stone and been given an insight into what some of their local community really thought, not only about war and peace, but about a whole host of issues of deep social concern. Some of the girls in the class had cried at the ending and more cried when they tried to argue with the boys and got shouted down.

That split in the audience, between bloodthirsty boys playing soldiers, and sympathetic girls playing nurses or mothers, mirrors the gender split in the play itself, between Michael and (to some extent) Thomas, on the one hand, and Sarah, on the other – although Sarah doesn't cry. Instead, she's actually the strongest character in the play, the one quietly in charge, who decides what course of action they should take: 'It's all a silly game. No one's killing anyone, got it? We've got to save this soldier, nothing else. He's cold and hungry and wounded. We've got to save his life.' Even Michael, whom she describes as a 'bloodthirsty little devil' and a 'nutcase' comes round to Sarah's way of thinking in the final episode. Before that happens, though, he's determined to kill the Argentinian soldier, calling the others 'Chicken' and recycling the vengeful and macho language he's imbibed from his father and the radio: 'I'm a patriot. We've got to do our bit. It's our duty to be ready.' He attacks Sarah's 'female logic', calls Thomas 'Weedikins', and wishes he had 'a real commando knife' with which to kill the Argentinian: 'I'd stick it in his neck and pull. It'd be sharp as sharp. I'd slice it through his jugular and watch the blood squirt. I could do it.'

These vengeful fantasies are exposed as such at the end of the second episode, and the start of the third, where the soldier drops his rifle, and passes out in front of Michael. Like a mini-Hamlet faced with a praying Claudius ('Now I might do it pat'), Michael has his chance ('I'll kill you, you bastard'). Yet despite being 'furious with himself, and confused, and ashamed', he finds he can't do it: 'I can't on my own, it's not fair on the others!' In the final scene, he confesses his failure to Sarah: 'Look, Sarah … we can't … I mean. I tried to shoo … I got the rifle but…' And she answers: 'You daft devil, of course you couldn't … We understand completely.'

By contrast, my classmates do *not* understand. To them, Michael has let the side down, and by the end of the TV programme, all three main characters are branded 'Weedikins' by male and female pupils alike. There is no gender split in my class, merely a near-unanimous response of frustration and disgust. This becomes apparent when Mrs Dee pauses the video, the final close-up of the soldier's agonised face twitching centre-frame, and turns to the audience: 'So, children, what would *you* do if you found a soldier like this?' It doesn't seem very likely that we'd find a runaway soldier from Argentina in the middle of Stoke-on-Trent. But my classmates willingly suspend their disbelief in order to unleash a torrent of bellicose disgust on Mrs Dee – lovely, kind Mrs Dee, who teaches modern dance, who wears kaftans and scarves, who encourages her pupils to express themselves in painting, stories, poetry, who cries in front of her class at the drop of a political hat.

'The kids on this are stupid. Chickens. *Weedikins.*'

'Michael should've shot him or stabbed him when he got the chance.'

'I'd have shot him. *Bang bang*. I'm getting a gun for Christmas.'

'At least the British Army'll shoot him now.'

'The British Army are the best.'

'Or the other farmers'll get him and kill him.'

'He deserves it.'

'Argie scum. That's what my dad calls them.'

'They deserve everything they get. Shouldn't have invaded in the first place. It's ours. *Our* land.'

'My dad says they're all weeds anyway. Thatcher sorted them out.'

'Yeah, let's tell Thatcher. Phone her up!'

'She'd blow him up in a tank.'

'Hang him.'

'Drop a stone on his head, like they were going to. Smash his brains in.'

'Stab him.'

'Eat him,' says Lee Hardwick, my primary-school nemesis. There's a scattering of laughter.

'Now, Lee,' says Mrs Dee. 'Now, everyone...'

I put up my hand. 'Yes, Jonathan?'

'I think ... I think they did the right thing. I don't think they should kill him.'

There's a groan around me. Lee Hardwick puts his fingers down his throat, pretending to be sick: 'Oh my God...'

'Lee!' says Mrs Dee, 'no language like that. Jonathan, go on.'

'It's like what Sarah in the play says: he's a human person. Just because he's from Argentina doesn't mean he's not like us. He's hurt and scared.'

Everyone looks at me with wide eyes, stupefied, as if they're looking at a corpse – a talking corpse. There's a silence, then the bubble bursts, and Mrs Dee momentarily loses control of the class, as they all round on me: 'What're you going on about?'

'Shurrup, Jonny. You're talking rubbish. He's the enemy, remember?'

'A "ruinator" and "rapist". That's what they call him on the programme.'

'And they'd call *you* an idiot.'

'Or a traitor. You can get hung for being a traitor, y'know. Executed. My dad says so.'

'Traitor.'

'God, you're so wet.'

'You're a *girl*.'

'Your name is *Sarah*.'

'Or weirdo.'

'My dad'd sort you out.'

'Go and live in Argentina. See how you like it.'

The anger is real, mingled with needling and laughter, *Schadenfreude* at Argentina's defeat. The whole country, top to bottom, is still angry – all the fury and joy of so-called 'victory' boiling away everywhere, from the House of Commons to a class of provincial ten- and eleven-year-olds. Carl Jung says somewhere that 'the psychology of the individual is reflected in the psychology of the nation'. Perhaps he should have said: 'the psychology of the nation is reflected in the psychology of the classroom'. The class as a whole is baying for more Argentinian blood.

Yet, later on, when Mrs Dee speaks to her pupils individually about the TV show, most of them change their tune, just as Michael does in the play itself. At the moment of crisis, he declares that he 'can't do it on [his] ... own', he can only kill the Argentinian soldier 'together ... [with] the others'. Only together, only as a group can the children conceive of killing another human being. Scapegoating is always a collective act.

'He's a *human being*,' I say to everybody and nobody. 'He's hurt, and you should look after people, whoever they are. War is a *bad thing*.'

The boy sitting next to me pushes me.

'That's enough,' says Mrs Dee, trying ineffectually to calm the class from the front. No one's listening to her.

'Kill him,' says Lee Hardwick. I don't know whether he's referring to me, or the soldier frozen on the screen, paralysed, jerking with interference.

'*Kill him kill him kill him*,' chant a couple of Lee's sidekicks.

'Be quiet, Lee, everyone!' shouts Mrs Dee. Her voice is wobbly, and she turns back to the video recorder.

A week later, it's parents' evening. My mother – who's basically a liberal pacifist like Mrs Dee, though her aversion to violence is as much aesthetic as it is ethical ('Switch that off, it *looks* horrible') – returns from school beaming, and tells me she really likes my new teacher. 'She says you stood up to the whole class in a debate about the Falklands War. She says even though the whole class was saying something different, you stuck to your guns' – which seems a rather inapposite metaphor in the circumstances. 'I think she likes children who are odd-ones-out, who don't go along with the crowd. I do too.'

If you think about it, that might seem a peculiarly undemocratic attitude for two quasi-hippy-liberal-pacifists. The idea that an odd-one-out might be right, the rest wrong, would probably not have crossed Mr Sugden's and Mr Yorwin's minds. In that sense, you could say they're the real democrats. It's they who believe in the inherent rightness, or righteousness, of the majority.

That belief, though, sometimes conjures up scapegoats, pariahs, whole victimised groups, who must, by definition, be in the wrong, simply because they are in the minority. This is what nineteenth-century political theorist Alexis de Tocqueville calls 'the tyranny of the majority' in his influential critique of American democracy. On a macro-political scale, you might say there have been some pretty compelling illustrations of the tyranny of the majority in recent years. I couldn't possibly comment. All I know is how it works on a micro-scale, in a classroom or workplace.

And maybe the point is that classrooms and workplaces aren't genuine democracies, anyway, even when they pretend to be. Nor is the tyranny of the majority my idea of true democracy. Instead, part of me likes to dream that perhaps there might exist an alternative model of (educational) democracy, one which substitutes for crude majority rule something more utopian-individualistic, something less murderous towards injured Argentinian soldiers – in a word, something more *Dee-ian.*

The problem, of course, with apparently individualistic behaviour is that it doesn't come from nowhere. Individualism is never simply itself. Rather, it is made – and often made *for*, rather than *by*, the pupil or pupils at the centre of it. In *The Prime of Miss Jean Brodie*, the so-called individualism of the 'Brodie set' is obviously made, in part, by Miss Brodie herself, forged by her 'as the leader of the set, ... as a Roman matron.' 'I am putting old heads on your young shoulders,' she declares, when her favourites are eleven. 'I would make of you the crème de la crème.' Later, she proclaims: 'You are mine ... of my stamp and cut.' Miss Brodie's stamp and cut are what 'set them apart' from the other pupils, and ultimately, 'it was impossible to escape from the Brodie set because they were the Brodie set in the eyes of the school.' The Brodie set's individualism is hence not only formed by Miss Brodie herself, but also by 'the eyes of the school.' This puts them in an 'enviable' position, such that 'everyone thought the Brodie set had more fun than anyone else.'

All too often, though, being set apart in 'the eyes of the school' is much less fun, more a matter of ostracism than envy. In Fleur Jaeggy's strange novel about a Swiss girls' boarding school, *Sweet Days of Discipline* (1989), the narrator describes, in almost mystical terms, the process by which one pupil is ostracised, becoming the school 'pariah':

> By tacit agreement and right from the beginning the girls in a school will choose their pariah with careless affection. Not because one passes the word to the others: it's a general impulse. It's the evil eye, like a divining rod, seeking out its victim. With no real reason to explain the choice but bad luck.

In the case of the narrator's current school, the 'victim' who gains the status of pariah is a 'black girl [who] did nothing but wrap herself in it, give it an aura of truth, as though imposed by destiny'

There are other reasons behind this destiny than mere bad luck: an obvious yet unspoken racism, for one, along with class envy, concerning the girl's parents' wealth and status. As the 'daughter of an African head of state', the black girl is 'received with all honours' on arrival at the school. The other pupils are 'lined up ... standing to attention to receive the President, the wife of the

President and the little girl.' This initial grand reception causes resentment among her peers:

The other pupils felt those honours were excessive.... As far as most of the girls were concerned she was the President's daughter, and they made her pay for that.... If a girl is received, as the black girl was, with flags and pomp of every variety, and if there is applause for an African head of state, then that applause will be held against her.

The headteacher of the school makes the situation worse, when she openly treats the black girl as a favourite,

holding her hand and taking her for walks.... *Mein Kind, mein Kind*, she whispered and caressed her hair, her thin pigtails.... She counted the fingers of her hand as if she were a doll. The girl let herself be caressed like a corpse.

To be a teacher's pet is to be a kind of doll, a corpse, a zombie, according to the narrator: 'It was as though I were looking at someone already dead.' That's exactly how I felt my classmates were looking at me, when I suggested Argentinians might be human too. The school's 'evil eye' brings the scapegoat-pariah into being, and simultaneously kills (or tries to kill) him or her off. Something similar happens in *A Game of Soldiers*: Michael excitedly fantasises about finding an Argentinian soldier, as though conjuring one into being, and then dreams of executing him.

So pariahs are conjured into being by those who want to kill them. But they're also conjured into being 'with careless affection' by those who treat them as favourites: parents, teachers, and so on. In my last year of primary school, I was certainly marked out, rightly or wrongly, as both a teacher's and mother's pet.

To put all this in slightly more positive terms: my own so-called 'individualism' in Mrs Dee's class was, in part, conjured up by my parents' attitudes. I can't claim any special insight of my own about the Falklands War. Just as Michael in *A Game of Soldiers* imbibes and regurgitates the jingoistic language of his father, his community, the radio, so I'd no doubt semi-consciously imbibed my father's scepticism, my mother's pacificism – and had vomited these things back up in response to my classmates' bloodthirstiness.

There was also another emetic behind my political regurgitation: Lee Hardwick. His gleeful invocation of violence ('Eat him!') had been a final straw, a red rag to a fey bull. Anything he said annoyed me, made me want to think and say the opposite.

It had all started a year before, in the previous class, when Lee and his sidekicks somehow discovered that I'd once had ballet classes:

'Did you wear a tutu? Pink and frilly, like? Did you? *Did you*?'

'What?'

'Did you wear a tutu – when you did ballet?'

'I didn't do ballet.'

'Yes, you did. When you were a little kid. D'you still do it now?'

'No, I don't.'

'Ah, so you admit that you *used* to do it.'

'I don't. Didn't.'

We're in the classroom at lunch break. Ten minutes before, I'd snuck in here to hide from Lee and his sidekicks, but they've discovered me. There's Lee and two sidekicks – which seems to be a popular, near-optimum number of sidekicks. While Lee interrogates me about ballet, one of the sidekicks is behind me, one of them is barring my passage to the exit.

I have no idea how they've found out that I took ballet lessons when I was three, four, possibly five. I wouldn't have said anything about it. Perhaps they've heard about it via the parental grapevine. Or perhaps my best friend has betrayed a confidence. I don't know. All I know is that, for some reason I can't put into words at this stage, ballet seems like the most shameful thing in the world.

Yet I myself can barely remember it. I remember standing in a line with girls in leotards, all of us pretending to be airplanes, holding our arms out straight, waving them around to the piano music coming from one corner ('Those Magnificent Men in Their Flying Machines'). I remember my mum making me a special shirt – pink with purple lilies on it – for the end-of-year show. I remember being spot-lit on stage, holding the teacher's hand, watching my feet carefully, the audience blacked out. I remember everyone afterwards squeezing my cheeks, telling me I was the star, as the only tiny boy there. Then, a few weeks later, I remember my mother driving me back to the dance class. We got stuck on the big roundabout near Hanley, and went round and round it because she kept missing the turn. The third time round, I said: 'I don't want to do ballet any more', and my mother found the exit for home.

Most of all, I remember the photo of me in the pink shirt with purple lilies that my mother keeps on her dressing table – a photo which, four or five years later, I pray Lee Hardwick never lays eyes on. Thank goodness, there's no Facebook in 1982.

'Did you wear a pink blouse with your tutu?' asks Lee. He's asking so many scatter-gun questions about my brief ballet career that some of them are bound to stick. For nine-year-old me, though, it feels like he's got some special psychic insight, which means he knows everything. This is bullying-as-apparent-omniscience. I'm scared. The hairs on the back of my neck prickle up. Lee's sidekicks snigger.

'No.'

'Did it have lots of frills and flowers on it?' Again: bullseye.

'No.'

'Weren't you embarrassed, like?'

'I didn't do it.'

'Come on, you don't need to lie to us, Taylor. We're not saying it's bad or anything' – he winks at his sidekicks, they snigger again – 'we're just, like, *interested*, y'know, in why a boy would do ballet. What *sort* of boy'd do it.'

Figure 2.1 This faded photo is all that remains of my short-lived career in ballet, c. 1977.

'Perhaps he wasn't,' says one of the sidekicks.

'Wasn't what?' asks Lee.

'A boy. Perhaps he wasn't a boy then. Perhaps he's not got the right bits.'

'We'd better check, then.'

The three of them close in, two of them pinning back my arms, Lee reaching down and grabbing my 'bits' through the trousers. 'Let's *feel* him,' says Lee. *Feeling* other boys' bits – through trousers, or more directly – is a craze going round school at present (if 'craze' is quite the right word). I confess I'd been willingly, if not happily, involved in it at times. No doubt it kills two birds with one stone: it causes pain to the other person (*tick*), and constitutes an early form of sexual exploration (*tick*).

Lee's grip is definitely causing me pain: 'Please, stop it, *please*!' I'm on the floor now, and the three boys are on top of me. Lee's sitting on my legs, unzipping my trousers, and squeezing what's inside.

'We'll stop when you admit you did ballet.'

'No.'

'Tell us.'

'Please stop.'

'Tell us.'

'I admit it. I did ballet. I did. But it was when I was little. *Please...*'

He squeezes harder and laughs. I see white spots in front of my eyes.

'Girl,' he says. It feels like he's pushing my testicle up into my mouth.

There's a silhouette at the door. Lee and his sidekicks scramble to their feet. It's the teacher, Mrs Marshalsea.

'What's going on? Why are you in here?'

'Ah, Miss,' says Lee, cough-laughing. 'Jonathan fell over. We were, like, helping him get up.'

Mrs Marshalsea steps into the room, glaring at us through narrowed eyes. I don't know what she thinks is happening, but she doesn't say anything about it. 'Get out of my classroom. You shouldn't be in here at lunchtime.' I stand, holding up my trousers with one hand, hoping she won't notice – as if it's my fault they're undone. As if I wanted to be 'felt'. I leave the room, red in the face, strangely guilty. Later, the guilt is compounded when Lee tells a girl I half-fancy that I like ballet and being felt by boys. My face burns with shame. It still is now, as I'm writing this.

The ballet-bullying continues, off and on, for a year. At times, it dies down, due to lack of fuel. It can't run on my balletic past alone, and needs new combustible material to keep it going.

It gains new fuel from the row over *A Game of Soldiers* ('You're a traitor', 'You're a girl', 'You'd make a better ballerina than soldier'), and finally reaches a kind of apotheosis a couple of weeks later – like the finale of *Swan Lake*, but less elegant.

I'm sat at a table with one of Lee's sidekicks and three other kids. Mrs Dee is talking about medical history, the invention of vaccines, anaesthetic, her own experiences of surgery.

'Who here has had an operation in a hospital?' she asks. Patient confidentiality doesn't seem to apply to primary-age kids.

Without thinking, I put up my hand. I love Mrs Dee, and I love answering her questions. 'I had one when I was seven.'

'Were you put to sleep?' she asks. I nod, thinking it sounds like what vets do when they can't cure sick animals. 'Tell the class what it was like.'

I'm relieved she doesn't ask 'What was it for?' because I'd struggle to answer. I know it was about my 'private bits' – my 'widgey' to use my dad's term (like many families, we struggle to find mum-friendly words for certain parts of the body). I also know the operation had something to do with my only having one where most boys have two. Beforehand, I had regular hospital appointments with a doctor, who'd take my trousers down, check out what was and wasn't there. He decided they should cut me open down there, to have a 'root around', as he delicately put it. He made surgery sound like a medicalised version of 'feeling' – a rather invasive version.

'Before the operation, they gave me something special to drink. I drank it, but I didn't go to sloop like they wanted. They put me on a trolley and told me to lie down. They said I should be asleep by now. But I always find it hard to go to sleep, even with medicine. I remember the nurses wheeling me down some corridors, into a lift. Then we were in a white shiny room, and doctors were looking down at me. One of them asked me if I was awake and I said "Yes", and he said: "Look at your wrist." So I looked down at my wrist. He said: "Can you see the butterflies?" And I said "No" – then "Yes", because lots of these colourful butterflies suddenly flew out of my wrist, like magic. Then I don't remember anything else.'

As I finish speaking, I notice the kids around me grumbling: 'So stupid', 'Butterflies can't fly out of your wrist, silly', 'What's Jonny going on about, Miss?' Lee Hardwick snorts: 'God, Taylor still believes in Santa and Tooth Fairies, and now it's magic butterflies too.' Everyone laughs, apart from Mrs Dee. She pats me on the head and says: 'That's beautiful, Jonathan. What a lovely dream. It's like one of your stories.'

Years later, I found out it was a *true* story: I really did see butterflies flying out of my wrist. It was a hallucination induced by a combination of the anaesthetic and the surgeon's suggestion.

After the butterfly hallucination and ensuing operation, I remember only flashes: my mother sitting by my bed, darkness, my father sitting by the bed, darkness, nurses chattering, a painful bath, darkness, my father holding my hand, showing me a little toy Daimler. 'It's for you,' he said. I didn't understand why he'd bought me a present. 'Because you've had an operation,' he said. For some reason, I couldn't connect the two things. Darkness. Pain. 'Thank you,' I said when I came to. He squeezed my hand, and said: 'Don't worry, boy. Absolutely everything's going to be all right now.'

Given what happened to him over the next twenty years, I think he might have overstated the case.

Meanwhile, just three years after the operation, Mrs Dee asks me one final (and possibly misjudged) question about my hospital experience: 'How did it feel when the anaesthetic wore off, Jonathan?'

'It felt funny, weird. And it hurt a lot. I found it really hard to walk. It was like I was a baby and had to learn how to walk again.'

To my right, I can almost see Lee's sidekick's ears prick up. He's suddenly sitting up straight, smirking, like he's some kind of TV detective, and I've inadvertently let something slip which has solved a case for him: *Bingo.* I'm trembling, and I don't know why.

I don't know what it is I've let out of the bag. But somehow, I know I'm going to pay for it.

Meanwhile, Mrs Dee rounds off what she's been saying about hospitals and operations, and sets us some work to do. Knowing her, it's probably a free choice between drawing a picture, writing a poem, or interpreting surgery through dance. My attention, though, is not on my work, but on what Lee's sidekick is hissing at me, across the table:

'What was the operation for?' asks Sidekick.

'Nothing,' I say. I feel my face reddening.

'It can't have been for nothing,' says a girl with a snub nose who's overheard, and who's sitting between Sidekick and myself. She's the girl I half-fancy, and I can feel myself going redder and redder.

'I don't want to talk about it anymore,' I whisper, trying to concentrate on the blank sheet of paper in front of me.

'Yes, you do,' says Sidekick. 'You obviously love talking about it – all those butterflies and stuff.'

'Shhh,' warns Mrs Dee from the front. There's a lull. I pray I've been let off the hook, and start scribbling something. But no.

'Come on, Taylor, tell us what it was for.'

'No.'

'I reckon I know anyway,' hisses Sidekick, like a mini-Hercule Poirot building up to an end-of-case revelation.

'Go on then, tell us,' whispers snub-nose girl.

'Yeah, tell us,' say a couple of others round the table.

'Shut up,' I say.

'I reckon,' says Sidekick, 'it was something down there. On your *balls*.'

Everyone around the table giggles. My face is only a few inches above the sheet of paper. 'Shut up.' I can't believe Sidekick's guessed correctly. Again, it feels like Lee and his sidekicks wield some telepathic ability, some kind of spooky omniscience. This is the *unheimlich* (uncanniness) of bullying. To a ten-year-old me, it seems at least as magical as Tooth Fairies or Wrist Butterflies. But Sidekick's uncanny insight concerns balls, not teeth or wrists, and hence is much more embarrassing.

'It was your balls, wasn't it?'

'No, it wasn't.'

'I bet it was.'

'How d'you know?' asks the girl I half-fancy.

'Well,' explains Sidekick proudly, 'one of my cousins had an operation on his balls a while back. And he couldn't walk afterwards too. So it *must* be the same thing.'

'Oh,' says the girl, impressed by his deductive abilities.

Sidekick turns back to me: 'You don't, like, need to be embarrassed, Taylor. We just wanna know. What did they *do* to your balls?'

'Nothing. It wasn't *there*. It was on ... my legs.'

'Oh come on, don't be stupid. That's a fib. Just tell us about it. What really happened. Between friends, like.'

'No.'

'Tell us.'

'No.'

'Tell us.'

The argument goes round in circles for a few minutes: *Tell-us-no-tell-us-no-tell-us-no-tell-us-no....*

'Shhh...' says Mrs Dee.

Sidekick leans across the desk. 'Did they cut them off?'

'What?'

'Did they cut off your balls?'

The girl I half-fancy laughs. Everyone round my table is giggling, apart from me. I'm desperately trying not to cry, because I know that'll make the giggling worse.

'Are you crying?' asks Sidekick.

'No.'

'Yes, you are. Hey, Lee' – he calls across the classroom, and somehow Mrs Dee doesn't hear – 'you were right. His balls are funny. Not sure he's got any, or they cut one off or summit.'

Suppressed laughter spreads from my table to the whole classroom.

'He's got no balls,' says Lee. 'Thought so.'

'Like Hitler,' says someone else.

'He kept his in the Albert Hall,' says someone else.

'Do you keep yours in the Albert Hall?' asks Sidekick, 'with Hitler's?'

'I didn't have an operation on my balls.'

'You did,' says Sidekick. 'Admit it.' He kicks me under the table.

'I won't.'

Yes-you-did-no-I-didn't-yes-you-did-no-I-didn't-admit-it-no-admit-it-I-won't-admit-anything-I-won't...

This bad pantomime carries on all day and into the next, the tone varying from insistent, to derisive, to concerned paternalistic ('Come on, Jonathan, don't worry, you don't need to be shy about it...'), back to insistent. Every gap in the lesson, every time Mrs Dee is distracted, or looking at the blackboard, Sidekick whispers: 'It was your balls, wasn't it? Wasn't it? *Wasn't it?*' According to many influential definitions of bullying, repetition is one of its principal characteristics. It is also one of its principal weapons. 'They operated on your balls, didn't they? Your-balls-your-balls-your-balls-balls-balls-your-balls-your-balls-your-balls-balls-balls...' Bullying can be a kind of poetry, with its sing-song refrains, its rhymes, rhythms and cadences, its strange distortions of everyday language.

At playtime on the third day, I'm hiding from the poetry behind one of the mobile huts, alone. My best friend has disappeared to the toilet. Lee and his two sidekicks come round one corner of the building; another boy – a tank of a boy called The Feeler – sidles round the other.

'Don't be scared,' says Lee. 'We only want a little chat with you.' It's entirely psychosomatic, but the scar left by my operation burns when he says this – as if it were a prototype for Harry Potter's scar, albeit in a more embarrassing place. It would hardly have been as picturesque if Harry's scar had been on his groin.

And Lee Hardwick is no Voldemort or Draco Malfoy, however awful his behaviour seems back in 1983. 'Look,' he says, reasonable, placatory, 'I'm not *that* bad, you know. But you and me, we never seem to get on. I dunno why.'

'You're bullying me,' I say.

Lee snorts: 'Don't be silly. We're just very different. It doesn't have to be like this, y'know. We can be okay – you do your thing, I'll do mine. I'm not a bully.'

Bullying always erases itself, covers its tracks, denies its own existence. No one (or almost no one) openly admits to being a bully, at least not while it's happening. Malfoy never holds up his hands and confesses to the teachers: 'Yes, of course, it was me what done it. I was horribly bullying Harry Potter and his friends across all seven books.' Bullying exists only in denial, in self-erasure (*I didn't do nuffin', Miss*), which is one reason why it's so difficult to diagnose, name, pinpoint.

Indeed, bullying often goes further than self-erasure, and radiates the fault outwards, such that it becomes the bullied person's fault that they are being victimised: 'You know,' says Lee, 'things could be different between us, Taylor. Jonathan. *Jonny.* You don't have to treat me as your enemy. I dunno why you think that, why you don't like me. You take everything too seriously. If you wanted, we could be friends.' He glances around. 'I mean, you could obviously do with more friends. I tell y'what, let's shake on it – no more aggro.' He holds out his hand. I stare down at it. 'Go on,' he says. I take it.

He pulls me towards him, as though to embrace me – and then trips me up, pushes me to the ground. While he watches, the others pile on top of me, one pinning my arms down, one holding my feet, The Feeler sitting on my legs. He pulls down my trousers while I try to writhe free.

'Let's see what they did to your balls,' says one sidekick.

'If he's got any left,' says The Feeler. 'We'll give him a good *feel* to find out.'

At first – and I can hardly believe this, looking back – I can't stop laughing. It's partly out of shock, partly because what they're doing tickles. It feels like complicity. Then I'm laugh-crying because it hurts and tickles at the same time. It's tickle-torture, tickling-unto-death.

'See, he likes it,' says Lee.

'Get off me,' I laugh-cry-moan. I don't shout, because I don't want anyone else to find me like this, with my trousers round my knees. Gradually, the crying is taking over from hysterical laughter. 'Don't, *please*.'

'Calm down,' says Lee. 'We're only taking a look. It's, like, what doctors do. You cough, then they feel yer balls.'

'Go on then, cough,' laughs The Feeler. He's holding down my kicking legs, enjoying himself.

As his name suggests, The Feeler is seen as the expert, a kind of Feeling Doctor. He's felt every boy in school. He does it all the time, and we know not to be alone with him, and what it means if he turns up at someone else's house when you're visiting. He's huge and I can't get away – though that doesn't stop me trying. I keep wriggling, trying to push him and the sidekicks off.

'It's like Bucking Bronco,' says one.

'Like Alton Towers,' says another.

"Cos he's having fun,' says Lee. 'Aren't you, *Jonathan*?'

'I'm not. Geroff me.'

'He's enjoying it like a girl or ballerina or poofter would.'

'What's a poofter?' asks one of the sidekicks, distracted for a moment. I bite him: 'Ouch.'

'A poofter's a girl. Or a boy who's like a girl. That's what me brother says.'

'And you know what soldiers do to girls,' says The Feeler.

'What?'

'Y'know.'

'Nah, what?'

'That thing they said on the stupid programme we watched. They *rape* them.'

'*Please stop...*'

'Yeah! Let's do a rape!'

I'm scared: '*Please...*'

Given what happens in the next couple of minutes, it's clear in retrospect that my tormentors have, as yet, a rather imperfect grasp of what the r-word signifies – just as one of the sidekicks doesn't really know what the word 'poofter' means. We're still at an early stage of learning the language of sex, gender, and violence, picking up half-comprehended words from brothers, parents, teachers, TV. Bullying is always a linguistic phenomenon as well as a physical one, and often the linguistic element is primary, physical violence only the enactment of insults, promises, and threats. We're not native speakers yet, though, and only half-understand the terms.

In this instance, The Feeler's imperfect comprehension of the terms he uses saves me from something a lot worse than what actually happens. When the boys eventually get bored, throw me my trousers, and run off, I'm left with bruises, grazes, and furious tears which, for days, feel like clenched fists behind my eyes – but that's all. The Feeler doesn't understand (yet) how far the game (of feeling, of sexual violence, of soldiers) might be pursued. Thank God.

A similar kind of incomprehension saves the children in Needle's *A Game of Soldiers* from behaving as badly as the adults. While the grown-ups have reputedly executed a number of Argentinian 'despoilers' and 'rapists', the children can't kill the injured soldier they find, because their notions of these concepts are too hazy to withstand the reality of a flesh-and-blood 'human being'. 'Despoilers?!' says Michael in response to Thomas, who in turn has picked up the word from his father, 'That's a big word for a little twit. What does it mean?' By the end of the play, it has come to signify its apparent opposite for the children; that is, 'human being'. As Needle herself suggests, in the final episode, the 'three children ... come to understand' the Argentinian soldier 'in human terms rather than in terms of propaganda or simplistic moral labelling'. Michael, in particular, moves a long way from the language he's picked up – from, that is, the 'macho bravado' of propaganda, to understanding others in more 'human terms'.

No doubt it is 'macho bravado', along with its correlates, sexism, homophobia, and so on, that lurk behind much of Michael's language. A similar macho bravado lurked behind my own bullies' weaponised use of half-digested words like 'rape' and 'poofter', and, for that matter, 'balls', 'ballet', 'tutu', etc. At the time, my classmates had only a nascent grasp of the implications of these words. They just waved them around like kids who've found their dads' guns. And I was on an even lower rung of knowledge, so all the easier to threaten. As a nine- or ten-year-old, Lee Hardwick's discovery of my ballet past somehow seemed to me the most shameful thing in the world; but I couldn't have told you why. Like Queen Victoria, I'd never heard of homosexuality (or, indeed, heterosexuality), let alone consciously connected it – in some culturally contorted way – with ballet, and pink flowery shirts, and tutus.

That's what Lee's language implied: that I was gay, or female, or given the operation on my balls, less than fully male. Clearly, in an overwhelmingly patriarchal society, bullying will almost always imply the feminisation of the subordinate other. I was not a soldier: I was a girl, a poofter, a traitor, a 'Weedikins', a ballerina, a tutu-wearer, a potential rape victim, a corpse, a ball-less Hitler, a eunuch ... and more. The language of bullying is culturally promiscuous, omnivorous: it's possible to be all these things at once, linguistically speaking, even if, in reality, some of them might seem rather incongruous (a ballerina corpse? a tutu-wearing Hitler?). If the language used by bullies is sometimes poetic, this is a surrealist poetry, a poetry of incongruity that gleefully mixes its metaphors.

And there's another strange incongruity here. To be despised – to be a girl, poofter, etc. – is also to be desired. In *A Game of Soldiers*, Michael has a bit of a crush on Sarah, however much he dismisses her advice and despises her 'female logic'. 'I think your mum's fantastic,' he says to her, 'Just like you.' The link between desire and despisal is even clearer in *Sweet Days of Discipline*, where Jaeggy's narrator claims that school pariahs are chosen 'with careless affection'. Towards the end of the school year, the nature of this affection comes into focus, as the narrator is increasingly fascinated by the black girl who has been *persona non grata* up till now: 'I followed her around. Somebody so unhappy, I thought, won't notice that she's being spied on, and spy is what I did.... My attention was entirely concentrated on her, [and] on that one thing: [her] unhappiness.'

The scapegoat-pariah, the victim of bullying, is also, it seems, a subject of desire: someone who attracts and absorbs attention; someone who is singled out from the crowd, with careless affection; someone who is different, strange, an object of horror and fascination; someone who is a doll, a talking corpse, a zombie; someone who might be a subject of, or subjected to, poetry; someone to be followed around, spied on, gazed at, an engrossing spectacle; someone to be hurt, held down, sexually experimented on – someone to be felt or worse; someone to be conjured by desire into being, and simultaneously wished into non-being; someone both welcomed into Jerusalem as a conquering hero, and condemned to crucifixion as a criminal; someone to be kissed and betrayed at the same time; someone who is at once king and sacrifice, saviour and *pharmakos*; someone who is both centre and periphery, self and other; someone who, for bullies and their sidekicks, disconcertingly embodies the circularity of the emotional spectrum, the nightmarish place where opposite emotions, detestation and admiration, abjection and attraction, curve round and meet.

The relationship between bullies and their victims is shot through with such paradoxical feelings, with a repulsion that is also a repressed desire, a hatred that is also a kind of love. After all, one of the etymological roots of the modern word 'bully' is its apparent opposite – namely, the sixteenth-century Middle Dutch word '*boele*', meaning: '*lover*'.

3

Sex Ed

In this, as in other things, fearlessness is the essence of wisdom.
Bertrand Russell, *On Education*

Over the years, the craze for 'feeling' other boys gradually died out, as words like 'poofter', 'gay', and, indeed, 'sex' became more defined, and tough boys shied away from any behaviour which they belatedly realised might be branded homoerotic. Forms of violence morphed, bifurcated: 'doing a rape', as Lee Hardwick's sidekick put it, belonged to girls, fists to other boys.

This decade-long process can be illustrated by my infrequent but regular encounters with another boy known as Stu 'The Cabbage' Cubbage. He was what you might call a *beta*-tough-boy. Even in the infants, he always looked like he'd once been an *alpha*-tough-boy, but had run to seed – perhaps as a baby, or before he was born.

Once a year, like clockwork, Stu would appear out of nowhere, and pick a fight with me, for no apparent reason. It reminds me of Herbert Pocket (the 'pale young gentleman') in Dickens's *Great Expectations*, who turns up out of the blue, and picks fights with Pip:

'Come and fight,' said the pale young gentleman.

What could I do but follow him?.... His manner was so final, and I was so astonished, that I followed where he led, as if I had been under a spell.

'Stop a minute, though,' he said, wheeling round before we had gone many paces. 'I ought to give you a reason for fighting, too. There it is!' In a most irritating manner he instantly slapped his hands against one another, daintily flung one of his legs up behind him, pulled my hair, slapped his hands again, dipped his head, and butted it into my stomach.

For Pip and Herbert, the 'reason for fighting' is ... well, fighting, in what is strangely circular logic. Herbert slaps and head-butts Pip, so Pip has to hit Herbert. This is the circularity of bullying: the reason for bullying is bullying, the reason for fighting is fighting, the reason for violence, at all levels, is violence, etc.

The reason for my clockwork fights with Stu 'The Cabbage' Cubbage was similarly circular. We'd fought the year before, so we should fight again. Perhaps there never was a first time. Perhaps we'd always already had a fight the year before, in reception class, in playgroup, as babies, shaking fists at each other from our mothers' wombs, wrestling in the cloudy realms of pre-existence and previous incarnations...

In my current incarnation, the earliest wrestling match I can recall with Stu Cubbage was at nursery school. Miss was reading a story to everyone. Stu and I were sitting at the back with a girl called Ann. We were all showing our bits to each other ('You show me yours if I show you mine', as the saying goes). The teacher seemed unaware, engrossed as she was in tales of the Three-Cornered Village and Roger Red Hat.

Suddenly, Stu Cubbage reached over and pinched my 'Roger Red Hat', as it were – and then shoved me over, kicking out at me.

'What's that for?' I asked, trying to get up, tears welling.

'Just because,' said Stu.

I kicked back at him. 'Take that.'

'Shhh,' whispered Ann, pulling up her pants.

Too late: Miss had looked up from the book. 'What're you doing over there? Not you two again. Jonathan, sit up. Both of you, pull up your trousers, for heaven's sake, and stop being silly.'

But we didn't stop it. Annually, from then on, we'd have a meaningless fight. Over the years, the fights evolved from pinches and shoves, to feeling, and then, in high school, to fists and painful kicks in the testicle(s). Though it goes unmentioned in *Great Expectations*, one peculiar aspect of boyhood fighting is its fixation on the groin area. By high school, however, this fixation was expressed as straightforward violence, having apparently lost its earlier alloy of sexual exploration: *kicking* was the new *feeling*.

Even in our teens, the violence burnt itself out quite quickly. The fights would start with 'Taylor! I hate you! We all hate you! I'm gonna kill you 'cos you're a weed! A girl! A bumchum! You play with dolls! You write poems! You lick teachers' bottoms! You're spineless and no one likes you! Go down the garden and eat worms!' – or something of that ilk. Unlike Lee Hardwick, I don't think Stu Cubbage cared what insults he bandied around. There was something about me he didn't like, for which he couldn't find the words. So he reached for whatever terms came to hand, in order to justify what he really wanted: fisticuffs. The words he used were only a pretext, the opening titles to the main event.

My encounters with Stu Cubbage hence never affected me as much as those with Lee. They were almost as absurd as Pip's fight with Herbert Pocket, full of pathetic insults from Stu, and dainty bitch-slaps from me. If, in my experience, bullying has always been first and foremost a linguistic phenomenon – where violent language is the primary condition, violent action secondary – Stu's periodic attacks were laughable failures.

In fact, most of my experiences of bullying at high school were partial failures (if not always laughable). In that sense, I was pretty lucky, and my experiences were relatively tame in the grand scheme of things. This book is by no means about how uniquely terrible my school days were. Some memoirs are about exceptional lives, some about representative experiences; this book leans towards the latter. Mine were common-or-garden experiences, neither exceptionally bad nor great, just representative of the time – and, in a displaced way, representative of other times, too. Like many people's, they were a weird mixture of the banal and horrible, the absurd and nasty, the silly and serious.

Naturally, they didn't feel like that when I was young. Back then they didn't feel relatively tame or representative of anything. Rather, they seemed harrowingly exceptional. Nothing is relativistic to a child – who, for the most part, lacks points of comparison beyond their own perspective – and it's all too easy for adults to forget how intensely children feel.[1] I certainly felt things very deeply as a kid.

But now, having been an adult for quite a long time, I'm well aware that what happened to me could have been a lot worse. As a white boy in the UK, I was cushioned from many of the more extreme forms of bullying. I witnessed, but was (obviously) not subjected to the kind of politicised bullying that's motivated by misogyny or racism. In that context, my schoolhood experiences were examples of what is sometimes categorised as 'personal bullying' (i.e. bullying that has no obvious political or sociological cause).

If I can see now that these experiences were fairly tame, one of the things that put them into perspective was, oddly enough, the personal bullying I underwent as an adult. For me, it was as a grown up, in the workplace rather than school, that I had my worst experience of bullying. It felt much more cruel and sustained than anything Stu Cubbage or Lee Hardwick ever doled out.

More on that later. Meanwhile, back at school in the 1970s and 1980s, bullying and physical violence seemed omnipresent, endemic, like chronic illnesses. But I was good at ducking, running away, avoiding exposed areas – the middle of playgrounds, for example, where danger came in 360°. And anyway, I was such a 'soft target' that the tough boys quickly got bored of hitting me. Yes, now and then, they'd back a Taylor or Pi or Steed into a store cupboard and knock him down. But there was no resistance, no challenge to it. So they'd go and punch someone more interesting instead.

---

[1] See also Chapter 6, 'History', on this subject.

What might have bound their punches together – a sustained linguistic framework, a shared language – never fully coalesced, except in the limited form of a recurring epithet ('Spineless', 'Poof', 'Boffin'). Lee Hardwick's beautifully choreographed reign of terror, towards the end of primary school, had perfectly combined a linguistic and physical regime, flitting between the two with the agility of a prima ballerina. By high school, though, this unstable compound was breaking down. The physical violence fragmented, became like rubble underfoot, through which pupils picked their way; while linguistic violence seemed to separate from it, ending up, for the most part, the preserve of girls and 'weedy boffins' (that is, those weaker kids who were supposed to be on the same side, but never really were).

Of course, the separation was never total. Physical and verbal violence remained correlates, uneasy bedfellows, even where one greatly predominated. Physical and linguistic violence may *appear* separate at times, yet in truth they always haunt each other. Bullying is an unstable compound that invariably includes both elements, even where one is repressed, off-stage, a kind of absent presence. One cannot exist without the other.

Stu 'The Cabbage' Cubbage, inarticulate as he was, couldn't abandon language entirely in his regular quest for Cabbage-on-Taylor violence: 'Boffin! ... Bumchum! ... Twat! ... Dickhead! ... Whatever!' His insults were weak chat-up lines for what was to follow ('Do you come here often? Fancy a drink? Or shall we skip the drinks and shag – I mean, fight?').

Stu would then casually inaugurate the main event with a swipe in my general direction. I'd duck and whine: 'Stop it, Cabbage, I don't want to fight' – and start walking away. But he'd patter after me on pudgy paws, pulling my arm, pinching me, kicking me between the legs, until I turned round: 'What d'you call me, Taylor? Oi, Taylor! Listen to me! You're ugly and gay and ugly and ... shit. And so's your mum. Turn round and fight, y'wuss!' Other kids would get wind of what was going on, and swarm towards us, attracted by that siren call: *Fight! Fight! Fight!*

Finally, with twenty kids surrounding us – chanting, shoving us at each other, like kids bashing their dolls together – we'd throw a few weak punches, there'd be some pinching and poking, a 'Chinese burn' or two, a little more testicle-orientated violence, and so on. After two or three minutes of huffing and puffing, I'd collapse on the floor, Stu would kick me, spit, and the crowd would disperse, grumbling at the anti-climax. Most school fights were anti-climactic, full of sound and fury and chants of *Fight! Fight! Fight!*, ultimately signifying nothing. Especially ours: Stu always 'won', but winning hardly gained him a medal, given that absolutely anyone who fought me won. My sister's dolls could beat me up.

Stu continued his uninterrupted winning streak till I left school. A few months later, I was mugged by two or three lads. It was night-time, too dark to see their faces. The next day, someone muttered that they'd heard from someone else who'd heard from someone else that Stu 'The Cabbage' Cubbage may have been involved. I shook my head. I knew for certain none of the muggers was him: our annual fight wasn't due.

The muggers hadn't seemed to want anything. They didn't take any money, and hadn't said much apart from a few inarticulate grunts and giggles. Even more than the Cabbage-Taylor annual scrap, this was pre-verbal violence – and asexual as well, in that none of them kicked me between the legs, let alone 'felt' me. I think they were just having a bit of fun, experiencing the unalloyed pleasure of returning to an infantile, pre-verbal, pre-sexual violence. Babies knocking over bricks, or banging xylophones. I was that day's xylophone, making different noises according to which part of me they banged – as it were.

As it were: even the word 'banged' has sexual connotations; even in the attempt to describe a supposedly asexual act of violence, language betrays me, implies something I didn't think was there. Violence, once described, once it enters into the English language, always seems to bear traces of sex, whether consciously or unconsciously. Something similar might be said of bullying. Just as it always seems to meld both linguistic and physical violence, so it always seems haunted by the language and physicality of sex – even when these things appear, at first glance, to be entirely absent.

For example: despite appearances, certain aspects of Pip's and Herbert Pocket's fight, in *Great Expectations*, could be (mis-)read as implicitly homoerotic. Pip is first put under a 'spell' by Herbert Pocket, seduced into following him to a 'retired nook'; Herbert then takes off most of his clothes, 'pulling off, not only his jacket and waistcoat, but his shirt too, in a manner at once light-hearted, business-like, and bloodthirsty'; both combatants minutely appraise the other's body, Herbert 'eyeing' Pip's 'anatomy as if he were minutely choosing his bone'; Herbert repeatedly ends up 'lying on his back' and 'finally went on his knees' in front of Pip – who, post-coitally (*as it were*) 'regarded [himself] … while dressing as a species of savage young wolf or other wild beast'.

Afterwards, Pip is filled with shame at what has happened with Herbert, fantasising about 'the pale young gentleman on his back in various stages of puffy and incrimsoned countenance'. So Pip attempts to expunge all physical evidence of the encounter: 'The pale young gentleman's nose had stained my trousers,' he says, 'and I tried to wash out that evidence of my guilt in the dead of night.' Maybe we're meant to assume that the stain, the 'evidence of … guilt', is blood, but 'nose' has sometimes been used as a euphemism for penis, and Pip doesn't explicitly state that the stain is blood. It could be a different bodily fluid. Language sometimes mixes up bodily fluids.

Such fluidic and linguistic mix-ups are particularly common at Pip's age, in pre- or early adolescence. In early wet dreams, before anyone had told me what sex was, I thought I was pleasurably weeing, usually in public. The dreams had nothing to do with what I later found out about sex. Before I understood the words 'sex' or 'sexual', before I knew what a 'wet dream' was, my dreams were about everything and nothing, polymorphously perverse – weeing, fighting, play-fighting, car crashes, explosions, fast-moving clouds, grass blowing in the wind. In his weird dream memoir, *My Education* (1995), William Burroughs says something similar. After a dream about packing, he gets an erection and asks himself: '*Does sex have anything to do with sex*? The whole ritual of sex, courtship, desire itself, the panting and sweating and positions, a sham, while the actual buttons are pushed offstage?'

In this sense, sex education – to use the term in its widest sense – is the process of ritualising sex, labelling the *on-stage* buttons ('sex', 'courtship', 'desire', 'panting', 'sweating', 'positions'), and repressing the off-stage ones (packing, weeing, fast-moving clouds, and so on). The process of learning about sex is also the process of limiting its sphere, containing it. I mean, what adult gets turned on by clouds (well, apart from 'nephophiliacs')? As French philosopher Michel Foucault suggests, in modern sex education, 'a certain reasonable, limited, canonical, and truthful discourse on sex was prescribed for [the child] ... enclosing [them] ... in a web of discourses ... discourses that were interlocking, hierarchized, and all highly articulated around a cluster of power relations.'

In other words, we learn the 'canonical' language of sex, and that serves to delimit and determine our conscious desires, as adults-to-be. We are inaugurated into a 'cluster of power relations', which set the boundaries of our sexual urges. While still young, these boundaries are policed by bullying and fear of ridicule (*Get this, everyone: ball-less-ballerina-Taylor fancies clouds!*); as we get older, they're enforced by other disciplinary and self-disciplinary systems. Something is gained in the whole process; fast-moving clouds are lost.

*

I can vividly recall the first few times I heard the word 'sex', in the 'sexual intercourse' sense, rather than the 'tick male or female' sense.

For instance, December 1983: I'm in the last year of primary school, and still half-believe in Santa Claus. I'm standing in the middle of our classroom. A girl called Fee is changing in one corner for a dance lesson. There are a couple of her friends there, and a couple of boys. One of the boys, a loud-mouth called Croggers, is staring straight at Fee. 'I like yer bra,' he says.

'Ta,' she says. 'All lacy, innit?'

'Taylor, look at her bra,' Croggers says.

I've been looking anywhere and everywhere except at Fee and her bra. But now she says to me: 'Yeah, you can look too if you like, Jonathan. Everyone else has.' So I look. It's a bra.

'Oh,' I murmur, 'that's nice.' My eyes wander again.

'You mean: *Corr*, more like,' says Croggers. 'Why aren't you staring at her proper? That's what she's there for.'

'I don't want to.'

'But she's got big tits,' he says. 'Everyone likes big tits.'

'Do they?' I ask.

'Course they do. Me brother says so. 'Cos big tits, they make you want to, like, *do it*.'

'Do what?'

'You know – have it off. Have *sex*.' He places heavy emphasis on the enchanted word, every time he says it. 'Look, Taylor, don't you know what *sex* is?'

I shake and nod my head, somehow at the same time. 'Isn't it whether you're a girl or boy?'

'Fee, get this: Taylor don't even know what *sex* is!'

Fee laughs. Everyone laughs – some more confidently than others.

'D'you want me to tell you what it is?' he asks.

'I dunno,' I say, honestly.

He's not listening, and assumes I've said yes. I think he's proud of his inside knowledge, and wants to share it with anyone who'll listen. 'Look, *sex*,' he speaks quietly, slowly, as if he's explaining where the Holy Grail is hidden, '*sex* is in the dictionary. So it's definitely a real thing. They call it *sexual intercourse* in there. That's the posh word for it. It's when a man's willy goes into a woman's hole and lays an egg. The egg grows and then they have a baby.' He demonstrates the action with his fingers, forming an 'O' shape with the thumb and forefinger of one hand, and poking the forefinger of the other in and out of it.

'Gosh,' I say, open-mouthed, staring at Fee's bra with a new sense of curiosity. She smiles at me, kindly, as she might at a pet.

'Taylor, just look it up in the big dictionary. I did. You can find out all sorts of dirty things in there. It's why me brother calls it a *dick-tionary*, 'cos it's all about stuff like sex and willies and eggs.' He grins – to an eleven-year-old, this is a brand-new joke, so he repeats it: '*Dick*-tionary – y'know, like *dick* – gerrit?'

Fee giggles too. 'I don't want no boy's eggs in me.'

'Bet you do,' says Croggers. 'You've got the biggest tits in the school.'

'I don't, it's yucky,' says Fee. She's buttoning up her blouse now. Tits and bra are hidden once more, and we all wander off – me, newly enlightened by the Wisdom of Croggers, towards the class dictionary.

It's the start, for me, of what two of the Brodie set, in *The Prime of Miss Jean Brodie*, call their 'research' into the meaning of sex. Like my own, their research is triggered by lighting upon the words 'sexual intercourse', because 'the very phrase and its meaning were new', and constituted 'a stupendous thought'. Thereafter 'they ... embarked on a course of research which they called "research", piecing together clues from remembered conversations illicitly overheard, and passages from the big dictionaries.'

My own course of research took place fifty years after Sparks's novel is set, but similarly relied on overheard conversations and big dictionaries, to fill in ellipses in my linguistic knowledge ('Sex is...', 'An erection is...', 'Wet dreams are...'). Dictionaries became my go-to *Encyclopaedia Britannica of Sex*, my aphoristic *Kama Sutra*, for unfamiliar terms, acts, insults, in lieu of much information from either school or family. My family rather enjoyed keeping me in the dark – my mother because, understandably, she preferred me as a wide-eyed innocent, a pre-pubescent Peter Pan, my elder sister and brother because my ignorance provided the perfect opportunity for sibling needling.

To be fair, very few siblings the world over would pass up an opportunity like that, myself included. In general, the nuclear family is a little machine for bullying, which kicks in automatically when a good opportunity presents itself. This is bullying-as-automated-domestic-appliance: sometimes brutal, sometimes gentle-affectionate, sometimes overflowing with *Schadenfreude*, sometimes over-heating and blowing a fuse.

My own family's casual teasing about sex started even before I embarked on my course of 'research' – a few months prior to Croggers directing me to the big dictionary (or big *dick-tionary*)...

It's a spring evening in 1983. I'm up a bit later than usual, in the living room with my mum and elder sister Karen. My dad's snoring in his corner chair, put to sleep by a strange melange of *The Guardian* on his lap, and a *Dallas* re-run on TV.

On *Dallas*, Pamela Ewing is pregnant. Her brother-in-law, J. R., is jealous. Not that he wants to be pregnant – rather, he wants to father the firstborn of his generation, who'll presumably inherit the family fortune, ranch, oil, skyscrapers, and ten-gallon hats. So, drunk, he shoves Pam off a ledge at the top of the Ewing barn. Outside the TV, in our living room, my sister squeals: 'Ooh, I know what he's doing – he wants Pam to lose the baby!' Cue titles.

Figure 3.1 A hierarchy of siblings, long before I could read dictionaries, c. 1979.

Meanwhile, I'm doing some colouring-by-numbers, only half-watching Pam's involuntary abortion. As a nine-year-old Stoke boy, I'm not that interested in oil, ranches, pregnancy, wealth, big hats.

Still, Karen's 'Ooh' partly attracts my attention, and I mutter in response. 'It's a silly story, anyway. It doesn't make any sense. She *can't* be pregnant.'

'Erm ... why doesn't it make sense?' my mum asks tentatively, as though holding her breath for what's coming. My sister's already sniggering from the carpet, where she's sitting, cross-legged. My mum nudges her with her slipper: 'Shhh.'

'I mean,' I say, still colouring, trying to stay in the lines, 'how can that nice Pamela be having a baby?'

'Well...' says my mum, slowly, 'people do. Women do.'

'Not if they're not married. You said that once. I'm sure you did. You can't have a baby if you're not married.'

Karen snorts. 'How d'you think it happens then?'

Surprised by the question and the accompanying snort, I glance up from my colouring-by-numbers. 'It happens when people get married. The man and lady decide they want babies, wish and wish, and then the lady gets one in her tummy. Sometimes they have to wait a long time, depending how lucky they are. It just ... happens.'

My sister's laughing openly now: 'You're getting how Jesus was born mixed up with ordinary babies. They don't "just happen". Pam Ewing isn't, like, the Virgin Mary or summit.' Karen curls up her lip: 'Bet you don't even know what *Virgin* means. You are stupid.'

'Be quiet, Karen,' says my mother, who's trying to keep a straight face, trying not to join in with Karen's laughter. Even my dad's snore-laughing in his sleep. Bit rich, really: laughing at your offspring for not knowing about the Birds and Bees when you've not so much as addressed the rudiments with them.

'I don't get it,' I say. If I had to colour my face by numbers at this moment, it'd be a number 1: scarlet. I feel like crying (tears, number 7: grey-white) like I do in dreams, where I walk into an unfamiliar room full of adults, probably *sans* Y-fronts, and everyone points and laughs at me.

'That's not quite right,' says my mother, treading carefully. 'You *can* have a baby out of ... wedlock. It happens occasionally. But it's not a good idea. You'll understand soon enough.'

Karen blows a raspberry: 'Oh, mum, you're so old-fashioned. Fuddy-duddy.' She turns and points at me. 'And as for you, you're an idiot. A dumb baby. Grow up. Mum, he needs to know! He needs to know about $s - e - x$!'

I've had enough: 'I do know. I do know!' I shout, over and over. 'Shut up, Karen! I do know!'

But I don't, and no one ever really tells me. Maybe, at some profound level, I still don't know, despite having twin daughters (somehow). Like many people of my generation, knowledge of sex came about in a jumbled, piecemeal way – a lurid colour-by-numbers collage of 'research', of 'clues from remembered conversations', and definitions 'from the big dictionaries', of *Carry On* films, Frankie Howerd comedies, trails of complicated underwear on apartment floors in *Dallas*, playground rumours, dirty postcards in Torquay newsagents, lingerie sections in mail-order catalogues – all accompanied by sexy saxophone music and/or swanee whistles.

As for areas of this elliptical sex-collage that were coloured in by formal education, they were few and far between. In the second year of high school, we were taught the sex life of flowers in Biology: stigmas, stamens, styles, pistils, pollination. Four weeks in a row, we copied down the same diagrams of these things from the blackboard, each time promised that we'd graduate to insects the following lesson.

At first, there were giggles, dirty jokes, as though the flower diagrams were cryptic pornography. By the fourth week, though, even Croggers had got bored of laughing at his own joke (*'Corr –* look at the stigmas on that'), and there were grumbles among the ranks: 'Miss, when do we get to the tits?', 'Miss, we can't shag flowers.' But Miss wasn't listening. She was distracted, ill (which perhaps explains the ever-repeating lesson), and by the fifth week, off sick. Maybe she was on maternity leave, surprised by her husband's stamen. Whatever the case, that was the end of our sex education. The supply teachers who replaced her retreated to safer territory, in the form of prehistoric life, asexual dinosaurs – well, apart from one cover teacher, a part-time magistrate, who showed us his collection of flavoured condoms and told us we could get AIDS from (and I quote) 'gay toilets'. *I kid ye not*, as Frankie Howerd might have said.

Meanwhile, at home, things weren't much better on the sex-ed front. My father was too ill, and probably too shy, to talk to me about sex. He barely managed to show me how to shave. My sister enjoyed my ignorance too much to share her knowledge. And my mother was out of her depth with anything that potentially involved rude big-dictionary words. She struggled with 'damn', let alone, God forbid, 'stamen'. So I never got any kind of Birds and Bees talk – only gaps, ellipses, filled in with guesswork and self-directed research.

My ignorance of the language of sex was at odds with certain physical developments in my own body. I'd been the first boy in the school whose voice had broken. At the same time, I was also the shortest, stuck for years at 4'8. Inevitably, such vocal dissonance – a tiny boy with a stammering bass voice – was the source of great amusement to girls at school. Physical incongruity, that is, gave rise to a form of linguistic bullying. It often does. Ridicule and laughter, as many theorists have suggested, frequently arise from the perception of incongruity; and incongruities are everywhere in adolescence: incongruities of voice, height, knowledge, weight, shape, smell, clothing, make-up, hobbies, and any combination thereof – all ripe for the picking, for others' entertainment. Hence why puberty can be so emotionally turbulent.

My own comic incongruity of voice with size was compounded by a well-known naïvety. My voice had broken, yet I knew next to nothing about sex. I was regularly asked questions about sex, just so everyone could laugh at my stammered responses and red face. It's a common enough trick, to weaponise someone's lack of knowledge in this way. Ignorance may be bliss, but not for the ignorant themselves – rather, for the bullies, for those in the know.

For me, this kind of bullying (ribbing, really) was gentle, the ignorance merely mortifying. For others, and especially the vulnerable, sexual ignorance can be a dangerous thing, the bullying potentially horrendous. The knowledge provided by a proper sex education, whereby people are given a language with which to understand what's happening to them, what might happen – this can be a vital defence against the worst kinds of sexual bullying.

*

No doubt things have improved since the 1970s and 1980s regarding Sex Ed. It's at least easier to look up words than it used to be. You might say too easy, given what horrors might turn up on a simple Google search.

And perhaps, in the end, you can't really win, or not entirely, anyway. As Foucault suggests, spelling things out can sometimes be as linguistically violent as ignorance when it comes to sex. Whether your sex education is riddled with ellipses or fully coloured-in-by-numbers, the entry into sexual language, the opening of a big *dick-tionary*, is itself a moment of psychological violence. Dawning linguistic knowledge – however that knowledge is gained – is a violent (gradual or sudden) shock, particularly when accompanied by physiological changes.

This is because language, and especially the English language of sex, is neither neutral nor objective, but riddled with 'cluster[s] of power relations' and violent hierarchies. Language is violent in itself, and this is particularly the case when it comes to sex: if, as I've said, it's true that descriptions of violence almost always bear traces of sex, the reverse is true too – that our language of sex usually bears traces of violence.

Such language hurts, bullies, ridicules, belittles, controls, sometimes through conduits (other people), sometimes with a force of its own.[2] A bully can't really oppress someone without language, but language can oppress someone without a bully. In this sense, you might say language is the bully of bullies, the *über*-bully. It is the overarching condition for bullying, the atmosphere in which bullying lives and breathes. It is the oxygen that

---

[2]See the note in Chapter 9, 'Extra-Curricular: Thanks, Notes, Contexts', on Les Murray's essay 'The Culture of Hell' (1994) and what he calls 'erocide'.

individual bullies inhale and then exhale as barbed words or insults or jokes ('Bumchum! ... Twat! ... Dickhead! ... Whatever!'). It is the air that victims inhale, and then hold their breaths until they burst. It is what makes auto-bullying so easy: all you need do is internalise the violent words surrounding you, and then you can hurt yourself.[3]

Of course, words hurt most when they're new – as they are to those first entering into the language of sex. I think we should be kinder to adolescents for that very reason.

Part of us probably doesn't want to enter into this language, doesn't want to open the big dictionaries, while another part feels compelled to do so. Part of me still thinks it was all one big mistake – that the dictionaries, Croggers, Stu Cubbage, Frankie Howerd, the flower diagrams got it wrong. After all, when I rewatched *Dallas* many years later, I found out that Pamela Ewing *was* married at the time she got pregnant. Maybe my initial hypothesis had been correct all along, and everything else a mere ellipsis...

---

[3]On different kinds of auto- or self-bullying, see also Chapters 5, 'R.E.' and 6, 'History'.

4

Practical: The Cane and the Fist

Part I. Theories, Equipment, Methods

> He that spareth his rod hateth his son: but he that loveth him chasteneth him betimes.
>
> Proverbs 13:24

In *Education and the Social Order* (1932), Bertrand Russell recounts a bullying incident he witnessed while visiting a school:

> I found one day in school a boy of medium size ill-treating a smaller boy. I expostulated, but he replied: 'The bigs hit me, so I hit the babies; that's fair.' In these words, he epitomised the history of the human race.

Hyperbole notwithstanding, the boy's behaviour certainly epitomises the more straightforward forms of physical bullying that happen in schools. In my high school, hard boy Danny Beaker hit moderately-hard-but-a-bit-flabby boy Stu Cubbage who then (periodically) hit school wimps, such as me. This was a simple case of what Russell calls 'an aristocracy of the physically strong' – a feudal system of bullying. In fact, because corporal punishment was still legal in English state schools until 1986, there was another layer above Danny Beaker in the aristocratic hierarchy, a kind of royalty; namely, the teacher with a cane.

The cane complicates Russell's model somewhat. A teacher with a cane might be smaller, weaker, than 'the bigs' in school; but the cane means he or she still wins out. So the 'history of the human race' isn't merely a simple matter of bigs hitting middles hitting babies, because babies or middles can hit back with canes – or clubs, or knives, or guns, or bombs, for that matter. Babies with bombs become, in effect, bigs (or, indeed, 'big-bigs'). And there are other, more complex ways that babies and middles can hit back, too, in what Nietzsche calls the 'revenge of the powerless': they can band together in gangs or societies; they can weaponise language; they can create laws, punishment regimes, penal systems; they can form religions, economic units, educational systems; they can wear suits, use big words, speak in posh accents, develop a whole semiotics of authority.

Nonetheless, Russell's model still lurks behind all the modifications of it. All of them are variations on a Bertrand Russell theme; all are haunted by the primal violence of bigs hitting middles hitting babies. In some of the variations, physical violence might seem invisible, almost absent, yet it lingers as a ghost in the language, or a distant threat. In workplaces, for instance, it lingers in the terms used by employers – one set of 'bigs' – for redundancy (*fired*, *sacked*), or in the unspoken threats to middles or babies posed by redundancy (physical deprivation, mental anguish, illness, and, in some societies, starvation).

Sometimes, of course, the physical violence of bigs hitting middles hitting babies is neither unspoken nor distant, but right there, in front of our faces...

It's June 1984. This morning, we're visiting our high-school-to-be, which we'll be joining in three months' time. We're in the big hall, standing in rows. The hall is divided into two: on one side are pupils from The Priory, upright in blazers and ties; on the other are pupils from my primary school, Ash Green, slouching in t-shirts, sweatshirts, shorts or flared skirts – all of us aghast at what's on stage and what's coming out of its mouth.

On the stage, towering above us, is a bulging suit, striding up and down, academic gown flaring behind – thump-thump-thump *turn* thump-thump-thump *turn* – like the cartoon hammers in

Pink Floyd's *The Wall*. The bulging suit is swishing a cane (or at least I think it/he is: however vividly I can see and hear that cane now, in my mind's-eye and -ear, I wonder if it's all a bit too pat – if the cane is a false memory, retrospectively imposed on an already terrifying scene as a kind of finishing touch, the *pièce de résistance*). With every swish of the (real or imagined) cane, the bulging suit recites one of the Gradgrindian school rules:

'Never go the wrong way round the one-way system.' *Swish.* 'Don't use biros. I *hate* biros.' *Swish.* 'Stand up straight during assemblies and don't faint. We don't do chairs here.' *Swish.* 'Tuck your shirt in.' *Swish.* 'The knot in your tie shouldn't be too tight or too loose.' *Swish.* 'Polish your shoes. You can always tell what someone is like from the state of their shoes. It's the first thing employers notice in a job interview.' *Swish.* 'Call male teachers "Sir". Don't call female teachers "Miss".' *Swish swish.* 'Never answer back.' *Swish.* 'Never chew gum. No sweets or drinks in class.' *Swish.* 'Don't wear your bag over your shoulder. You are not allowed rucksacks. Pupils in this school develop curved backs and long arms, because they have to hold their heavy bags by the handles, low to the floor.'

Bulging Suit makes a strange gurgle-snorting noise, pauses his catechism for a moment, and turns to face us. Although I can't see the face atop the suit from where I am standing – near the stage, staring almost vertically upwards at polished shoes, pressed trousers, jacket – I'm guessing there's the ghost of a smirk hanging somewhere above those shoulders. 'Yes, boys and girls, you'll all look like Neanderthal Man by the time you've finished here' – five swishes of the cane – 'in five years.'

My heart sinks: *five years – nearly half my lifetime so far. Go to Gradgrind Jail. Do not pass Go. Do not go round the one-way system the wrong way. Do not collect £200. And when you finally come out of jail in five years' time, you'll be hairy, square-jawed, dragging your knuckles along the floor. An adolescent Captain Caveman...*

I wish I could go back to that little four-foot-something boy now and tell him: *It's okay, five years will pass, it's not forever, and one day, in hindsight, it might even seem funny. One day you might write about it in a memoir*. But that's the problem: you can't go back, and, in that respect, a memoir is a sign of failure. A memoir isn't a real time machine. You can't really return to comfort the self back then, only write them a letter they'll never receive: *Dear Small-me, don't listen to Mr Bulging Suit. You will get out one day, and it'll all seem rather absurd in retrospect.*

'You may think I'm joking,' continues Mr Bulging Suit – 'joking' not being quite the word which springs to my panicking-back-then-child-mind – 'but there is a serious point here. You will change mentally and physically over the next few years. In my day, you know, there was no such thing as a teenager.' I wonder whether Bulging Suit's generation somehow skipped ages thirteen to nineteen; or, as seems more likely, the suit has never been anything but old. He is definitely of the 'old school' in his disciplinary methods – a phrase, as Dickens points out, 'generally meaning any school that seems never to have been young.'

'Unfortunately,' Bulging Suit continues, 'teenagers now do exist, and we have to deal with you lot, with the idea that bodies and minds go through so-called "changes" during teenage years. Our job as teachers is to *manage* those changes. Keep you in check. Teenagers all-too-easily go off the rails and behave badly. Our job as teachers is to *mould* you, make you better.' As he says this, he curves the cane almost to breaking point, no doubt to illustrate how he intends on moulding us. (Or that's what I remember him doing: again, perhaps my memory subsequently exaggerated the scene out of childish terror, conjuring canes out of thin air. So often, discipline works through people terrifying themselves).[1]

---

[1] See, in particular, Chapter 6, 'History', on this subject.

To the terrified mini-me, Mr Bulging Suit seems to loom over us, casting a shadow over the two halves of his audience: 'And the first thing we have to do,' he declares, 'is *mould* you into one school, one body, not separate schools shoved together. Once you are here, you will forget your previous school, whether it be The Priory or' – he coughs – 'Ash Green, and everyone will mix with everyone else. Our school uniform and rules and one-way system will help you forget, and you will owe loyalty to this school, not your previous one.'

I reckon Mr Bulging Suit is laying such emphasis on school unity because of something that happened a few months before. My older brother had come home with a bloody shirt, following a massive fight between ex-Priory and ex-Ash Green pupils. Apparently, half the high school had joined in. Police had been called.

I sneak a glance around me, and find it hard to imagine my fellow pupils from Ash Green winning such a fight – and even harder to imagine kids from the two schools forming a homogeneous community. At this point in its history, Ash Green is still, in part, an arty, liberal, post-hippy school – a Michael Goveian nightmare – where the majority of pupils, boys and girls alike, do Modern Dance classes with the lovely Mrs Dee. We wear spandex, and put on shows across the country, frolicking to Pink Floyd, Kate Bush, and Fiddler's Dram. The children at The Priory, by contrast, do not frolic. They wear ties, say 'Sir', and do Maths. I can't help feeling they're going to be more at home in secondary school than us high-kicking-jazz-handing Ash Greeners. A few of The Priorians are nodding appreciatively at what Mr Bulging Suit is saying

He's wrapping things up, rocking backwards and forwards on the balls of his feet: 'So ... we will look forward to seeing you in September.' He flexes the (real or imaginary) cane one last time, and it crosses my mind that by 'we' he means 'The Cane and I.' He rocks forward and towers darkly above us. I think maybe he's going to take off like a huge bat, after the cordial welcome to high school is over. Before he does so, though, he adds, in his deepest voice: 'But just remember this, boys and girls, above all else: THE ONE-WAY SYSTEM. *Never ever* go the wrong way round the school corridors. Or...' *Swish.*

The very first afternoon at high school, I get confused, and go round the one-way system in the wrong direction. As if Mr Bulging Suit has some magical power, some innate one-way-system radar, or is somehow omnipresent in all school corridors at once, there he is, glowering at me, flexing his cane. 'You are going the wrong way round my system, boy. *And* you've got your bag on your shoulder.'

I'm at a T-junction in the corridor. He's to my left. I squeak with terror, and turn right. There's a swish, and he's in front of me again. 'You are STILL going the wrong way round the system, boy.'

I panic: how can both ways be wrong? I turn away, but somehow, he's still in front of me: 'Not that way either. This is NOT a good start, is it?'

I'm shaking, determined not to cry: 'No, Mr ... Sir.'

'Mr Sir? What kind of name is that, boy?'

I don't know how to answer, so stay quiet.

'What is *your* name, boy?' he asks.

I answer too quietly, too quickly.

'Speak up.'

'It'sJonathanSirit'sJonathanTaylorSirthankyouSirsorrySir.'

'Oh dear,' groans Mr Bulging Suit, 'dear-dear-me. Not *another* member of the Taylor clan. I should have known. The Mongol Horde. Harbingers of Chaos.' He looks me up and down (or, rather, down and further down, given our relative heights). 'I see we're onto the runts now.'

'Yes, Sir. No, Sir. I'm sorry, Sir.' I want to add: 'Pleasepleaseplease don't cane me. I didn't mean to go the wrong way round the corridors. It's my first day. I got lost. I promise I'll never do it again.' But nothing comes out when I try to open my mouth.

In the end, he supplies the words for me. '*Never* do this again. It's your first day, so, with some reluctance, I'll let you off.' He forcibly turns me round, and propels me back the way I'd originally come. 'It's that way. Remember it. Don't let me see you again today, *Taylor*.'

He doesn't see me again that day, nor the next, because I stay at home, pretending to be sick.

For the next three years, Mr Bulging Suit remained a dark presence in school – a silhouette at the end of corridors, a giant bat overshadowing assemblies, the Grand Inquisitor of the one-way system. Grown-ups used to say things like: 'He's not *that* bad. At least you know where you are with a Mr B. S. He's straight down the line, old school, harsh but fair. You know exactly where he stands.' To which my childish response was: *yes, everywhere.* He seemed to stand everywhere I looked.

For the disempowered, those above them can seem to wield uncanny, magical powers. Fear makes the powerful seem near-omnipotent, omnipresent. As sociologist Max Weber suggests, charismatic leaders are often seen as 'endowed with supernatural, … superhuman … [or] magical powers', especially in 'primitive circumstances'. Mr Bulging Suit, to primitive mini-me, was a disciplinary necromancer, ready to appear in a puff of smoke and rustle of gown anywhere in the school. Well, anywhere apart from actual classrooms: by and large, he didn't teach much. He was too busy policing the sacred one-way system.

Occasionally, though, he did swoop down to one of our lessons, to cover an absent colleague. Every time he did so, I think it stunted my growth for a month. I was a mummy's boy, really, who'd been taught by female teachers during primary school; and my father seemed, for the most part, gentle. So to be in close proximity with a big booming alpha male with a stick came as a bit of a shock.

'You'll be overjoyed to know you've got me for French today, class 2A3. I've got my faithful cane with me, and there won't be any messing around. Unlike usual.' *Swish*. 'Understand? First off, I'll have silence. *Now*.'

Silence.

'Which way did I see you come down that corridor, Taylor?'

'Pardon, Sir?'

'Did you come into this room from the left or the right?'

'From the l...' – his features cloud over, so I change my answer – 'I mean right, Sir.'

'Good. Glad to hear it, Taylor.' He towers over my desk. 'I wouldn't want to think you were up to your old tricks.'

'No, Sir.' I gulp. In his shadow, I can't remember how I got here, or indeed who I am.

Thankfully, he turns away, doesn't ask me anything else for now. Instead, he addresses the whole class: 'Today, I'm giving you maps of the Paris Métro. You will tell me, in French, how to get from one station to another.'

It's the only lesson he ever seems to teach, finding the way round the Paris Métro. This seems apt, given his preoccupation with the one-way system in school. Here is a man obsessed with directions, whose entire aesthetic sense seems to revolve around the smooth running of traffic (whether of children or trains): 'It is a beautiful thing, the Métro,' he says. 'Complex, like a maze. But also dangerous. If you get lost...' He shakes his head and bangs his cane against one boy's desk. The boy jumps. I gulp again. Years later, part of me still worries that if I take the wrong London Underground or Métro connection, it'll end in caning (as opposed to Canning).

Every question Mr Bulging Suit fires at the class similarly feels like it might end in caning: 'You, boy: tell me how to get from Saint-Augustin to the Tuileries.' 'That girl there: tell me how to get from Saint Lazare to Gare d'Orléans-Austerlitz.' 'Taylor: tell me how to get from *This Place You're So Panicked You Can't Find It on the Map* to *Gare Caning de Caningsville*.'

My friend Steed, who's sitting next to me, comes to my rescue and points out the first station with a trembling finger. I start to stammer: '*Monsieur, je vais en train sur le ligne cinq pour quatre gares et puis je change à...*' – or rather, more accurately, '*Me ... mesh-err, je ... je ... je vayz on trains sir le line sink poor cat-re garrs eh pweess je ... je change at ... at ...*'

'What's that meant to mean?' interrupts Mr Bulging Suit. 'What kind of accent is that?'

'French, Sir. *Fron-sayz, me-sherr*.'

'No, it's not. It's *Stench*, that's what it is: *Stoke-French*. There's nothing more I detest than *Stench*. Speak properly, Taylor. I've heard better French accents from *mon chien. Wouaf wouaf*!' He hits a desk with his cane and barks again: '*Wouaf wouaf*! That's how French dogs talk, you know. They have proper accents.'

Steed next to me giggles. Mr B. S. spins round and fixes him with a stare that would turn *chiens* to stone. He points the end of the cane at his new victim. '*You* can answer instead,' B. S. says, 'but it had better be in *un accent approprié*. Or' – he waves his cane – '*Wouaf wouaf*!'

I breathe a sigh of relief. It's no longer me on the spot, in the firing line. Okay, so it's my mate Steed, and he helped me a minute ago, and is now going an agonising red. But the hard truth is that this is every-pupil-for-themselves. This is Survival of the Fittest. Or Survival of the Least-Worst-Stench-Accent. Or Survival of the Pupil with the Best Sense of Direction. I can't help thinking Mr Bulging Suit's *chien* would win on all counts. Especially if it had *un bâton*.

This was the Darwinian Era of my schooldays. Until corporal punishment was officially banned, violence seemed to permeate the school, from teachers to 'bigs', to 'middles', to 'babies', and sometimes back again, in the great struggle for life. I'm not claiming it was an exceptionally rough school. It wasn't. By Stoke comprehensive school standards, it was quite decent, really, and I certainly didn't hate everything about it. No: the point is that an education system which uses corporal punishment is tacitly sanctioning physical violence at all levels. As Russell says, 'If the grown-ups exercise force in their dealings with the older children, the older children will, in turn, exercise force in their dealings with the smaller ones', and so on and so forth.

At my school, the two deputies were at the apex of this force-food-chain, as top predators – Mr Bulging Suit and his female counterpart, Mrs Formidable Bosom, who could telekinetically make my nose bleed just by entering a room. They caned misbehaving boys and girls respectively (only a woman could cane a girl, only a man could cane a boy, because homoerotic violence was, for some reason, more socially acceptable than heterosexual violence). Next down the chain from them were other teachers, who would occasionally throw board rubbers at kids, pick them up by their ears, or scrape their noses against walls. Caned, ear-stretched, or nose-scraped kids would then go on to hit other kids, who would hit smaller kids, and then they'd be caned too. And it wasn't all a one-way system, more a Paris Métro of interweaving lines of violence: occasionally, a Danny Beaker would lash out at a teacher, and be suspended for a little while. Or, at least, caned.

Up to a point, this Métro of violence was tolerated as part and parcel of growing up. In retrospect, it feels like different kinds of violence were everywhere in the 1970s and early 1980s, tying kids up in coloured lines, connecting up corporal punishment with playground bullying with home life with the Falklands War with miners' strikes – and even with children's comics and TV programmes. I mean, almost every story in *The Beano* ended with Dennis the Menace or The Bash Street Kids being beaten. As for TV programmes, well, there was *Jim'll Fix It*, which, it turns out, existed on a different plane of horror.

As a younger kid, I'd written to the programme, asking the kind white-haired gentleman who presented it for a ride in the *Chitty Chitty Bang Bang* car. Given what we now know of that presenter, it was a good job I never got an answer. In fact, I wonder if I only escaped a terrible fate because I misaddressed the letter. I thought his actual name was Jimll, so I'd started my letter, 'Dear Jimll'. In Chapter 3, I suggested that, since bullying is first and foremost a linguistic phenomenon, an inadequate grasp of language can sometimes alleviate its worst excesses.[2] In this (rather different) scenario, I can't help feeling that bad spelling might have saved my life.

Of course, *Jimll* was a uniquely horrific case, out on a terrible limb, the very final *gare* of a Métro line. Yet as such he was still part of a network, still distantly connected to a whole map, an entire traffic system of violence. *Jimll*'s violence was tolerated, even enabled, by that system for decades.

On a more general and more prosaic level, the system tolerated violence because it was, and sometimes still is, seen as 'character-building', as an education in itself. It helps prepare kids for the brutal dog-eat-dog reality of the grown-up world. Violence, bullying, bigs hitting middles hitting babies – these are transferable skills: the games of soldiers played by kids are preparation for the games of soldiers played by adults. The attitude still haunts education, sometimes in overt, sometimes in displaced forms. For example, in a notorious 2010 article, 'Sorry, But It Can Be GOOD for Children to Be Bullied', psychologist Helene Guldberg writes:

Stamping out bullying, saying no to bullying, zero tolerance on bullying ... are sentiments intended to protect pupils from every unpleasant playground experience.... But in reality they are robbing them of the opportunity to learn some of life's most valuable lessons.... The result across the country

---

[2]Conversely, this goes some way to explain why, at least in my experience, it's generally been intelligent and articulate adults who are the most adept bullies, given their sophisticated command of language. I discuss adult bullying in Chapter 7, 'Politics'.

is sanitised playgrounds where bullying is such a dirty word that disputes and incidents, which not so long ago would have formed an important part of childhood development, are being treated like capital crimes.... But most [children] benefit from a little exposure to the knocks that life will inevitably deliver.... Without the chance to fight their own corner, to find solutions and to make amends, today's children will lack fundamental social skills as adults.... It [all] implies that a person has the right to expect everyone they meet to be unfailingly pleasant and kind.... Children are growing up without the social skills or toughness to exist and compete in the adult world. To me, that seems far more damaging to their development and their relationships with each other than any fight or insult could ever be.

Guldberg's argument here, like that of many arguing for the 'character-building' model of school, lives or dies on one basic principle: namely, the assumption that the adult world is tough, competitive, nasty – that it is unreasonable to expect everyone you meet as a grown-up to be 'pleasant and kind'. Bullying, physical and psychological violence, it is assumed, are necessary in school because they provide children with the 'social skills and toughness' to deal with what is an even worse adult world. As psychologists Rosalyn Shute and Philip Slee put it, this is the idea that 'school bullying is just a reflection of normal human competitive behaviour, and children simply have to learn to deal with it'.

It's an all-too-familiar argument, and one, with its language of 'fighting your own corner', 'competitiveness', 'survival', that is informed by a casual Social Darwinism. Bullying is natural, inevitable; bullying is Survival of the Fittest; bullying in childhood is preparation for the brutal-every-person-for-themselves struggle for existence in the capitalist world beyond the playground.

The objections to this kind of argument are the same as the oft-rehearsed objections to Social Darwinism in general: namely, that there is nothing inherently 'natural' about modern capitalist society; that Survival of the Fittest isn't really about the sorts of linguistic, psychological, or financial competitiveness common in the human world; that the whole economic analogy is founded on a reductive reading of natural selection; and that nature, Darwinian or otherwise, is so infinitely varied, it can be pressed into service for all sorts of contradictory ideologies. This is especially the case when it comes to notions of the supposed naturalness, or otherwise, of bullying. As educationalist Ken Rigby writes,

It is sometimes said that bullying is a natural and indispensable feature of the way nature works. In Darwinian terms, it serves an evolutionary purpose: it ensures that the fittest survive.... Parallels are certainly there between some animal and human behaviours of the kind we can call bullying. But the conclusions we may draw are far from clear. Depending on where we look [in nature], ... we can find support for a variety of views: that bullying is good for us; that bullying is an unspeakable evil; that bullying is the means by which we can, and sometimes do, protect ourselves from 'outsiders'.

Unlike Guldberg, most modern psychologists and educationalists don't subscribe to the view that 'bullying is good for us.' For Shute and Slee, the idea 'that bullying is "character forming"' is 'dangerous ... as ... evidence about the effects of being bullied suggest that far from being advantageous, prolonged bullying is likely to damage "character"'. Instead of preparing kids for the adult world, it can cause long-term psychological damage. As Ellen Walser deLara suggests in her book, *Bullying Scars*, 'bullying, harassment, and hazing ... can have serious and lifelong implications' that are not 'left behind at graduation.... Research establishes that both bullies and victims can experience lifelong depression, anxiety, difficulties in relationships, ... an inability to trust others [and] ... post-traumatic stress disorder [PTSD].'

Many literary authors have understood the lifelong effects of bullying, and have explored them in stories, poetry, and drama. The 1970s and 1980s TV series *Tales of the Unexpected*, for instance, is full of middle-aged men (and it is usually men) haunted by violent schoolboy traumas. In an episode called 'The Stinker' (1980), Denholm Elliott experiences flashbacks to his long-gone schooldays, and eventually takes (misplaced) revenge on his former bully. In the episode 'Galloping Foxley' (1979), based on a Roald Dahl story, an ageing commuter becomes convinced that the man sitting opposite him on the train is the prefect who, long ago, mercilessly tortured him at Repton. The trauma of those days returns with full force, decades later.

One poet who comprehends both the immediate trauma *and* long-term effects of bullying is Adrian Mitchell. In his poem 'Back in the Playground Blues' (1982), Mitchell brilliantly satirises the kinds of opinions espoused by Guldberg *et al.* He turns her Social Darwinist assumptions on their head: rather than school bullying being a (relatively mild) training ground for the brutal competitiveness of adulthood, for him, it is the playground world that is worse. It is the playground world which is explicitly violent, prejudiced, lawless, in a way that far surpasses the adult world, however bad the latter might be:

I dreamed I was back in the playground, I was about four feet high
Yes dreamed I was back in the playground, standing about four feet high
Well the playground was three miles long and the playground was five
    miles wide

It was broken black tarmac with a high wire fence all around
Broken black dusty tarmac with a high fence running all around
And it had a special name to it, they called it The Killing Ground

Got a mother and a father, they're one thousand years away
The rulers of The Killing Ground are coming out to play
Everybody thinking: 'Who they going to play with today?'

                Well you get it for being Jewish
                And you get it for being black
                You get it for being chicken
                And you get it for fighting back
                You get it for being big and fat

Get it for being small
Oh those who get it get it and get it
For any damn thing at all

Sometimes they take a beetle, tear off its six legs one by one
Beetle on its black back, rocking in the lunchtime sun
But a beetle can't beg for mercy, a beetle's not half the fun

I heard a deep voice talking, it had that iceberg sound
'It prepares them for Life' – but I have never found
Any place in my life worse than The Killing Ground.[3]

*

For me, The Killing Ground was as much the classroom as the playground. While at primary school it was other kids who caused me most hassle, at secondary school, by contrast, I lived in fear of the teachers. Of course, break times were scary; of course, I haunted the corners of playgrounds, kept my back against the fence, so nothing could come at me from behind; of course, there were insults, and punches, and kicks; but these things were the white noise of school, the incidental music to a monster movie. The real terrors – Mr Bulging Suit, Mrs Formidable Bosom, and other frightening teachers – stalked the classrooms, gigantic, inexorable, like stop-motion prehistoric beasts. Yes, the kids had fists and invective, but the big-big beasts possessed *The Cane*. And, like a primitive in the film *One Million Years B.C.*, I'd developed a fetishistic reverence for The Cane, an abject fear of its totemic power.

Maybe that's one reason why, for some, the cane (or The Cane) becomes a *sexual* fetish in later life: it symbolises an uncanny flashback to the magical beliefs of childhood. Sadomasochism, as Freud suggests, can represent the exciting revival in adulthood of 'primitive' childish terrors and idolatries. This is especially the case in

---

[3]'Back in the Playground Blues' is cited here in full with the kind permission of the Estate of Adrian Mitchell, granted by United Agents Ltd.

England, where use of the cane was, until recently, so widespread that it led the French to term it 'The English Vice', and George Bernard Shaw to claim that the English suffered from '*flagellomania*':

We are tainted with *flagellomania* from our childhood.... It has always been a vice, craved for on any pretext by those depraved by it.... Other methods and other punishments were always available: the choice of this one betrayed the sensual impulse which makes the practice an abomination.

According to Shaw, that is, the choice of caning as the dominant form of punishment was determined by a 'sensual impulse', first shaped in childhood, for inflicting and receiving pain. Brutally caned ('tainted') as children, the English grew up to enjoy inflicting that same pain on the next generation, and so on, and so forth. For Shaw, the English were stuck in a self-perpetuating cycle of child abuse, of sadomasochistic *flagellomania*.

Notwithstanding the cane's demise as a centre of gravity, I wonder if the English remain, in many ways, a nation of sadomasochists. After all, what is the class system if not a system of institutionalised sadomasochism? Deep down, it seems to me, the English want pain, want to be bullied, and often seem to embrace these things, in education, as in politics, as in the weather.

I don't quite get it myself. Despite my own Englishness, sadomasochism isn't my chosen vice (believe it or not). I personally can't see the attraction of being beaten, or beating someone else, with a stick. Perhaps I was just *too* straightforwardly terrified by the cane for it to become a playful symbol of sexual excitation, for it to gain ambivalence enough to work both as an object of pain and a bringer of pleasure. Perhaps because it remained for me a terrible yet unrealised threat, its power was never circumscribed by reality, never diminished by experience, to the extent that it might become exciting. Perhaps somewhere, deep inside, I'm still terrified of the cane, still a trembling eleven-year-old boy, prostrating myself before this magical totem of disciplinary power. Or perhaps I'm lying to myself and/or to you. Who knows?

What I do know now is that the cane or The Cane was the magical totem, the wooden phallus, of a whole system of (for me, primarily patriarchal) violence. It was the central symbol of an institutionalised hierarchy of bullying: teachers caning bigs hitting middles hitting babies. To be on the wrong end of The Cane was the constant threat and ultimate punishment; to wield The Cane was to possess ultimate power in the tribe – think of a tool-using ape brandishing the first bludgeon among his defenceless peers. All discipline in the school-tribe led back to The Cane: who had it, who was threatened with it, who was beaten with it.

The problem with all this is that it's hard to balance an entire disciplinary system on one narrow stick. The system's liable to totter, fall off. In a tribe where only one ape has a bludgeon, eventually the other apes will try to nab it.

Something similar can happen in schools – as is the case in a famous scene in Dickens's *Nicholas Nickleby* (1838-9), where the hero intervenes on his friend Smike's behalf, and wrests the cane from the despotic headteacher of Dotheboys Hall, Wackford Squeers. The latter has just threatened to 'flog' the drudge Smike to 'within an inch of [his] ... life':

Squeers caught the boy firmly in his grip; one desperate cut had fallen on his body – he was wincing from the lash and uttering a scream of pain – it was raised again, and again about to fall – when Nicholas Nickleby suddenly starting up, cried 'Stop!' in a voice that made the rafters ring.

'Who cried stop?' said Squeers, turning savagely round.

'I,' said Nicholas, stepping forward. 'This must not go on.... I will not stand by!'...

He had scarcely spoken, when Squeers, in a violent outbreak of wrath, and with a cry like the howl of a wild beast, spat upon him, and struck him a blow across the face with his instrument of torture, which raised up a bar of livid flesh as it was inflicted. Smarting with the agony of the blow, and concentrating into that one moment all his feelings of rage, scorn, and indignation, Nicholas sprang upon him, wrested the weapon from his hand, and pinning him by the throat, beat the ruffian till he roared for mercy.

Without his 'instrument of torture', Squeers is powerless. He begs for mercy, and is ultimately rendered 'stunned and motionless'. The cane is his one and only means of maintaining authority – he has no other form of discipline, no intellect, no reciprocal respect from the schoolboys, who 'move … not, hand or foot' to help him.

Unlike, say, intellect or respect, the cane all too easily changes hands. The cane is fickle, promiscuous. And, above all, the cane is ambivalent – at once a potent symbol of authority, an 'instrument of torture', and also a symbol of instability, even weakness. At the moment of caning, the moment the cane is held aloft, the moment when the Wackfords of the World might *seem* to be at their most powerful, other dangerous, revolutionary possibilities open up: a Nickleby might just intervene, shout 'Stop!', wrest the cane from the caner's grip, turn the cane on the caner.

For me, first coming across this scene in *Nicholas Nickleby* was a revelatory and liberating experience. It helped to dispel, or destabilise, my childish idolatry, my unquestioning faith in The Cane's straightforward omnipotence.

There's a 1950s pessimistic replay of the Nickleby-Squeers scene in Alan Sillitoe's short story, 'Mr Raynor the Schoolteacher' (1959). Sillitoe's teacher is more interested in ogling female assistants in the shop opposite his classroom, than in teaching R.E. to the school kids. This gives the latter licence to misbehave while his attention is distracted, and a disruptive pupil with the apt name of Bullivant (*Bully-much*) starts 'thumping the boy at the desk in front with all his might'. As the pupil's denotive name might suggest, the story is almost an allegory of bullying. It stages a school power struggle, where the 'big' (Bullivant) hits the 'middle', and is then, in turn, hit by the teacher (the 'big-big').

In the latter half of the story, Mr Raynor finally takes notice of Bullivant's behaviour, and tells him to come out to the front:

Bullivant slouched out between rows of apprehensive boys. ''e 'it me first,' he said, nearing the blackboard.

'And now I'm going to hit you,' Mr Raynor retorted, lifting the lid of his desk and taking out a stick....

'Y'aren't gooin' ter 'it me,' [Bullivant] ... said. 'I ain't dun owt to get 'it, yer know.'

'Hold out your hand,' Mr Raynor said....

No hand was extended towards him as it should have been. Bullivant stood still, and Mr Raynor repeated his order....

'Y'aren't gooin' ter 'it me wi' that,' Bullivant said again....

[Mr Raynor] stepped to Bullivant's side and struck him several times across the shoulders with the stick, crashing each blow down with all his force. 'Take that,' he cried out, 'you stupid defiant oaf.'

Bullivant shied away, and before any more blows could fall, and before Mr Raynor realised that such a thing was possible, Bullivant lashed back with his fists, and they were locked in a battle of strength.... 'You ain't 'itting me like that,' Bullivant gasped between his teeth. 'Oo do yo' think yo' are?'

The fight ends in a kind of 'truce', whereby neither Mr Raynor nor Bullivant come out on top, and the lesson resumes. Mr Raynor reassures himself: 'What did it matter, really? Bullivant and most of the others would be leaving in two months.'

Nonetheless, in the meantime, Raynor has lost his authority with both Bullivant and the class as a whole. He's been asked: 'Oo do yo' think yo' are?', and the cane he uses to 'keep [the boys] ... in check' has been challenged, demystified. It's no longer the infallible symbol of power it was prior to the confrontation. In a straight fight between Mr Raynor and his cane, on the one hand, and Bullivant and his fists, on the other, there has been no outright winner.

Perhaps there never are outright winners in school; perhaps it's almost always a matter of uneasy truces, stand-offs, between Raynors and Bullivants. In Sillitoe's story, the two characters come to an unspoken agreement in not 'spinning out trouble to its logical conclusion', in not pursuing the confrontation to its bitter end – unlike, say, the fight between Nickleby and Squeers, where the former does knock the latter out, nearly kills him. Their fight ends in 'Squeers striking his head' on a bench, and Nicholas has to 'ascertain ... that Squeers was only stunned, and not dead (upon which point he had had some unpleasant doubts at first).'

This is the 'logical conclusion' of confrontation in a school like Dotheboys Hall: the potential death of teacher or pupil. As Russell puts it, in an education system founded on a 'struggle for power', on the violence of bigs hitting middles hitting smalls, 'moral training [has] ... homicide as the apex of a virtuous life, to which everything else leads up'. Writing as he was between two world wars, Russell is ostensibly talking about ways in which education trains people for the 'legal' homicide of warfare *after* school. At the same time, though, he's also implying something about the role of homicide *within* school – namely, that 'moral training' points the way towards homicide, that homicide is the unspoken apex of 'virtuous' education. School, in other words, is potentially murderous.

This is most obvious in an education system like the one envisioned by Helene Guldberg, where violence is tolerated or even morally sanctioned ('It Can Be GOOD for Children to Be Bullied'). Guldberg complains that, in the 'sanitised' education system of today, 'disputes and incidents, which not so long ago would have formed an important part of childhood development, are being treated like *capital crimes*'. She tries to downplay the 'little ... knocks' that children receive at school; but what Dickens, Russell, Sillitoe, and Mitchell all suggest is that there is an element of school violence which is implicitly homicidal, which might just tip over into a 'capital crime'.

Anti-bullying activist Michele Elliot points out that common perceptions of bullying range across a whole spectrum, from
'harmless fun' to 'murder'. While Guldberg clearly leans towards
the former attitude, Dickens, Russell, Sillitoe, and Mitchell see
murder as the 'logical conclusion' of bullying and its correlate,
corporal punishment. Bullying might just become a capital crime;
corporal punishment might shade into capital punishment. *I'll kill
you, Taylor*: this is the ultimate threat posed by institutionalised
violence. If a cycle of bullying is not arrested in time, if blind eyes
are turned, the cycle might become a spiral, ending in homicide or
suicide. Homicide haunts the so-called 'play' in Mitchell's poem,
where the playground is 'The *Killing* Ground' (my italics), and
where beetle vivisection is compared to childhood cruelty; it is the
unspoken possibility that lies behind Bullivant's 'battle of strength'
with Mr Raynor; it is the threat made by Squeers to Smike, and one
possible outcome of Nickleby's fight with Squeers.

In some other texts, the outcome of bullying is literally death.
There's William Golding's still terrifying *Lord of the Flies* (1954);
there's Susan Hill's claustrophobic *I'm the King of the Castle*
(1970); there's J. D. Salinger's 1951 novel, *The Catcher in the Rye*,
where one boy throws himself out of a school window after being
bullied; and there's the 1989 movie *Dead Poets Society*, where one
of the characters kills himself, partly because of a bullying father.
As well as fictional casualties, there have been a number of notorious real-life cases of school bullying which have ended in murder
or suicide. The massacre at Columbine High School (Colorado) in
1999, which involved both mass murder and suicide, was seen by
many as the vengeful end-point of a cycle (or spiral) of bullying.

No doubt such cases are rare(ish). For the most part, the murderous promise of bullying remains metaphorical (as in Mitchell's
poem), unspoken (as in Sillitoe's story), or unfulfilled, a matter
of almost-but-not-quite (as in Dickens's novel, where Nickleby
doesn't *quite* kill Squeers, and Squeers flogs Smike to 'within
an inch of ... [his] life' [my italics]). It exists, to a lesser or greater

extent, as an unrealised threat. If it were realised – if, say, Bullivant did kill Mr Raynor, or vice versa – then the 'struggle for power' would presumably be over. Power struggles, disciplinary systems, and abusive relationships depend on the survival of both parties. It's hard to imagine bullying carrying on after a victim is dead; a corpse presumably can't bully or be bullied. In that sense, murder is the absent presence implied by bullying – the ever-present-but-generally-never-realised threat within it.

Philosophy: An Interlude

German philosopher G. W. F. Hegel says something similar in his famous 'Master and Slave Dialectic' – a short passage in his book *Phenomenology of Spirit* (1807), which might be (mis-)read as an abstract paradigm, an archetypal pattern, for bullying. Using characteristically obscure but suggestive language, the dialectic posits two 'self-conscious individuals' engaging in a 'life-and-death struggle', in which 'each stakes his own life, [and] … each must seek the other's death'. This primal struggle results in the victor enslaving the other – that is, one becoming master (a.k.a., for our purposes, bully), one slave (a.k.a. victim). In other words, the master-slave (or bully-victim) relationship depends for its existence on an odd kind of struggle that is both murderous and not *really* murderous – not spun out to its logical conclusion.

If pursued to its bitter end, Hegel suggests, the 'trial by death … does away with the truth which was supposed to issue from it', leaving those 'who survived this struggle' alone, 'without the required significance of recognition' from another. For Hegel, 'death is the natural negation of consciousness', and this applies *both* to the dead *and* the living: the latter are stranded in a kind of limbo, without the limited 'recognition' afforded by an underling.

Hence it is in the master's interest to keep the underling alive, and not pursue the struggle to its murderous conclusion. The same goes for the bully-victim relationship: the bully might threaten the victim with homicide (literal or metaphorical – *I'm gonna kill you, Taylor!*), but it's generally an empty threat. If the bully actually kills the victim, the former loses their status: you can't carry on being a bully without a live victim. As French psychoanalyst Jacques Lacan puts it, 'in the end, the loser [of the life-and-death struggle] must not perish if he is to become a slave'.

The inevitable result, according to Lacan, is some kind of 'pact', whereby the master agrees not to kill the slave, in return for the latter's subjugation. This pact is analogous with the 'truce' between Bullivant and Mr Raynor. The two of them tacitly agree not to pursue their 'battle of strength' to its conclusion; and this agreement restores the illusion of hierarchical equilibrium, whereby they resume, albeit superficially and temporarily, their teacher-pupil relationship. Mr Raynor, in particular, needs the truce in order to maintain his position as schoolmaster. Otherwise, he or Bullivant might end up dead, and either outcome would clearly destroy his authority. The master keeps the victim alive, in order, as Hegel says, to achieve 'recognition through another consciousness'.

What is the nature of the 'recognition' gained by the master or bully from the victim? Hegel claims, again in typically abstract language, that it consists in witnessing 'that the other consciousness sets aside its own being-for-self, and in so doing itself does what the first does to it'. To put this another way: the bully gains a sense of satisfaction from the victim's acknowledgement of his or her power, and corresponding self-debasement. In that sense, the bully's form of recognition might be understood as a kind of sadistic pleasure. This is most obvious in Mitchell's poem, where the bullies 'sometimes ... take a beetle, tear off its six legs one by one', but 'a beetle can't beg for mercy, [so] a beetle's not half the fun'. In begging for mercy, the victims are providing the bullies with sadistic 'fun'.

This type of sadistic recognition belongs not only to playground bullies, but also to some 'parents and schoolmasters'.

As Bertrand Russell suggests, they experience the 'pleasures ... derived from inflicting chastisement' – pleasures which reinforce the 'adult's convenience and sense of power'. In a word: *flagellomania*. Smike, in *Nicholas Nickleby*, provides Mr and Mrs Squeers with just such a sadistic form of recognition, when he begs for mercy:

'Spare me, sir!' cried Smike.

'Oh! that's all, is it?' said Squeers. 'Yes, I'll flog you within an inch of your life, and spare you that.'

'Ha, ha, ha,' laughed Mrs Squeers, 'that's a good 'un!'

Mrs Squeers is clearly enjoying herself in witnessing Smike's physical debasement, his abject plea for mercy. Paradoxically, her *flagellomanic* pleasure also depends on Smike's plea being accepted: Mr Squeers agrees 'magnanimously' (and humorously, in Mrs Squeers's opinion) to spare Smike's life. Her sadistic pleasure, that is, depends on both Smike's torture *and* on his survival. Otherwise, it would be homicide, not bullying, and that would presumably not be so funny. All that separates one from the other is, as Mr Squeers states, 'an inch'.

That inch has been important to other sadistic torturers throughout history. According to the Roman historian Suetonius, several of the Caesars deliberately kept their victims alive, so they could enjoy witnessing their pain, their pleas for mercy. Emperor Tiberius enjoyed inflicting 'prolonged and exquisite tortures', and

used to punish with life those who wished to die. He regarded death as a comparatively light affliction.... Once, during a jail inspection, a prisoner begged to be put out of his misery; Tiberius replied, 'No; we are not yet friends again.'

Similarly, Tiberius's successor, Gaius Caligula, enjoyed watching victims stabbed with 'numerous small wounds, avoiding the

A Physical Education

prisoner's vital organs, and his familiar order "Make him feel that he is dying!" soon became proverbial'. In one instance, he 'watched the manager of his gladiatorial and wild-beast shows being flogged with chains for several days running, and had him killed only when the smell of suppurating brains became insupportable'.

It may well seem over the top to compare school bullying with the near-apocalyptic cruelty of a Caligula. But Squeers's flogging of Smike does come close to Caligula's treatment of the gladiatorial show manager. And if this Yorkshire Caligula's cruelty is *physically* close to the Ancient Roman model, the violence captured in Mitchell's poem is *metaphorically* close to it: tearing a beetle's legs off one by one is a kind of 'prolonged and exquisite torture', which inflicts pain without the insect actually dying. Again, Mitchell's metaphor, like my Caligula analogy, may seem hyperbolic to an adult reader. But maybe the point is that it wouldn't seem so hyperbolic to a child 'four foot high' who is stuck on The Killing Ground 'one thousand years away' from his or her parents. To him or her, it might seem all too real.

It can sometimes seem all too real to an adult too. In my first permanent teaching job, I knew someone who, at least to me, was a kind of Caligula, ruling her own micro-Roman Empire with sadistic glee. There was no physical violence, but psychologically I got the impression she wanted to flog me to within an inch of my life – and no further. Professor Caligula didn't want me to die; she didn't even want me to leave. She wanted me there, alive, at the centre of her Killing Ground, begging for mercy, a legless beetle on its back.

More on that lovely subject in Chapter 7. For now, though, what I want to emphasise is how Hegel's abstract paradigm helps me to understand my own beetle-like experiences, and how those experiences might relate to other bully-victim scenarios. Just as the term 'bullying' can be used in all sorts of different contexts, for all kinds of abusive relationships, so Hegel's 'Master-Slave Dialectic' provides a framework which can encompass (and connect) everything from Caligulian tyranny to so-called 'office politics' – everything from physical torture to corporal punishment to playground bullying. And these things *are* connected, at the same time as being very different. After all, Wackford Squeers himself likens his role as brutal headmaster to that of 'a slave driver in the West Indies.'

It's not a matter of saying that these things (slave driving, headmastering, bullying, tyrannising) are the same, or of comparing them – I mean, how can you compare or rank different levels of cruelty anyway? There's no objective scale on which you can compare manifestations of bullying with each other. What to one person is mere everyday joshing is to another breakdown-inducing abuse. To the near-suicidal victim of workplace bullying, it hardly matters that Gaius Caligula might have been an even worse boss than the one who's driving them round the bend. 'Worse' is pretty meaningless in this subjective context (*Her wounds are worse than his wounds! Caligula was worse than Tiberius! Nero was worse than Caligula! This form of abuse is worse than that form of abuse!*, etc., etc.). Instead, what Hegel's model allows us to do is to trace commonalities between very different kinds of bully-victim relationships, without equating or comparing them. Hegel's abstract model, that is, points up recurring patterns – regarding struggles, threats, pacts, forms of recognition, and sadomasochism – which are shared by bully-victim relationships, across divergent contexts.

One of the more optimistic aspects of Hegel's model is that the slave-victim doesn't remain a slave-victim forever. This is the promise Hegel holds out: that the slave-victim will eventually liberate him- or herself, and overturn the relationship, so that the slave becomes the master, the master the slave. Over time, the 'inch' the master initially gives the slave becomes a mile:

The truth of the independent consciousness [of the lord or master] is accordingly the servile consciousness of the bondsman.... Just as lordship showed that its essential nature is the reverse of what it wants to be, so too servitude in its consummation will really turn into the opposite of what it immediately is.

According to Hegel, this 'consummation' happens because the master-slave (or bully-victim) relationship is, by definition, unstable. For a start, the sadistic recognition the master receives from the slave can only ever be 'one-sided and unequal'. It cannot provide real 'independent' validation of their existence, and the 'satisfaction' it accords 'is ... only a fleeting one'. At the same time, the slave gradually works towards independence, gaining a sense of self through work and 'fear of death': 'fear', writes Hegel, 'is the beginning of wisdom [and] ... through work ... the bondsman becomes conscious of what he truly is.... In his work, ... he acquires a mind of his own.' While the master's satisfaction is merely fleeting, the slave realises a long-lasting sense of recognition, because

work ... is desire held in check, fleetingness staved off; in other words, work forms and shapes the thing. The negative relation to the object becomes its *form* and something *permanent*.... This ... formative *activity* is at the same time the individuality or pure being-for-self of consciousness which now, in the work outside of it, acquires an element of permanence.... Consciousness, *qua* worker, comes to see in the independent being [of the object] its *own* independence.... In fashioning the thing, [the bondsman] ... becomes aware that ... he himself exists essentially and actually in his own right.

Now, the idea that a slave can attain his or her independence through work has, understandably, been much criticised. After all, real-life slave systems are not renowned for providing slaves with rewarding work; and nor is, or was, manumission common for slaves good at their jobs. Still, there are other, more psychological ways of looking at Hegel's model, which might help us reclaim its happy ending, at least for the bully-victim relationship, if not that of master and slave.

Speaking personally, for instance, I understand the idea of working towards freedom, in the sense that, ever since childhood, my own reading and writing have represented an antidote to the violence of everyday life – an escape route, in which I found, and continue to find, an 'independent ... mind of [my] ... own'. By later high school, I was relatively good (according to school measurements) at reading and writing, while most of the kids who punched me were not. I even liked doing these things in my own time. They represented both a space in which I gained an independent consciousness, and, on a more prosaic level, one in which I enjoyed a mental ascendancy over those whose physical ascendancy I could never challenge. This was reading-as-both-escape-route-and-displaced-weapon (*I read, you don't, so I may not be as strong as you, but at least I've got brains*). I'm not condoning my adolescent intellectual elitism here; I'm just explaining how I felt at the time – that reading and writing represented a space beyond the dialectics of The Killing Ground[s], beyond bigs hitting middles hitting babies. Clearly, I'm not alone in this: literature is full of oppressed David Copperfields and Matildas who try and read (and sometimes write) their way out of victimhood. Such characters mirror back the real-world experiences of many an avid reader, and vice versa.

If, on occasion, reading fails to live up to its promise (as is the case for Jude in Thomas Hardy's *Jude the Obscure*, for example), there are other alternatives available, other escape routes from oppressive relationships. In *A Kestrel for a Knave*, Billy Casper doesn't read much, but through falconry he gains a glimpse of something beyond a human world in which he's bottom of the pecking order. In Kes, he finds something that has 'a kind of pride, and ... independence, ... a satisfaction with its own beauty and prowess.'

If Billy finds his escape route from the pecking order in the natural world, Harry Potter finds his in the supernatural realm, as apprentice magician. This, though, turns out to be a rather double-edged sword (or wand). During the school year, it gets him out of the Dursleys' home in Privet Drive, but it puts him in the way of Lord Voldemort. Swings and roundabouts, Muggles and Dark Lords.

Reading and writing were, for me, similarly ambivalent forms of magic, double-edged wands – at one and the same time both an escape route from school bullying, *and* a reason to be bullied ('Swot', 'Boffin', 'Geek', 'Arse-licker', 'Poofter', etc.). Reading and writing were what philosophers call the '*pharmakon*': Greek for cure and poison at the same time. Many of the supposed escape routes from bullying are similarly double-natured, and I'll talk more about that towards the end of this book.[4]

Despite Hegel's claims, 'work' is often a *pharmakon* for the victim-slave. In Sillitoe's short story, Bullivant's ultimate escape from Mr Raynor's cane will literally be work: Bullivant and his classmates are two months away from leaving school for employment. But this may well be a matter of swapping one oppressive regime for another. It's all too often the case: Harry Potter swaps the Dursleys for Hogwarts and Voldemort; I swap physical subjugation on the playground for an academic hierarchy which, it turns out, can be even more savage. Only the visionary Billy Casper truly escapes, because he glimpses something beyond human hierarchies in the animal kingdom. Or, at least, he does so until the human world, in the person of his brother, intervenes again, and destroys that escape route.

Maybe one reason why so many escape routes partly fail is that they don't do anything to alter the original bully-victim scenario. Literal, psychological, and metaphorical escape routes can,

---

of course, be immensely valuable to victims of bullying (let alone slaves); but they don't necessarily change the fundamental situation. They represent valuable spaces away from The Killing Grounds, but don't magic away those Killing Grounds, don't directly challenge the bullies' dominance therein.

Hegel doesn't talk about escape routes, as such. Rather, his confrontational model suggests that the bully-victim relationship can be overturned from within, the bully's dominance overthrown through the victim's work. In this respect, Hegel's ideal of work is not so much an escape route, but rather something that causes radical change. Work is rebellion, revolution, fighting back. Work is war.

Both Nicholas Nickleby and, to a lesser extent, Bullivant seem aware of this, insofar as they both confront their respective bullies head-on. Bullivant challenges Mr Raynor and his cane with his fists; Nickleby wrests Mr Squeers's cane from him, and proceeds to beat him, just as Squeers had intended beating Smike. Nickleby literally inverts the hierarchy: the caner has become the caned. As Hegel might expect, Nickleby gains control of the 'object' or 'thing' (*das Ding*, in German) – in this case, the cane – and hence gains ascendancy over the master, Wackford Squeers. To gain control of *das Ding* – the 'weapon', the 'instrument of torture' – is to gain control of the school, if not the world.

The ultimate example of the caned taking control of the masters' weapons is the infamous 1968 film *If...*, directed by Lindsay Anderson. Malcolm McDowell and his friends are brutally caned by prefects, and subsequently take savage revenge on them and the whole school. They bypass canes and go straight to a cache of rifles, grenades, and automatic weapons conveniently stored in the school's basement. The result is full-scale bloody revolution.

In Sillitoe's short story, Bullivant threatens Mr Raynor with bloody revenge from his elder brother: 'I'll bring our big kid up to settle yo.' In the present of the story, though, he never quite reaches Nickleby's ascendancy over the teacher, let alone the murderous revolution in *If...*, because he doesn't gain control of the necessary weaponry (*das Ding*). He doesn't manage to wrest the cane from the schoolmaster's grip, so doesn't wholly overturn the teacher-pupil relationship. Immediately after the fight, Bullivant slouches back to his desk, and Mr Raynor returns to his 'high stool'.

Still, things have changed. Bullivant has challenged the cane's sacred authority with his fists, and this act of resistance has altered his relationship with both cane and Raynor forever. Rather than remaining a victim-slave, Bullivant is now almost, but not quite, the teacher's equal. The truce resulting from the 'battle of strength' between Bullivant and Raynor both temporarily upholds the latter's authority and undermines it. What separates them now is no wider than an inch, the width of a stick. And if Bullivant's brother has a longer stick, or knife, or gun...

Part II. Results, Conclusions

> He's not a sadist, like one or two of the other ... masters.... He wouldn't
> be so frightening if he were.
>
> Terence Rattigan, *The Browning Version*

A direct 'battle of strength' isn't a viable option for most victims of bullies, let alone victims of stick-wielding teachers. So, more often than not, neither Nickleby's near-homicidal victory, nor Bullivant's uneasy truce are attainable outcomes of the bully-victim relationship. The diminutive Billy Casper is never going to win any trials of strength, and nor was my 4'8 thirteen-year-old self. We are the victims left behind by life-and-death struggles, the spectators who look on, while Nickleby and Squeers flog each other; we are the lesser classmates excluded from Bullivantian truces; we are the students and, for that matter, teachers who are stuck in the middle, who are neither Bullivants nor Raynors, Danny Beakers nor Bulging Suits. We are the teachers who do not cane, the pupils who try not to use fists. We get it from all sides.

What we get as pupils is pretty obvious. As Russell writes, at worst, we are subjected to 'a reign of terror, in which the strong [keep] ... the weak trembling and miserable'. But there are parallel effects on the more liberal teachers as well. Put it this way: it's a well-known phenomenon, among schoolteachers, that working alongside a strict disciplinarian can be difficult, unless you are a strict disciplinarian too. Otherwise, the contrast becomes marked, and the kids exploit the softer teacher, more out of a sense of relief, of hydraulic pressure being released, than malice. As my eleven-year-old daughter said one afternoon, returning from a traumatic third day at secondary school: 'Why do the nice teachers get all the stick?' The same thing applied back in the day. Metaphorically speaking, it wasn't only the kids who got 'the stick'.

There were occasional incidents of gentler teachers being punched or head-butted by Bullivants or Beakers ('This is where you can stick your homework, Sir'). For the most part, though, pupil-teacher bullying was verbal, psychological, and none the less merciless for that. If schools had been less harsh at the top, maybe the revenge of kids on gentler teachers wouldn't have been so ghastly. The kids' mercilessness reflected the management's mercilessness: educational institutions can be halls of mirrors, everyone reflecting everyone else, sometimes grotesquely, sometimes terrifyingly, sometimes comically.

It's 1985. We're in a Science lesson with the gentle Mr Trog. He's a member of the Campaign for Nuclear Disarmament and Friends of the Earth, so he doesn't own a car. Instead, he trudges every day to school with the kids, staring at the ground in front of his feet. Bent over like Atlas, he seems to bear the weight of the violent world on his shoulders.

In this lesson, we're meant to be conducting experiments with Bunsen burners. My mate Steed and I are using a Bunsen burner to conduct our own experiment on a plastic-based substance – specifically, our friend Pi's ruler – an experiment we'll write up in the usual way. Our working *Hypothesis* is that Pi's ruler will melt. Our *Equipment* is simple: a Bunsen burner and Pi's beloved 30 cm shatterproof ruler, which he has been waving around, boasting: 'It's the best ruler in the class!' It is his miniature-totem, his mini-cane – and, indeed, while waving it around, he accidentally on purpose hits me across the knuckles with it. I grab it off him, and Steed and I hold it over a flame, to observe what happens. this is our *Method*. Pi is desperately trying to grab it back, but we keep pushing him away with our free hands. The *Result* of exposing the ruler to heat is that the ruler melts at one end, as predicted in our original *Hypothesis*. In addition to the expected outcome, there are two unexpected side effects: Pi cries, and I feel bad. The *Conclusion* of our experiment? – that cruelty, violence, bullying persist even at the lowest levels, even among the 'babies', the dweebs of a school. There's no honour among boffins.

Meanwhile, Mr Trog hasn't noticed our experiment, or Pi's crying, because his attention has been distracted by cruelty on a slightly higher level – although he doesn't yet recognise it as such. The school tearaway, a boy with carrot-coloured hair, has wandered to the front, winking theatrically back at the class. You'd have thought the wink and barely suppressed grin might have given the game away, even before it began. But Mr Trog is extremely shortsighted – squints dimly through jam-jar NHS specs – so doesn't notice winks or grins any more than he sees what we've been doing to Pi's ruler. He only notices the boy with carrot hair at all after the latter has been waiting patiently, in front of his desk, for a minute or so. 'Yes? Can I help you, boy?'

Carrot Hair addresses Mr Trog in a loud voice, so the whole class, his audience, can hear: 'I have a bit of a problem, *Sir*.'

'What's the problem?' asks Mr Trog. 'Shouldn't you be doing your ex...'

'I want to do my experiment, Sir. I *really* do. Y'know I love Science. But something's getting in my way, ruining my concentration, like. Funnily enough, Sir, it's something you were talking about last week. Something you're a bit of an expert on, if you don't mind me saying.'

Mr Trog clears his throat bashfully: 'Well, hmmm, let me know what it is, and I'll see what I can do.'

'It's this,' says Carrot Hair, nodding downwards at his right hand. Mr Trog's myopic gaze follows the direction of the nod. Carrot Hair's thumb and forefinger are pinched together, as though holding onto something, about eight or nine inches from his school jumper. 'It's really getting on my nerves, Sir.'

Mr Trog squints. 'I can't see anything, boy.'

'It's this,' says Carrot Hair, 'this thread coming out of my jumper. Me mum'll kill me if the jumper, like, unravels.'

Mr Trog bends down, his forehead lined, shakes his head. 'I still can't see anything.'

'It's really bothering me. And it's right up your street, Sir. That lesson on tension last week. One-dimensional string tension. Newton and all that sh... *jazz*. You seem like a bit of an *expert* on it. I thought you might know what to do. But if not...'

Mr Trog doesn't want to let the boy down – doesn't get many compliments on his lessons or expertise – so he interrupts: 'It's all right, boy. I'm sure we can find a simple way of dealing with the issue.' He thinks for a moment, and then slowly – he only ever moves slowly, deliberately – slides off his stool, and plods over to a chest of drawers in the corner. He opens one drawer, then another, rooting around. In the meantime, Carrot Hair looks back at his audience, putting on a dumb show, twirling a finger round in the air by the side of his head, sticking his tongue into the bottom of his mouth – both offensive gestures indicating imbecility on the part of an unwitting victim. There's giggling around the room.

'Shush, class,' says Mr Trog, still rooting through the drawers. 'We'll sort out this complex problem in string tension soon enough.' He smiles at his own half-joke, pulls out a pair of scissors. 'Aha!'

He shuffles back over to Carrot Hair. 'Hold the thread out tight,' he says, 'so it is of uniform tension.' Carrot Hair pretends to do so, and Mr Trog tries to snip through the thread, once, twice, three times.

'No good,' says Carrot Hair. 'It's still there, Sir.'

'It's like cutting the Gordian Knot, isn't it?'

'More like the Emperor's New Clothes,' someone pipes up behind me.

'Y'what, Sir?' asks Carrot Hair. 'What's a Gordian Knot when it's at home?'

Mr Trog doesn't answer. His concentration is fully focussed on the non-existent thread. He tries again and again with the scissors – snip, snip, snip – each time leaning in closer, squinting through thick glasses, his brow furrowed, his tongue out. 'I can't seem to get it,' he says, exasperated. Snip, snip, snip.

'No good,' says Carrot Hair. 'I'm doomed. Me mother's going to belt me one.'

Mr Trog shakes his head, concerned, sympathetic. 'I wouldn't want that to happen. As you know, I'm a bit of a pacifist myself.' He glances up at the class: 'Can anyone else help us?'

A couple of big boys, not even bothering to conceal their laughter, step forwards to volunteer their assistance: 'Anything to help a mate out, Sir.' Elsewhere in the classroom, there's more laughter, chatter. One girl shouts out helpful advice, while Mr Trog snips again at the thread: 'You're missing by a mile, Sir! To your left! No, your right! Up a bit! Warmer! Colder! Oh, you're dead hot, Sir!' The whole lesson is collapsing around us – which, of course, is the aim of the enterprise. One or two kids feel sorry for Mr Trog: 'Oh come on, stop it, give him a break,' but no one is listening.

The two volunteers take turns with Mr Trog's scissors, pretending to try and cut the invisible thread. 'Oh dear, Sir, missed it,' says one, now snipping the air nowhere near Carrot Hair – now snipping Mr Trog's notes by mistake – now trying to snip his tie: 'Oops, sorry, Sir.'

Carrot Hair is still holding the mythical thread between thumb and forefinger. He shakes his head, stoically accepting defeat: 'Nothing's gonna work, Sir.'

Mr Trog is not ready to give up, though, and has another idea: 'I know,' he says, 'I'll go and fetch Mr Bulging Suit from next door. He'll know what to do.' The laughter in the classroom stops dead, cut like a thread. *O-oh.*

Carrot Hair says hurriedly: 'No need, Sir, honestly. I'm sure it'll be okay, I think I can get it, Sir, I think...' But it's too late. Mr Trog has left the classroom. Carrot Hair remains standing at the front, paralysed, holding the imaginary thread in his fingers. The other two boys dump the scissors and scarper back to their chairs.

Everyone's quiet, suddenly engrossed in experiments which don't include rulers or invisible threads.

Mr Bulging Suit breezes in, the *deus ex machina* to any failed lesson. Mr Trog trails in his wake, trying to explain the situation. Mr B. S., though, doesn't need any explanation. He only needs to take one look at Carrot Hair and his 'thread' to understand what's going on. If there's one thing Mr B. S. can spot, it's, well, B. S.

There's a pause. Something seems to twitch on the side of Mr Bulging Suit's mouth. It's a fleeting thing – I might have imagined it – and then his face sets into its usual concrete expression, its state-school stare. 'I see what the problem is,' he growls. 'I see very well.' He takes the pair of scissors from the desk, and cuts decisively through the air next to Carrot Hair's jumper. 'There you go,' he says to Carrot Hair. 'That's all right now, boy, *isn't it*?'

Carrot Hair looks down, gulps, nods: 'Yessir, all sorted, Sir. Like new.'

'Right then, now you can get back to work. Can't you?'

'Yes, Sir. Certainly, Sir.' Carrot Hair scampers back to his chair, head down, like he's evading gunfire.

Bulging Suit turns on his heels. 'All sorted, Mr Trog,' he says.

He strides to the door, opens it. Carrot Hair can't believe his luck, thinks he might have got away with it. We all know that Mr Bulging Suit knows that it was one big lesson-destroying hoax; we all know that he knows that we know he only pretended to cut the thread to spare Mr Trog's blushes; but, despite all this, we wonder if, for once, he's going to let a kid off the hook. The kid in question, Carrot Hair, is holding in a breath, ready to breathe it out when the door closes...

But Mr Bulging Suit has nothing if not timing. On the threshold, his head turns, with reptilian slowness, in Carrot Hair's direction, and fixes the latter with his stare. There's another torturous pause. And then, sounding all the world like a Comprehensive Columbo, Mr B. S. says: 'Oh, just one more thing, *boy*. One more, minor thing. Please come to my office at your earliest convenience during breaktime, so we can discuss sartorial matters further.'

'Yes, Sir,' says Carrot Hair meekly.

Bulging Suit addresses the whole class: 'And I'll see the rest of you after school for a special lesson I'd like to give on tension theory. I call it *de-tension*.' Again, that twitch at the side of his mouth, and then he's gone, his gown following him like a shadow. As soon as the door slams shut, there's a general groan – a release, as it were, of tension. Someone kicks Carrot Hair off his stool, hisses: 'It's all your bloody fault.'

But in a way, it wasn't *all* Carrot Hair's fault: it was everybody's fault – the kids', Mr Bulging Suit's, the whole system's, balanced as it was precariously on a stick. In a system where the ultimate sanction was an object, a thing (*das Ding*), those who didn't wield the thing seemed stripped bare of power. So the only means for pupils to gain a modicum of power was through trickery, subterfuge; and one of the only means of maintaining authority for teachers who didn't use violence was to call on someone who did. Mr Trog's only way of re-establishing order in his class was to fetch Mr Bulging Suit and (by extension, or ex-*tension*) the cane. In other words, maybe the only way for the non-violent to maintain any authority in a system based on violence (or the threat thereof) is by indirect recourse to that violence. Mr Trog may have been a self-proclaimed pacifist, a gentle soul, but the system besieged, undermined that gentleness, rendered it laughable.

Up to a point, I'd thought my father was one of the gentler ones, a Trog rather than a Bulging Suit. Though I knew he was headmaster of a huge school in a scary part of Stoke, I never thought he might be a different person there, that he might behave differently towards other kids. As young as five, I was dimly aware that school headmasters sometimes used corporal punishment – 'the pump' or 'the cane' or 'the strap' or another instrument of torture – yet I never equated that abstract knowledge with my own father.

Admittedly, he did smack us now and then, if we got him angry. I remember yelping, as his smacks chased me up the stairs, some hitting the target, stinging my legs, some of them wide of the mark because I was nimbler than him, practised at evasive manoeuvres. I'd scamper into the bedroom, slam the door, and cower in the corner, sobbing. For some reason, the bedroom was sanctuary, and he wouldn't come in. The raised voices and smacks would evaporate. An hour or so later, my mother would quietly open the door, and sit down on the bed with me for a chat. 'You were being a naughty boy,' she'd say.

'But he smacked me!' I'd say, bottom lip protruding, still resentful.

'You're lucky,' she'd say.

'Lucky?'

'Yes, once, before you were born, he showed your brother a belt. He didn't use it. But showing it that one time was enough.' The belt-showing incident was always spoken of in a reverential tone. It was a kind of family myth, although the first time I heard it, when I was very young, I didn't understand the implication: why would Daddy show Robin a belt? Was it a particularly nice belt? Did it have Cowboys and Indians on it like my belt?

Anyway, at home, my father never got beyond belt-showing and a few half-hearted smacks. Otherwise, he was sedate, kind, often taking our side when we argued with mum, much to her frustration ('Yes, darling, but he only wants *one* more toy car,' 'Yes, darling, but you know he doesn't like your gravy – I mean, *any* gravy,' 'Yes, darling, but surely we can let him off the sprouts this one time?'). With the blind faith of childhood, I assumed that was what he was like everywhere, at all times, past, present, future.

Then, one day, I came across a cane in the corner of his school office.

When we were little, my father would occasionally take us to his school for a morning during the holidays. For him, no doubt, it was work. For me and my elder siblings, Robin and Karen, it was an exciting day-trip to the exotic Orient of East Stoke. To visit our own schools during the holidays would have been torment; but as it was his school, we rampaged joyfully round it, treating it like a vast fun-house, all to ourselves. The corridors were empty, and we could play World War II or Cowboys and Indians or hide and seek. We could pile up chairs in classrooms, turning them into dens. We could draw rude pictures on the blackboards, for the kids to see when they returned from their holidays. The school secretary had a typewriter – *a typewriter, no less* – on which we could write news flashes and insulting messages to each other. My father's office connected with that of his secretary via a stable door, so you could swing open the top half, and keep the bottom half bolted. That way, you could pretend Jonathan was a trapped piglet in a cattle market, feed him pencil shavings from the wastepaper basket, slam the top half shut in his face, or clamber over the bottom half when it was time to slaughter him.

One morning – probably the last morning we ever went to my father's school, when I was nine – my brother slammed the top half of the door too quickly, and banged the piglet's (i.e. my) nose. I squealed and started crying, in a piglety way. I heard my father's voice telling my brother off on the other side of the door, and then the bolt being shot across. My father stepped through the door, scooped me up, and sat me on his lap, next to his desk. 'It's okay, boy,' he said, looking at my nose. 'No blood, just a bit red.' He grinned. 'Look, perhaps if I smack your ear, like this, the hurt in your nose will go away.' He tapped my ear, and the tap turned my head just enough for me to see something propped up, in the corner of the room. Something long, thin, and wooden.

I stared at it, open-mouthed: 'What's that?' I asked, forgetting about the tears.

'What?' my father asked.

'That,' I pointed.

'It's a stick,' he said. He paused. 'A cane.'

I got off my father's lap, and went to pick it up. He didn't stop me.

It was an actual garden cane, like the ones you tie up beans with, not like the curved and polished walking sticks usually associated with old-school disciplinarians. I wondered if he'd nicked it from my mum's vegetable patch. Typical dad, I think now: he couldn't be bothered to fork out on a proper cane.

I cut the air with it. It made a pleasing swooshing noise. 'Careful with that,' said my dad, but he didn't take it off me.

I swooshed it again. 'Daddy?'

'Y-e-s?' he asked, drawing the word out, probably guessing what was coming.

'Do you ... use this? Do you cane kids at your school?'

'Yes,' he said, in a measured way. 'Not often, but yes, I do. As a last resort, if a boy has been very, very naughty. Some of the children here, you see...'

At that moment, Robin and Karen rushed in – having decided my nose must be better by now – and saw me with the cane. Robin grappled it off me, and started chasing Karen and me round and round the desk: swish, swish, swish: 'I'll beat your bottoms!'

Eventually, my father elegantly reached down, as my brother was passing him for the third time, and took the blurred cane away. He looked a little embarrassed. 'Let's put this back, shall we?' he said, and propped it up in the corner, in shadow.

Shadow or no shadow, I couldn't help glancing back at it as we left his office for the last time. If I close my eyes, I can still see it there now, years after his death and the school's demolition: a warning, a fetish, a symbol of something lost.

What was lost?

As a child, I'd always dreamt my father into the shoes of Danny's father in *Danny the Champion of the World* (1975) – the

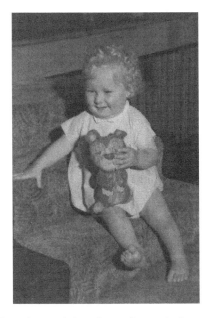

Figure 4.1 The only remaining photo of me enjoying myself at my father's school, long before the discovery of his cane, c. 1975.

father Roald Dahl describes as 'the most marvellous and exciting father any boy ever had.... Plots and plans and new ideas came flying off him like sparks from a grindstone.' He makes kites and fire-balloons; he builds tree-houses and soap-box cars; he takes Danny poaching. He is 'sparky', as Dahl puts it, fun and loving.

By contrast, Danny's teacher Captain Lancaster is 'a horrid man, ... a violent man', and the schoolchildren are 'all terrified of him'. The violence is expressed through caning, and eventually he canes Danny. For me, reading the book as a child close to Danny's age, the visceral description of his caning seemed as close as writing could come to communicating actual physical pain. I felt I was being caned too. And perhaps so did the author: Dahl himself had considerable first-hand and, indeed, first-bottom experience of corporal punishment during his school years (doled out by various sadists, including one future Archbishop of Canterbury). Hence, at this climactic moment in *Danny the Champion of the World*, it seemed to me that the author's, narrator's, and reader's experiences converged on the page, and we all shared the same pain and outrage:

It was almost impossible to believe that this man was about to injure me physically and in cold blood.... The long white cane went up high in the air and came down on my hand with a crack like a rifle going off. I heard the crack first and about two seconds later I felt the pain. Never had I felt a pain such as that in my whole life. It was as though someone were pressing a red-hot poker against my palm and holding it there.... Oh that fearful searing burning pain across my hand!

The caning leaves a 'long ugly mark about half an inch wide running right across the palm,' which is 'raised up in the middle and the raised part was pure white, with red on both sides.' Later, Danny's father spots the mark, and is furious at Captain Lancaster: '*I'll kill him!.... I swear I'll kill him!*' As with Bullivant and Raynor, Nickleby and Squeers, school violence escalates quickly, exponentially: Smike is caned by Squeers, who is in turn almost killed by Nickleby; Danny is caned by Captain Lancaster, who might then be killed by Danny's father.

In the event, Danny talks his father out of murdering his teacher. Once again, homicide remains an unrealised threat, a ghost in the education system. Danny's father's rage subsides, and he returns to being a 'gentle lovely man' who, instead of murdering Captain Lancaster, arranges a midnight feast and chatters to his son about their poaching plans.

I'd thought of my father as a 'gentle lovely man'. I'd dreamt of him as Danny's father. Okay, he wasn't always 'sparky', especially as he got older, but he did play with us, did enjoy being with us. Okay, he didn't build kites or soap-box cars from scratch, but he did take us kite-flying, did buy me a faulty go-cart. Okay, he didn't poach pheasants, was neurotically terrified of the police, but he did take us on country walks and picnics. So overall, my father had been much more like Danny's father than not, while I was very young. I know how lucky I was with both my parents.

But then – funnily enough, at the very moment things were teetering on the brink of change, when he was starting to get ill, though we didn't know it at the time – I came across the cane in his office. Then I glimpsed a different father, one who existed in a different dimension to us, one who might seem more Captain Lancaster to the kids he caned, than Danny's father. In the years to come, there were other glimpses too. When, many years later, I met my father's long-lost first son, he said his early memories of my father were of a 'stern, mean man, an old-school disciplinarian' – again, more Captain Lancaster than Danny's father.

Still, no doubt most fathers are part Danny's father, part Captain Lancaster, to different degrees and in different contexts. I didn't understand that back then when I found my dad's cane, or later when I met my half-brother. Since becoming a father myself, though, I see it more clearly. I want to be Danny's father, but there are moments when an inside-Captain-Lancaster takes over.

It can happen to all of us: *I guess we are all guilty of everything.* In hierarchical systems like parenthood or school where there's a radical power imbalance, it's all too easy for Captain Lancaster to possess anyone who isn't right at the bottom of the heap. As Dickens says, '[T]he abuse of irresponsible power [is] ... of all earthly temptations the most difficult to be resisted.' The only answer is to try and shape systems which don't confer irresponsible power, where our inner Captain Lancasters are regulated, controlled, kept within certain disciplinary bounds. Otherwise, however non-violent we think we are, self-control can break down, the temptation of ingrained *flagellomania* temporarily winning out...

*

It's 2010. Our twins, Miranda and Rosie, are two years old. Our living room is a fortress, a toy-filled jail. There are child-proof fences everywhere: a gate at the bottom of the stairs, a gate at the kitchen doorway, a play-pen, two fences awkwardly joined together round the fireplace and TV. There are safety guards on all the electric sockets. Toys are strewn across the carpet like rubble, dead bodies. Everywhere you step, a squealing soft toy, an electronic nursery rhyme, goes off.

My wife Maria is out for the afternoon. The twins are on the rampage with the superhuman energy of toddlers, testing the fences for weaknesses (to paraphrase *Jurassic Park*), setting off all the toys at once. I'm encircled by a polytonal fugue of 'Mary, Mary, Quite Contrary', 'Twinkle, Twinkle', Tchaikovksy's 'Waltz of the Flowers', steam trains, car horns, mingled with screaming, laughing, crying. Miranda's thrown one of Rosie's musical steam engines over the fence by the fireplace. Rosie's shrieking, squeezing in the gap between two fences to retrieve it. I pull her back, tell her not to go near the fireplace – the fire isn't lit, but the fire-surround is jagged concrete, asking for trouble from two-year-old heads. I pick up the steam engine, give it to Rosie, tell Miranda off.

Miranda throws it back over the fence. Rosie squeezes between the bars to get it. I scoop her up, pick up the steam engine, hand it to Rosie, tell Miranda off. Miranda throws it back over the fence. Laughs. It's a circular, never-ending game of fetch, a joke on Daddy: *Fetch, Daddy Dog, fetch!*

I'm exhausted. I don't find the joke funny. I tell Miranda off, get the toy, put it out of reach on the mantelpiece: 'I'm taking this away.' Rosie cries. I harden my heart and shout: 'You've got to learn. You MUSTN'T go near the fireplace!' Rosie looks up at me uncomprehendingly, as if I'm a silent movie, and she missed the intertitle. 'It's dangerous and you'll get hurt.'

I go into the kitchen to make their tea. I hear a crash and a cry. I step back into the living room to find Rosie head-down between the fences, having fallen trying to reach up for the steam engine.

I scoop her up, push the fences together, return to the kitchen. I hear a crash and a cry. I go back into the living room, to find Rosie head-down between the fences, having found another gap between them. I shout: 'Don't go near the fireplace!', then relent, get the steam engine down, and give it to Rosie: '*Please* don't go near the fireplace.'

I seal up the gaps in the so-called 'child-proof' fences, step into the kitchen. I hear a crash and a cry. I go back into the living room. Rosie's prised the fences apart, and is retrieving her steam engine, which, of course, Miranda has thrown onto the fireplace. I shout. Tchaikovsky, Waltzes, Flowers, Mary, Mary, Twinkle, Twinkle all shout with me. I shout louder, as if volume means anything to twins who don't understand what I'm saying: 'Stop it! Stop throwing it, Miranda! Don't go near the fireplace, Rosie! *Please* stop it!'

'Shtop it, Wosie!' echoes Miranda, giggling. 'Shtopitshtopit!'

I ignore the echo, and adjust the useless fences, cursing them under my breath, swearing I'll buy new ones, or maybe sledgehammer the whole bloody fireplace. I return to the kitchen. There's a crash, a thud, a cry. I run back into the living room, trip over a Fisher Price telephone. Rosie's squeezed behind the fences again, to retrieve her steam engine. Miranda's at the other side of the room, so this time it must have been Rosie herself who threw the toy over. Rosie's crying and laughing hysterically at the same time, as though blowing raspberries at me: *Look at me, I'm behind the fence, I'm doing what you said I shouldn't do, I'm in charge, and you're not! Haha! Silly Daddy!*

Now Miranda's laughing hysterically too, and so are Tchaikovsky's Flowers, Mary, Mary, Twinkle, Twinkle and Little Star, all of them laughing at me – and my head's ringing, and I've had enough, and I scoop Rosie up, and I smack her, hard, on the legs, like my dad used to, and I yell at her, at Miranda, at the toys, at myself: 'Stopitstopitstopit! I've-told-you-not-to-go-behind-the-fences-for-fuck's-sake-stop-it!'

Everything – even the toys, it seems, even the Waltzing Flowers and Mary, Mary – everything goes quiet for a moment. Miranda stares up at me, open-mouthed, like I once stared at a cane in my father's office. Rosie's shaking, red-faced, holding in her breath. When I put her down on the floor, she finally lets it out in a huge, elongated scream. She cries and cries, backing away when I go near her. There's a red mark on her leg. I start crying too, as does Miranda.

The front door opens and closes. Maria comes into the living room, finding us all on the floor, in a chaos of sobbing. 'What on Earth is going on?' she asks.

'I smacked Rosie,' I manage to say. 'I smacked her, and I'm never going to smack her again.'

And I haven't. But that doesn't take away the unending guilt I feel for that one terrible time. I still feel that failure, still see Captain Lancaster when I look in the mirror. I want to say sorry to Rosie, if she ever reads this, at some point in the future. In parenthood, there are moments of failure – of temper or disconnection or dismissiveness – we can never take back, however much we want to, and this was one of them.

Above all, the moment makes me feel like a bloody hypocrite. Years of cane-terror, years of detesting corporal punishment at school, yet here I was, doling it out myself, to my own daughter. She and Miranda were only doing the sorts of things all two-year-olds do: winding each other up, winding their parents up, endlessly repeating the same actions, seeking attention, testing parents for weaknesses. All of us did these things when we were two, three, four. Yet, as parents or teachers, we get exasperated, and end up punishing kids for echoing back our own infantile misbehaviour. In that sense, parenthood and teachership are institutionalised hypocrisy, discipline a displaced and belated kind of guilt, self-hatred radiated outwards: *I hate what you're doing because I hate*

*myself for doing it once upon a time to my own parents and/or
teachers.* And what's more, this is double hypocrisy: *I'll punish you
for doing what I once did in precisely the way I hated as a kid: the
smack, the fist, the belt, the cane.* As Shaw claims, we are tainted by
flagellomania from childhood.[5]

The hypocritical circularity of all this, with each generation
echoing the last's behaviour and punishment, might bring to mind
Philip Larkin's well-known poem 'This Be the Verse': 'They fuck
you up, your mum and dad.... / But they were fucked up in their
turn.' By all accounts, my dad was belted by his biological father,
who in turn had suffered as a soldier in World War I. There's a sense
of inevitability and futility here, whereby 'Man hands on misery to
man.' Larkin, of course, didn't have children, and his poem is, in
part, absurdly reductive, a virtuosic pot-boiler. Or perhaps, to be
more precise, it resembles a distorted playground rhyme, the kind
that accompanies hop-scotch or, indeed, certain forms of bullying.[6]
As such, for those of us who *do* have children, it is also deeply frightening, a kind of curse, an invocation of deterministic futility.

I felt that futility at its most intense when I smacked Rosie.
It seemed so pointless. All the smack achieved was useless pain
on her part, which she didn't understand, and an overwhelming
sense of failure on my own.

Naturally, that's not how corporal punishment is always seen.
There's a long tradition of representations of physical discipline
that might be summed up in the short phrase *That'll teach 'em* – in
other words, the idea that physical violence is somehow ameliorative, enlightening, a lesson in itself. The cane is the teacher's magic
wand, conjuring up higher-calibre kids. The cane, as Mr Bulging
Suit suggested in our 'Welcome to School' assembly, might help
teachers 'to *mould*' kids, to 'make them better'.

---

[5]On teaching as institutionalised hypocrisy, see also Chapter 5, 'R.E.'.
[6]On the poetics of bullying, see Chapter 2, 'Playtime: Games of Soldiers'.

Other teachers have thought along similar lines. In Sillitoe's short story, for instance, Mr Raynor thinks that, by caning Bullivant, he can 'get these Teddy-boy ideas out of his head in a few seconds'. In his 1984 memoir, *Boy*, the young Roald Dahl is brutally caned by the headmaster, while another female teacher looks on, 'exhorting [him] ... to greater and still greater efforts'. 'She was bounding up and down with excitement', writes Dahl: '"Lay it into 'im!" she was shrieking. "Let 'im 'ave it! Teach 'im a lesson!"' This sadism by proxy is pre-echoed in *Nicholas Nickleby*, where the stepmother of one of the pupils at Dotheboys Hall 'hopes Mr Squeers will flog [her stepson] ... into a happier state of mind'. You can be beaten into happiness as well as goodness, it seems.

We've come a long way since Dotheboys Hall. And yet, despite the demise of the cane, the idea that harsh quasi-militaristic discipline makes school kids better still persists, in multifarious guises. In place of corporal punishment is corporal control, a discipline that affects the body in different ways (*stand up straight, sit up straight, wear the right uniform, don't chew gum, don't smoke, don't vape, smile at teachers, sit down, shut up, go to isolation, go to detention*). All of this, we're told, is beneficial to kids, a good in itself. But I can't help feeling that discipline for its own sake has no inherent meaning; that discipline for its own sake is no different to the exercise of power for its own sake; that discipline for its own sake is, at worst, a self-justifying form of sadism; that discipline is not an end, but a means; that discipline only has a point when it's the same thing as care. In this, I'm with controversial paediatrician Benjamin Spock, who suggests that 'good discipline' should be 'based on love', and its 'main source is ... being loved'.

Such a claim might seem pretty startling and far-fetched to some – especially to past victims of corporal punishment. However ameliorative disciplinarians in the 1980s felt the cane to be, it's a big ask to persuade someone who's being beaten that the cane-wielder's really doing it for their own good, out of love.

Nonetheless, the idea that harsh discipline is ameliorative has a very long tradition. The scenes in Dickens and Sillitoe have a prehistory, back to an Ancient Greek comedic text called *The Mimes* of Herodas, from the third century BCE. In a short scene called 'The Schoolmaster', a boy's mother asks his teacher that he 'be thrashed until his last miserable breath hangs only on his lips'. The very embodiment of *flagellomania*, she wants her son flogged 'as many [times] as [his] ... wicked hide can stand ... until the sun goes down'. Only this, she claims, might cure him of his gambling habit, and teach him a lesson: 'He does not even know the letter Alpha, unless someone shouts it at him five times.'

The schoolmaster asks for his 'cutting-switch', and says that, by the time he's finished with the boy, he'll be 'more reticent than a girl', when it comes to gambling. Flogged till he is 'striped like a water-snake', the boy begs not to be murdered. He swears that he will never again go gambling. The schoolmaster is satisfied, declaring that 'we will have him bent over a book ... read[ing] better than Klio herself'. The ferocious beating seems to have worked, in both moral and educational terms.

Or it does so till right at the end of the piece. Then the boy shouts: 'Yah!' and presumably runs off, cocking a snook at both schoolmaster and mother. Even 2,300 years ago, in a text that seems to extol the educational efficacy of a near-homicidal corporal punishment – a text that seems to revel in its own comic sadism – the ultimate implication is that it doesn't work; that, however brutal it is, thrashing signally fails to teach anybody a lesson. The idea that flogging is an exercise in futility, the only fruit of which is short-lived sadistic pleasure on the part of adults, is as old, it seems, as the idea of its pedagogical efficacy.

Since Herodas, the sense of corporal punishment's futility has often haunted teachers and educational theorists alike. In his influential 1693 treatise, *Some Thoughts Concerning Education*, Enlightenment philosopher John Locke claims that 'threats and blows ... lose their force when once grown common' – to the point that '*punishment* will by familiarity ... lose all its influence: offending, being chastised, and then forgiven will be thought as natural and necessary as noon, night, and morning following one another'. This cyclical sense of punishment (offence-chastisement-forgiveness-then-back-to-offence) has troubled many educators over the years – not least those who *seem*, like Herodas, most vehemently in favour of corporal punishment.

Mr Raynor the schoolteacher is a case in point. Despite his apparent belief in the cane, the question he asks himself, 'What did it matter, really?', following the tussle with Bullivant, implies its own answer: *nothing*. After all, 'Bullivant and most of the others would be leaving in two months', so all he needs to do is 'keep them in check for that short time'. Mr Raynor's cane has achieved nothing, intellectually or morally. It has not beaten the 'Teddy-boy ideas' out of Bullivant's head; it cannot make anyone 'better'; it can only keep his pupils in check for a short time, maintain an uneasy truce.

In Hines's *Kestrel for a Knave*, the cane's failure to make anyone better – its failure, that is, as a totem, or magic wand – is even more obvious to the world-weary headmaster, Mr Gryce. Confronted by a line of boys who've been caught smoking (or, in Billy's case, sleeping), he declares:

'I'm sick of you boys, you'll be the death of me. Not a day goes by without me having to deal with a line of boys. I can't remember a day ... in ... ten years, and the school's no better now than it was on the day it opened.... It ... makes me feel ... like it's a waste of time standing here talking to you boys, because you won't take a blind bit of notice what I'm saying.... As far as I can see there's been no advance at all in discipline, decency, manners or morals. And do you know how I know this? Well, I'll tell you. Because I still have to use this every day.'

He brought the stick round from behind his back for the boys to have a look at.

'It's fantastic isn't it, that in this day and age, in this super-scientific, all-things-bright-and-splendiferous age, that the only way of running this school efficiently is by the rule of the cane…. So for want of a better solution I continue using the cane, knowing full well that you'll be back time and time again for some more. Knowing that when you smokers leave this room wringing your hands, you'll carry on smoking just the same.'

For Gryce, punishment is 'a waste of time' because it is a never-ending cycle: he has to keep using the cane, day in, day out, year in, year out, while the boys keep smoking and misbehaving, so he has to keep using his cane, while the boys keep smoking and misbehaving, so he has to… The rule of the cane doesn't stop the boys doing anything, doesn't change anything, can't foster any 'advance' in terms of 'discipline, decency, manners or morals'. All it can do is keep the boys in check, keep the school 'running … efficiently' round and round in disciplinary circles.

At least everyone in this system knows what everyone else is meant to be doing, over and over again, like repetitive automata. Headteachers are meant to cane, kids are meant to smoke and misbehave, big kids are meant to bully smaller kids. And when those smaller kids become bigger kids, they in turn will take up smoking, get caned by the headteacher, pick on the new 'babies'. This model of education is stuck in an ever-repeating loop, as is discipline, as is bullying.

Victims of bullying often go on to bully others, in what is known by psychologists as the 'bully-victim-bully cycle'. Bullying is often defined as repetitive abusive behaviour, and, as such, it's always in danger of becoming a repetition compulsion, a trau-matic loop. If, as Russell claims, school seems to replay in minia-ture 'the history of the human race', this is a circular history that never gets anywhere, never advances – not unlike Larkin's view in 'This Be the Verse', where every generation compulsively repeats the violence and misery of the generation before it.

It is also the circularity of The Wall. In the video to Pink Floyd's famous 1979 single 'Another Brick in the Wall (Part 2)', the cartoon wall curves round to form a circle. The wall built by education is a circular prison cell, the cane-brandishing teacher just 'Another Brick in the Wall'. Indeed, the teachers are as trapped by the circular wall as the pupils: another (rather misogynistic) song from the same album, 'The Happiest Days of Our Lives', suggests that the bitterest teachers are only recycling the violence they experience at home from their wives.

My father loved 'Another Brick in the Wall', which seemed a bit of a departure for a Beethoven fan, let alone a life-long teacher. But like Mr Gryce, I think he'd come to understand the more pessimistic views of the teaching profession, the more futile aspects of school discipline. After his death, I happened across some papers from a training course he'd attended; and the famous quotation, often attributed to George Bernard Shaw, kept recurring like a refrain among his elegantly scrawled notes: 'My education was only interrupted by my schooling.' In the final phase of his doomed headmastership, I think he'd come to feel, in part, that school was a dead end, and he was another brick in the wall. A lot of teachers feel that kind of pessimism, some time or other. A lot of teachers, including myself, are fans of Pink Floyd, loving the very songs that lambast them.

Still, despite the pessimism, once a teacher, always a teacher: much as my father enjoyed Pink Floyd's song, he couldn't help interrupting his own humming when the chorus came along, in order to criticise the syntax. 'I don't want to be pedantic about it,' he'd say, 'but the chorus is all double negatives. So actually it's saying we *do* need education. Which is probably true, given their poor grasp of grammar.'

*

In the Library: An Epilogue

By the mid-1980s, quite a few of the older generation of teachers were unsure whether or not they needed (no) education any longer. When corporal punishment was finally banned in English state schools in 1986, some teachers, including our very own Mr Bulging Suit, took early retirement, unable to reconcile themselves to the new dispensation. Others carried on regardless: Mrs Formidable Bosom hardly needed the cane, when she could make kids' noses bleed spontaneously at ten paces. And still others neither retired nor adjusted to the new regime, but were stuck in a kind of limbo, believers in a defunct religion.

One of these was a Mr Chandler, who seemed to live in the school library. Every time I walked past the open door of the library, a mournful voice would intone from within: 'I'll cane you, boy' – the word 'b-o-o-o-o-y' elongated, with an upward flourish at the end, like a serif. It reminded me of nothing more than the 'strange, remote wailing' of dying Martians towards the end of H. G. Wells's *The War of the Worlds*: 'Ulla, ulla, ulla, ulla', a voice for the school's 'fear and solitude'.

'All I do is walk past,' I said to my elder sister, 'and he starts howling, "*I'll cane you, boy*."'

'Oh, don't worry about Mr Chandler. He threatens it to everyone.'

'Why?'

'The cane's all he ever goes on about. He's an old fuddy-duddy. He's stuck in the library 'cos he's, like, almost retired, and they don't want him beating up kids any more. I think he's allowed to teach a CSE English set sometimes. But that's it. No one wants him any more.'

'Oh,' I said, 'that's a bit sad as well as scary' – rather like the dying Martians in their derelict fighting machines, I thought.

'Don't be so wet,' said my sister. 'He's just a loser. A bastard.'

For the next couple of years, Mr Chandler's sad and scary refrain, 'I'll cane you, b-o-o-o-o-y', echoed down the corridors, following me round school, just as '*Ulla, ulla*' haunts Wells's journalist round dead London. At home, the two calls mingled in my nightmares: 'I'll cane you, boy, *Ulla, ulla.*'

As we got a bit older, and were sure that corporal punishment was gone for good, we also got braver. We started experimenting on Mr Chandler. Sometimes we'd deliberately walk past the library door more than once, to see if he'd repeat his catchphrase – like apprentice DJs scratching a record: 'I'll cane you, boy, cane you, c-c-c-cane you.' Or we'd run past the door, to see if he'd say it really quickly: 'I'llcaneyouboy.' Or we'd reverse, to see if he'd say it backwards, Yoda-like: 'Boy, you cane will I.'

Occasionally, at the end of the school day, I'd glimpse Mr Chandler from a distance, dressed head to toe in beige, beige hair, beige face. He'd emerge from the library – which, surprisingly enough, wasn't his actual home – and glide slowly down the corridors, out of the building, out of the school gates, a ghost leaving the building.

Then one day, towards the end of my high-school years, I was sent to the library to pick up a book about Vikings, and Mr Chandler was there, right in front of me, ensconced in his armchair. On the bookshelf opposite him was a small TV, showing a test match. I was tiptoeing around, hoping he wasn't going to threaten me with the cane. But he didn't. Instead, for the first time ever in my hearing, he said something different: 'Do you like the cricket, b-o-o-o-o-y?'

'I don't know,' I said.

He patted the chair next to him and said: 'Well, come and watch it with me. I need someone to explain it to. No one likes cricket in Stoke. And the wife gets bored when I go on.'

I sat down, and for the next half hour or so, I watched the cricket with him, lessons and errand forgotten. He explained the rules to me, bemoaning England's ineptitude, the 'lolloping fatness' of its captain. To my surprise, he seemed gentle and soft-spoken – that is, Mr Chandler, not the England captain. I liked him a lot.

Eventually, I told him I had to go back to my lesson. He gave me a sports biscuit, and I got up to leave. I glanced back at him from the doorway. His head was following the ball's trajectory on the TV, as the England bowler was hit for six. To me, he looked ancient. I thought again of the wrecked fighting machines dotted round Primrose Hill, at the end of *The War of the Worlds*.

That was one of the last times I ever saw (or heard) him. By the final year of school, he was gone, and even the echoes down the corridor – 'I'll cane you b-o-o-o-o-y, *Ulla, ulla*' – died away.

The rule of the cane, like that of the Martians' heat-ray, was over.

5

R.E.

Woe unto you, scribes and Pharisees, hypocrites! for ye make clean the outside of the cup and of the platter, but within they are full of extortion and excess.

Matthew, 23:25

If the cane ruled British schools of the 1970s and early 1980s, it didn't reign alone. As I've said, physical violence is rarely if ever just itself, when it comes to bullying; it's almost always intertwined with language in some way. Mr Bulging Suit might stalk the corridors wielding his cane, but our R.E. teacher wielded an equally terrifying, linguistic power, in the form of Christianity.

In many ways, the two teachers had a lot in common, even if one was much more efficient than the other. For a start, both relied more on the threat of violence than its actualisation. While Mr Bulging Suit's terror inhered in the idea that he *might* use the cane, the R.E. teacher played a much longer game, constantly threatening the violence of the hereafter. Power, of course, relies heavily, often solely, on threats. Actual violence can sometimes be anti-climactic by comparison.

Oddly enough, it turned out in the long run that it was the *über*-Christian R.E. teacher who was far more (anti-climactically and hypocritically) violent than Mr B. S., despite appearances, and despite the latter's cane. Above all, the whole sorry tale reminds me of one of the bitterest indictments of teachers, by American novelist Kathy Acker: 'A scholar is a top cop.... Teachers replace living dangerous creatings with dead ideas and teach these ideas as the history and meaning of the world.... [They] teach you intricate ways of saying one thing and doing something else.'

*

Mr Nerritt is one of two R.E. teachers at my high school. The other is mumsy Mrs Jones, who has a big bottom, and whom I fancy. I don't fancy Mr Nerritt, even though he wears denim, looks a bit like David Essex, and plays the guitar – all of which would seem to be in his favour, marking him out as the apparent opposite of Mr Bulging Suit.

Occasionally, Mr Nerritt leads school assembly and, instead of everyone mumbling along to 'Thine Be the Glory' or 'We Plough the Seeds and Scatter', we watch in sniggering embarrassment as he strums his guitar and sings praise music to us. His repertoire generally consists of modified pop hits, such as 'We Love You, Jesus, Yeah Yeah Yeah', 'I Wanna Hold Christ's Hand', and an alternative version of 'Imagine', where, instead of 'no religion', there's only one: his own.

Between songs, born-again-hippy Mr Nerritt provides short commentaries while he turns the pages on the music stand. These improvised, laid-back, fire-and-brimstone mini-sermons sound like God and Satan are sharing a spliff, like Hieronymus Bosch has turned up to paint Woodstock. They mingle words like 'cool' and 'ace' with shreds of Scripture, and threats of eternal damnation for more or less everybody. In Mr Nerritt's hands, that is, the Bible is at once 'very cool' and a gigantic *How to* manual of bullying – God bullying Job, Joseph's brothers bullying Joseph, Judas bullying Jesus, St Paul bullying women, homosexuals, children, heathens, and, for that matter, other Christians.

'Yeah, man,' proclaims our school's resident St Paul, sounding all the world like Dylan the Rabbit from *The Magic Roundabout*: 'I'm afraid most of you are on the broad road to hell. As good ol' St John says in Revelations: "All liars shall have their part in the lake which burns with fire and brimstone, which is the second death."' He tuts, as if to say: 'Oh well, never mind,' and strums a chord. 'But still, God is love, so do join me if you like in the next song, "All You Need Is Christ".'

No one joins in, not even with the half-hearted grumble-singing usually reserved for assemblies. 'Christ on a bike,' mutters loud-mouth Croggers, who's standing next to me. 'I'd rather have "All Things Shite and Beautiful" than this bollocks.'

Mr Nerritt finishes his song, alone, with a flourish, and props up the guitar next to him. 'That's all, folks, for today,' he says.

'Thank Christ,' says Croggers, in chorus with half a dozen others round the hall. Mr Nerritt overhears, mistaking relief for spiritual transport.

'Indeed: thank Christ!' he declares, clapping his hands. 'Alleluia! Say it with me: *Alleluia!*'

No one says anything.

'Come on, with me: *Alleluia!*'

There's a scattering of muttered 'Alleluias' round the hall. Most of us just open our mouths and shut them again, like fish. Some of the kids stretch out the word like a dirge: '*All-el-ooooou-ia*', as if it's a comment on their morning: 'Halle-fucking-lujah.'

'That's not good enough. Shout it loud and proud! *Alleluia*! Thank the Lord! You can hold up your hands too if you want.'

I feel like we're in a pantomime, or an episode of *Hi-de-Hi!*, a 1980s sitcom about a Butlin's-esque holiday camp, where the first utterance of any catchphrase is always followed by an exhortation to shout more loudly. 'I didn't hear you the first time! All together now: *Hi-de-Hi!*'

There's a louder grunt around the hall, which makes 'Alleluia!' sound like a swear word. Bad boy Danny Beaker cups his mouth and shouts out '*Alleluia!*' with all his might. 'Alleluia, Sir! *Alleluia*! Praise the Lordy Lord!' Everyone except Mr Nerritt knows he's taking the piss.

'Wow,' says Mr Nerritt, 'that's just great. *Cool.*'

There's a sudden thud from the front row. Greg, a tall boy with a big head, has keeled over, fainted. It's hot in here, we're squashed together, and we've been standing for half an hour. There are no seats in the assembly hall. A couple of pupils usually pass out every morning – sometimes genuinely, sometimes as a cunning exit strategy.

Greg's one of the genuine cases. Two teachers rush over from the side to drag him out. While they're doing so, one of them glances up at the stage, frowns, but doesn't say anything. It's never crossed my mind before that the teachers might feel as uncomfortable as the pupils in Mr Nerritt's assemblies – or, indeed, that the teachers, their stone-like faces ranged round the perimeter of the hall, might be thinking anything whatsoever. Theirs is clearly a practised impassivity, which Greg, Croggers, Danny, and, of course, Mr Nerritt do not share. He happily salutes the unconscious Greg and the teachers carrying him out, whistling: 'Wowee, that's cool. Looks like the Holy Spirit really moved that boy. *Alleluia*.'

'Greg faints every assembly, Sir,' Croggers calls out. Sir doesn't – or doesn't seem to – hear, and picks up his guitar again. There's a general groan. We thought it was over.

'To celebrate, let's have a short encore, shall we?' asks Mr Nerritt. He pauses, waiting for an enthusiastic 'Yes!' that never arrives. So he supplies it himself: 'Yeah, man!'

He strums his guitar, tuning it. 'This one's about Jesus's love. It's about how that infinite love is in all of us, in our minds and bodies, and about how, if you shut your heart to it, you're joining the ranks of the Damned. As it says in Corinthians: "Your body is the temple of the Holy Ghost which is in you, which ye have of God." You need to open the doors of God's temple. You need to welcome into your heart the grace of Jesus Christ, just like that boy who fainted. If you don't, you're defiling His temple, man. You're putting yourself on a level with' – he strums a chord for each group of sinners he lists, in a kind of mini-recitative – 'thieves, liars, murderers, and self-abusers.'

The last chord – or, to be more specific, last lyric – elicits a mixed response among the assembled pupils: some snigger, others look blank, and others, like me, go bright red. *Oh God, he's found me out.* Whether 'he' refers to God, Jesus Christ, or Mr Nerritt is unclear in my mind. But it doesn't matter. All that matters is that, ever since I lost my virginity at eleven to my teddy-giraffe, I've been convinced I'm pretty much damned, well on my way to hell, wrapped up in a tissue. I want to stop, but there's no escape route, no confessional absolution available in my form of Christianity; and besides, the shapely fluffiness of my giraffe's calves keeps seducing me back to 'the rank sweat of an enseamèd bed', as Hamlet says.

According to the Nerrittian Creed, there seems little chance of escape from the 'enseamèd bed' anyway. Even if you don't *physically* abuse 'God's temple' (i.e. your own body), merely think-ing about it is enough to damn you. 'You see, that's the wonder of Jesus's new covenant,' claims Mr Nerritt. 'The Ark of the Covenant is now inside us all. If it so much as crosses your mind to steal, covet another guy's ass, or commit adultery, you're desecrating your own Ark.'

I steal a glance at Mrs Jones, who's standing to the far left of my row, and silently apologise to God for coveting another man's wife's ass, breaking at least two commandments for the price of one. On top of that, I'm also guilty of objectifying her, and bearing false witness to Croggers, who accused me of staring at her bot-tom: 'No, I wasn't, honest.'

'I guess we are all guilty of everything,' suggests William Burroughs – or, as Fyodor Dostoevsky puts it, 'each single one of us is indubitably guilty in respect of all creatures and all things upon the earth.' Mr Nerritt certainly makes it feel that way, even if he hasn't quite mastered Dostoevsky's turn of phrase. I'm rid-dled with guilt like woodworm, and there's no one around to cure it. There are no adults reassuring me: 'Don't worry, it's fine, it's just your hormones, teenage lust for teachers' bottoms is perfectly natural.' Instead, even the most laid-back, apparently 'right-on' adult I know, Mr Nerritt, threatens me with eternal damnation. I know I'm going to hell. Or perhaps I'm already there: sometimes, my own adolescent consciousness seems like a 'lake which burns with fire and brimstone'. 'The mind is its own place, and in itself / Can make a Heav'n of Hell, a Hell of Heav'n', as Milton says.

Our society is all too happy, it seems to me, to condemn adolescents to a mental hell in multifarious ways (nowadays with added social media). This is partly because many grown-ups – Mr Bulging Suit and Mr Nerritt included – subscribe to a notion of what one might call Teenage Original Sin, such that teenagers somehow deserve hellish punishment. They seem to believe that kids, and particularly older kids, are inherently bad, and school is there to manage them, contain them, spiritually or literally beat the badness out of them. Puberty, on this (il)logic, is the Fall where kids eat the forbidden hormonal fruit. Teenagers are bad because of an inevitable biological process.

Despite the demise of Mr Bulging Suit's corporal methods, I think the attitude persists in a wider sense – namely, that teenagers, and sometimes children in general, are necessarily in the wrong, and need harsh disciplinary systems to keep them in check. In 2021, Katharine Birbalsingh, headteacher and chair of the government's Social Mobility Commission, responded favourably to a tweet on Twitter that read: 'We are all born "bad", that is why it is so important to be morally educated.' Birbalsingh answered: 'Exactly. Original Sin. Children need to be taught right from wrong and then habituated into choosing good over evil.' In an education system based on Original Sin, it seems *we are [always already] guilty of everything*.

If this is the case for children generally, it's particularly adolescents who get it in the neck. Birbalsingh was co-founder and headteacher of Michaela Community School, a notoriously strict secondary school; and it's in secondary schools that the idea of

Original Sin really flourishes. Adolescents are inherently suspect, always on the verge of transgressing, unless strictly policed – if no longer with the cane, then with anything else disciplinarians can get their hands on. Adults flood the perceived moral gap between themselves and high-school kids with detentions, seclusions, referrals, uniforms, assemblies, pep talks, lectures, anger, disappointment, rhetoric, even religion. Maybe they're not merely suspicious of teenagers, but scared of them too.

Fear and suspicion radiate beyond school walls as well. Anyone who's been on the school run might have witnessed the near-murderous feelings some drivers seem to exhibit towards teenagers, putting their foot down as soon as the latter try to cross the road. They hoot at them, they swear at them. The British seem to have a problem with adolescents, treating them as both children-gone-wrong and pre-failed-adults. I reckon it's born of an unconscious jealousy of youth, or something like that.

It doesn't have to be like this. There is an alternative, non-murderous, and maybe idealistic view available: that if you treat teenagers as good, decent, kind human beings, the vast majority will live up to that expectation. In other words, there is an idea that disciplinary systems are self-fulfilling prophecies, which serve to shape the behaviour of those trapped within them. If you chuck children without preparation into an unforgiving environment, which is at least as bad as the adult world; if your system is dominated by threats and punishments, and rewards are the exception; if children imbibe suspicion to the extent that they come to suspect themselves, then the inevitable result is that they will flail, maybe lash out, and then you will have to punish them more, and then they will flail more, and then you'll have to up the punishments, and so on, and so forth, in a hellish cycle.

If, by contrast, you ease kids into an environment full of rewards, encouragement, and understanding, then maybe the cycle will work out differently. It sounds obvious, perhaps. But however obvious, it remains, in our sadomasochistic, crypto-Puritanical society, terribly rare. We don't seem to believe that organisations might be based on ideals of love, trust, and kindness, as opposed to omnipresent suspicion. We seem determined to aim for dystopia rather than utopia when it comes to education. We can't conceive, at least on a national level, of a disciplinary system that can do anything but make hells of kids' minds.

When Mr Nerritt's final number starts, it certainly makes a hell of the assembly hall. Like an interminable Last Trump, it's more extended medley than short encore, more EP than 48 single – a many-headed beast of 'Jesus Christ's Lonely Sinners' Band', 'It's Been a Hard Hell's Night', and 'Hey, Jesus'. While the elongated coda of the third song is going on (*Na-na-na-nananana*), Danny Beaker holds his hands in the air, enraptured, and starts swaying side to side – as an excuse to knock down the boys in his row like dominoes. Mr Nerritt smiles from the stage, happy to see such enthusiasm among his flock. He builds to a grand peroration: '*Amen-Alleluia-Amen!*'

Afterwards, as all the embarrassed Damned sigh, yawn, and shuffle, readying themselves to file out, Danny is the only one to applaud. He puts two fingers in his mouth and wolf-whistles. 'Wow, Sir,' he calls out, 'that was *cool*. You've really, like, inspired us, *man*.'

The nature of Danny's inspiration becomes all too clear that lunchtime, as he stalks the playground making crosses in the air – then smacking kids on the forehead, knocking them to the ground. 'The power of Christ compels you!' he declares, chucking liquid over them from a flask he's carrying. He claims the liquid is holy water. It's yellow. 'Alleluia!' he shouts. 'Stay *cool* in hell, man!'

He's seen a bootleg version of *The Exorcist*, and is mixing up the movie with Mr Nerritt. He's also mixing up denominations, Catholic and low-church Protestant, but I don't think that bothers Danny too much. He's creating a patched-together, Frankenstein's Monster of a religion, ideal for a new mode of bullying: 'Stay-cool-man-god-bless-you-the-power-of-Christ-compels-you-*la-plume-de-ma-tante*-alle-fucking-luia-amen.'

Denominationally speaking, Mr Nerritt's form of Christianity is what our parents would call 'Pentecostal', and what my elder brother terms 'tambourine-bashing-happy-clappy'.

Still, despite the tambourine bashing and mangled Beatles songs, Mr Nerritt claims he's arrived at his faith through reason, and is very balanced about it all – to the extent that, in R.E. lessons this term, he's decided he's going to discuss the origins of the world according to 'many different theories and cultures', giving each one its due weight. That way, he says, we can decide for ourselves, as he has. He wouldn't want to impose his own faith on his pupils. Oh no. That wouldn't be *cool*.

Nevertheless, the claim that he'll discuss 'many different theories and cultures' turns out to be somewhat of an exaggeration, in that most of his lessons boil down to a straightforward comparison of Biblical Creationism versus Darwinian evolution. No other theories or cultures seem to have reached R.E. lessons in 1980s Stoke. 'I'll deal with the different theories fairly and in a balanced way,' Mr Nerritt declares, clicking onto an overhead projector (O.H.P.) image of a bearded man – whom we assume is God, but might equally be Darwin – holding the Earth in His hands.

Over the next few weeks, in a *balanced* way, his O.H.P.s flick through the seven-day Creation, Adam and Eve (who always have conveniently placed shrubbery to hand), the story of Cain and Abel (which we discover is not a TV mini-series by Jeffrey Archer), the Land of Nod (which has nothing to do with Big Ears) – and then, finally and most memorably, Noah and the Great Flood.

From behind the O.H.P. machine, Mr Nerritt clicks onto an image of the Earth surrounded by a gigantic halo of water. 'This, you see, kids, is the canopy that's mentioned in Genesis. It's like a huge balloon of water surrounding the Earth. All God had to do is burst it for the Great Flood to happen. Then – *wallop*.' He claps his hands together with the *wallop*, and grins. I think he's enjoying the apocalypse-by-water-balloon. 'Wow, man, *cool.*'

My friend Carrot Hair, who's a self-proclaimed atheist, pipes up: 'But, Sir, how did the sun get through to Adam and Eve if there was, like, a big balloon round the Earth?'

Mr Nerritt isn't fazed: 'Because of *science*. Light and heat can pass through balloons and water. It's another example of how science and Christianity are compatible with each other. You see that, don't you, after everything we've talked about? Science and religion can be friends. They share the same vibes, man.'

Mr Nerritt nods, as if agreeing with himself, acknowledging his own wisdom. I nod too, taken in for the moment by his unique teaching style, its incongruous intermingling of wheedling informality and bully-boy fundamentalist rhetoric. He hectors and seduces, sometimes in the same sentence. As I pointed out in Chapters 1 and 2, certain types of bullying are packed full of incongruities, inconsistencies, paradoxes – and that's what makes them so slippery, so dangerous. It's why Mr Nerritt occasionally wins me over, in a way that the all-too-consistent Bulging Suit will never do. No doubt he exercised a not dissimilar, if more damaging, effect on some of his later victims, shall we say.

More on them later. As for myself, I sometimes wander home in a daze after Mr Nerritt's lessons, and tell my family what he's said, as if it's gospel truth – at which point my elder siblings helpfully scoff me out of my credulity: 'You're so gormless and gullible, Jonathan. You'd believe the Earth is flat if a teacher told you so. Sucker.'

Mr Nerritt preys on suckers, or tries to, often seeming to single out one pupil for special attention. In his lesson on the Great Flood, his chosen victim is Carrot Hair, on whom he's smiling down with the hypnotic expression of one who's benevolently bestowing wisdom on a simple child: *Bless you, my son. Stay cool.* In this regard, he's like a hip version of one of Dickens's vicars – the Rev. Chadband in *Bleak House*, for instance, who is said to have a pulpit habit of fixing some member of his congregation with his eye, and fatly arguing his points with that particular person; who is understood to be expected to be moved to an occasional grunt, groan, gasp, or other audible expression of inward working; which expression of inward working, being echoed by some elderly lady in the next pew, and so communicated, like a game of forfeits, through a circle of the more fermentable sinners present, serves the purpose of parliamentary cheering, and gets Mr Chadband's steam up.

Though he fixes his eye on an 'ill-starred' individual, the Rev. Chadband is really addressing the entire 'circle of ... sinners' – that is, those assembled as a whole, whom he calls 'My friends!' Mr Nerritt does something similar: in blessing Carrot Hair with his superior knowledge, it feels like he's addressing everyone by proxy. Even when ostensibly focussed on a particular pupil, that is, Mr Nerritt's pulpit-benedictions are really directed towards us all, the Damned Kids *en masse*. The 'immediate recipient of his discourse' is less a specific or named individual, more a representative, a conduit, a foil. Like Chadband ('My friends!'), Mr Nerritt never uses real names for anyone, never seems to see any of us as individuals.

'Look,' he says to his current foil, 'I'll give you another *cool* example where, like, science and religion meet.' He clicks onto the next O.H.P. It's an image of the Ark, with measurements round it (300 cubits x 50 cubits x 30 cubits), along with line drawings of some of the animals therein (lions, bears, aardvarks, super-size ants), and their width and length measurements. 'Here, you can see, it's been worked out by proper scientists; all the animals would've fitted onto the Ark quite easily. Honestly, look at the diagram. It's simple Maths. If you measured all the different species end to end and doubled it (because, y'know, they went in two-by-two), you'd still have plenty of room on the Ark for Noah's family, belongings, and maybe for species that don't exist any more.'

'You mean like dinosaurs, Sir?' asks Carrot Hair. 'What happened to them?'

'Ah, it's funny you should ask that, because that's explained on my next slide.' Mr Nerritt clicks the button, and we're faced with a felt-tipped image of the Deluge coming down like Niagara. The Ark is in the foreground, riding high on a wave, while Tyrannosauruses, Brontosauruses, Triceratops are in the background, flailing, a tangle of legs, and torsos, and teeth. It looks like they've missed the bus and are trying to flag it down: *Stop, wait, we were only a couple of minutes late, Noah, you drink-driving bastard.*

Mr Nerritt steps away from the projector, and stands in front of us, next to the image, gesturing at it like a TV weatherperson in front of a map. He's obviously taken a long time colouring in this picture, and is proud of it. 'This shows you what happened,' he declares, as if the picture were photographic evidence, or drawn live at the scene. 'What we now call "dinosaurs" is just the name for animals that Noah left behind. It says in Genesis that there were giants roaming the Earth before the Great Flood. That's the Biblical term for dinosaurs. But they were wiped out, like everything else that wasn't on the Ark: "And all flesh died that moved upon the earth, both of fowl, and of cattle, and of beast, and of every creeping thing that creepeth upon the earth, and every man."'

'Why did Noah leave them behind, Sir?' asks Carrot Hair. 'I mean, it must be pretty hard to forget a Tyrannosaurus Rex, or summit as big as that.' Carrot Hair's having fun baiting Nerritt. He turns round to face everyone, to share his enjoyment: 'What was he like, Sir? "*Durr*, I knew I was missing summit."' There's scattered laughter round the room. From the back, Croggers makes a noise that's meant to sound like someone (presumably Noah) getting the wrong answer on a quiz show. Carrot Hair grins.

Unlike the Rev. Chadband, whose message is 'communicated' via his foil 'like a game of forfeits, through a circle of the more fermentable sinners present', Mr Nerritt seems to have hit upon the wrong foil. Instead of his message, it seems to be Carrot Hair's that is connecting with the fermentable classroom of sinners. He's doing his very best to burst, or at least deflate, Mr Nerritt's rhetorical balloon. Many of the kids are openly jeering now, egging Carrot Hair on. It's turning into one of those micro-carnivalesque moments in school when trickery and laughter temporarily destabilise the *status quo* – when it's unclear who's in charge of the lesson, who's bullying whom.

Not that Mr Nerritt is necessarily aware of the trickery or laughter. He's too busy thinking through his answer to Carrot Hair's question. 'Well,' he says slowly, drawing out the word, 'Noah was known to have a few too many drinks.'

'So he was, like, drunk driving, Sir? No wonder he saw two of every animal.' Cue more sinful sniggers round the classroom.

'Maybe, maybe not. Simmer down, please, everyone.' Mr Nerritt waves his hands up and down, like he's calming flood-waters. 'Maybe he felt the dinosaurs were too big for the Ark – although, as I explained, there was plenty of space to go around. Or maybe God told him that the dinosaurs deserved to be destroyed, along with all the human sinners. I mean, dinosaurs were pretty horrible. Not *cool*. Or maybe Noah was worried they'd eat the other animals on board.' Mr Nerritt smiles half-heartedly, though it's unclear whether he's joking or not. 'So as you can see, there are many *rational* explanations concerning the extinction of dinosaurs.'

Having almost been thrown off for a moment, he mutters 'Cool' under his breath a few times, and gets back on track: 'Of course, it's been shown over and over by palaeontologists that fossils – fossils of dinosaurs, and plants, and stuff – bear traces of the Great Flood. The evidence is there, *man*, in the geological remains. It shows how Creation can easily be reconciled with modern science.'

'But what about carbon dating, Sir?' asks Carrot Hair. We've been discussing carbon dating in a recent Physics lesson.

'What about it?' asks Mr Nerritt.

'Carbon dating says the fossils are millions of years old. That dinosaurs lived millions of years before people. That the world wasn't, like, made in seven days.'

Mr Nerritt is ready for this objection: 'Don't worry about that. A lot of people think fossils and rocks have a kind of in-built age. They were put there by God already old.'

'But why would God do that, Sir? To take the p... I mean, to trick us? Like a practical joke?'

'Not exactly. More to test our faith, I think. To challenge us to find ways to reconcile God's Word with the physical evidence. I've shown today how you can do that' – we're heading towards the end of the lesson, so he's trying to wrap up the pseudo-debate – 'for instance, how the Great Flood can explain the extinction of the dinosaurs, and...'

'What about the dinosaurs that could swim?' Carrot Hair asks suddenly.

'Pardon?'

'The dinosaurs that could swim – you know, Ichthyosauruses-es-es and stuff. Oh, and the ones that could fly too – you know, Pterodactyl-osauruses-es-es.' I'm not sure whether the stammer is genuine, or if Carrot Hair's deliberately elongating the dino-names for comedic effect. 'What about swimming-o-sauruses-es-es? They wouldn't have drowned, Sir.'

Mr Nerritt's mouth opens and closes for a moment, like a flailing Ichthyosaur. He repeats the word 'Cool' under his breath, perhaps reassuring himself, or gearing up to answer. Apart from that, there's a strange silence – unusual in his lessons – until the bell goes for break, and we never learn what happened to prehistoric aquatic or aerial life in the Great Flood.

Next week's R.E. lesson, Mr Nerritt is off ill, so we're with the lovely Mrs Jones instead. For a while, it feels like heaven, half-watching her tracksuited bottom, half-designing pretend-tabloid headlines about Moses and the Plagues of Egypt: *Locusts Ate My Hamster, Moses Burnt My Bush, Topless Frogs on Page 3*, etc.

Then something catches the corner of my eye, and I glance to my right. A blue and orange flame (yes, a flame) shoots past my table, up the aisle, towards the front – where Mrs Jones is writing 'Pestilence' on the blackboard, her back to the class. The flame doesn't quite reach Mrs Jones's bottom.

For a second, I wonder if the flame's from the fiery pit, finally come to swallow me and my lascivious fantasies up. Then it's gone, and I wonder if I'm seeing things. Perhaps Mrs Jones's bottom has gone to my head, as it were.

She turns round and smiles at us, says something about dead first-borns and water turning to blood, then turns back to the board. Another flame shoots past me.

I swivel round to see where it's coming from. Danny Beaker is at the back of the room, holding a lighter in front of an aerosol can, using it as a flamethrower. 'It's the eleventh plague,' says Danny. 'Spontaneous combustion.'

'Aim for her bottom,' whispers Croggers, who's sitting next to him. 'It's a big enough target, that.'

Danny shoots a third flame towards the target. He misses, because Mrs Jones ducks down at the last minute, to write 'Exodus' in one corner of the blackboard. 'Carry on children,' she says, unaware of the imminent danger to her posterior.

'Stop it,' I hiss at Danny. But he grins demonically, and shoots another flame, this time narrowly missing me. He's turning Mrs Jones's wonderful lesson into a miniature inferno. The classroom is its own place, and in itself can make a Heav'n of Hell, a Hell of Heav'n – as Milton didn't quite say.

If my own teenage mind sometimes made a Hell of Heav'n, I can't really blame the kind of Christianity into which I was baptised. Anglican Christianity – at least, the corner of it I knew – didn't seem to have much to say about hell or heaven, and generally avoided those subjects, as a little tasteless. As a child, I went to church and my mum's Sunday School regularly, destroyed Egypt with fuzzy felt locusts, built a model Garden of Gethsemane with Easter Eggs in place of disciples, ran my cars *brum-brum-brum* up and down pews during tedious sermons, played roly-polies in the vicarage while my parents and the vicar sipped tea – tea and cake being, as many have pointed out, the true Anglican Eucharist. But, despite all this, I rarely if ever heard the word 'hell' in sermons, Bible readings, or even casual swearing. When I asked my mother, one day, what she thought hell was, her answer was flippant, though also telling: 'A place where you can't get a good cup of tea.'

Nor did anyone seem quite sure who might be sent to this tea-less place. While murder, robbery, adultery, covetousness, overt homosexuality, feminism, swearing, pop stardom, dislike of tea, and pre-marital sex with cuddly toys were all, no doubt, *sins*, no one ever dared say outright that you'd go to hell if guilty of any of them. Condemnation, judgemental absolutism, in this respect, were also a little tasteless.

Maybe this haziness on the question of what qualified you for heaven or hell made my own adolescent terrors worse, not better. At least with the Mr Nerritts you knew where you were, or rather where you were going, as a thief, liar, or self-abuser. With my church, there was no such sense of direction. So, in the end, I read all signposts as pointing downwards: *This way to the fiery pit, sans tea*. In lieu of Chadbands or Nerritts, let alone Bosches or Dantes, I invented my own hells, and populated them with copies of myself. I terrorised myself – my own accused and accuser, my own Nerritt and the Damned, my own bully and victim in one. It's the spiritual acme of bullying, bullying-as-solipsism – the end-point of Protestantism's emancipation of the individual conscience, as Milton and others have recognised. Protestantism is the internalisation of bullying. And not only that: you end up internalising priest, congregation, judge, sinner, heaven, hell, God, Satan, in one almighty playground scrap of the soul. It gets quite busy in there.[1]

Whenever there were playground scraps at our high school, most kids naturally ran towards them, sucked in like gravity by the call: *Fight! Fight! Fight!* Just a few of us would do the opposite, deliberately wandering off in the opposite direction, suddenly inheriting the rest of the playground as our own space – if only for a few precious minutes.

   A lot of twentieth- and twenty-first-century memoirs do something analogous in spiritual terms: that is, they tell the story of people who wander away from Christianity's playground scrap of the soul, resisting its gravitational pull. There are many such 'deconversion' narratives, from Edmund Gosse's genre-defining memoir, *Father and Son* (1907), to Jeanette Winterson's semi-autobiographical novel, *Oranges Are Not the Only Fruit* (1985) and her subsequent memoir, *Why Be Happy When You Could Be Normal?* (2011), to Tara Westover's *Educated* (2018). If one of the roots of modern autobiographical writing is in Christian conversion testimonies – by, for instance, St Augustine or Margery Kempe – many memoirs of the last two centuries have reversed these narratives. In place of a Road to Damascus, modern memoirs tell the more ambivalent story of the road away from it, often during adolescence or early adulthood. Their protagonists choose to walk away from Damascene Revelation, turning their backs on a bully-God and His earthly mediators (i.e. domineering parents or priests). In doing so, you could say these narratives set out to celebrate Teenage Original

---

[1]On the internalisation of bullying and discipline in a more secular sense, see also Chapter 6, 'History'.

Sin, rather than deploring it, transmuting it into something willed, positive.

In Winterson's novel, the road away from Damascus is literal *and* theological: the narrator ends up moving away from both Accrington and her mother's non-conformist Christianity. Prior to this, her childhood is dominated by the church; and, although my childhood was by no means overshadowed by religion to the same degree, there are certain elements of her early experience with which I do identify – for example, the fuzzy felts:

There was some Fuzzy Felt to make Bible scenes with, and I was just beginning to enjoy a rewrite of Daniel in the lions' den when Pastor Finch appeared. I put my hands into my pockets and looked at the lino.

'Little girl,' he began, then he caught sight of the Fuzzy Felt.

'What's that?'

'Daniel,' I answered.

'But that's not right,' he said, aghast. 'Don't you know that Daniel escaped? In your picture the lions are swallowing him'....

'I got mixed up.'

He smiled. 'Let's put it right, shall we?' And he carefully rearranged the lions in one corner, and Daniel in the other. 'What about Nebuchadnezzar? Let's do the Astonishment at Dawn scene next.' He started to root through the Fuzzy Felt, looking for a king....

I left him to it. When I came back into the hall somebody asked me if I'd seen Pastor Finch.

'He's in the Sunday School Room playing with the Fuzzy Felt,' I replied.

'Don't be fanciful, Jeanette,' said the voice.

For me, this doesn't seem 'fanciful' at all – rather, entirely realistic. *Of course* the vicar might be in the Sunday School playing with fuzzy felts. In fact, in my experience, he's far more likely to be doing that – along with sipping tea, eating Battenberg cake, manning the tombola at the summer fête – than he is to be delivering fire-and-brimstone sermons.

By contrast, Winterson's evangelical Pastor Finch does give fire-and-brimstone sermons, as well as playing with fuzzy felts. He has no problem declaring that he is 'afraid of Hell, of eternal damnation', both for himself and others; he claims the narrator is full of demons because of her homosexuality, and attempts an exorcism on her; and he drives a mini-bus, an 'old Bedford van' with

the terrified damned painted on one side and the heavenly host painted on the other. On the back doors and front bonnet he'd inscribed in green lettering, HEAVEN OR HELL? IT'S YOUR CHOICE. He was very proud of the bus, and told of the many miracles worked inside and out. Inside had six seats, so that the choir could travel with him, leaving enough room for musical instruments and a large first-aid kit in case the demon combusted somebody.

'What do you do about the flames?' we asked.

'I use an extinguisher,' he explained.

No doubt the Alan Bennettish humour in this passage is all about incongruity – incongruity of language (apocalyptic language mixed with the quotidian), incongruity of context (the terrified damned appearing on an old Bedford van in Accrington), and incongruity of message (demonic combustion regulated by proto-Health and Safety provisions, including a fire extinguisher and a first-aid kit). For me, though, these incongruities are softened by inside knowledge of what Protestant Christianity is like in provincial England. There seems nothing fanciful in Winterson's description of the old Bedford van. It all seems totally commonplace to someone brought up in a Potteries church full of fuzzy felts and Battenbergs, to someone whose R.E. teacher mingled the language of the Book of Revelation with that of the Beatles. Perhaps this clash of languages is inevitable in a provincial, post-industrial, and essentially pagan England where Christianity always seems out of place.

Though the narrator eventually moves away from Accrington and her mother's church, Winterson's novel doesn't neatly resolve its clashing incongruities. The narrator escapes to the University of Oxford, but this merely adds a new layer of incongruity, the 'two realities' of past and present. All the incongruities persist within her, whether she's in Oxford or Accrington. 'I came to this city to escape', she says, but there are still 'threads that intend to bring you back. Mind turns to the pull, it's hard to pull away'. The religious past persists in mental echoes, wherever you are. Ultimately, you no longer need the Pastor Finches or Mr Nerritts, because your own mind does the job for them, carrying their echoes, incongruities, condemnations everywhere. 'If the demons lie within', Winterson declares, sounding rather like Milton, 'they travel with you'.

And sometimes, the demonic incongruities don't just travel with you: they derail you, crash the Bedford van. This is the case for one of the pastors in *Oranges Are Not the Only Fruit*. At the end of the novel, the well-respected Rev. Eli Bone, secretary of the 'Society for the Lost' in Morecambe, is unveiled as a fraudster, fornicator, and adulterer, who has embezzled 'most of the [society's] money ... to pay ... gambling debts' and 'his wife's maintenance. His estranged wife. The woman he lived with was his girlfriend'.

Something similar happens in *Bleak House* to the Rev. Chadband. By the end of Dickens's novel, he is exposed as not only a glutton and free-loader, but also an extortionist, who attempts to blackmail the aristocrat, Sir Leicester Dedlock, over his wife's 'sinful secret'. Ever the preacher, Chadband manages to make extortion sound (incongruously) like a religious sermon:

'My friends, we are now ... in the mansions of the rich and great. Why are we now in the mansions of the rich and great, my friends? Is it because we are invited? Because we are bidden to feast with them, because we are bidden to rejoice with them, because we are bidden to play the lute with them, because we are bidden to dance with them? No. Then why are we here, my friends? Are we in possession of a sinful secret, and do we require corn, and wine, and oil, or what is much the same thing, money, for the keeping thereof? Probably so, my friends.'

If sinful secrets, fornication, and money all feature in both the Rev. Chadband's and the Rev. Bone's stories, they did too in Mr Nerritt's – to a degree undreamt of in *Bleak House* or *Oranges Are Not the Only Fruit*. Mr Nerritt's story trumps them both, in terms of its demonic incongruity. Twenty-five years after the lesson on the Great Flood, I read his subsequent story in a tabloid newspaper (not unlike the ones we used to make in R.E.), a cutting of which was sent to me by Carrot Hair.

It turned out that Mr Nerritt – pictured next to the article, older, balder, his denim faded – had got caught out, in his own self-made Deluge of Sin. He'd been found guilty of keeping a brothel in Birmingham ('City Sparklers'), and possession of Class-A drugs. Apparently, he'd also been conducting an affair with a married woman and her teenage daughter in Spain, and had allegedly beaten up the latter. There were hints of other nefarious elements to the tale: gaslighting, grooming, coercive control, who knows what else. His was a physical, linguistic, and psychological violence, all wrapped up in a bullying hypocrisy.

In sum, it was quite the tabloid field-day: *R.E. Teacher, Lay Preacher, and Brothel Keeper Attacked My Daughter*. Mr Nerritt had, it seems, been a busy man. I still have no idea how he'd managed to balance a teaching job with his trans-continental extra-curricular activities. I wonder if he'd ever got his guitar out, as it were, for the punters in City Sparklers: 'Hey, man, d'you fancy a quick song, "Jesus's Fields Forever", before you...?' Then again, that might have put a dampener on the sparklers

For me, it put a dampener on fiction. Carrot Hair suggested I turn Mr Nerritt into a novel, but I felt that his near-antediluvian level of hypocrisy was more than fiction could bear. Winterson's pastors, Dickens's comic sermonisers are one thing; but Nerritt is quite another, and his tabloid-style story would surely drown a novel. 'That's ridiculous', the critics would declare, 'unbelievable, caricatured, absurd.'

If, in this respect, reality is stranger than fiction, it is also at least as absurd as religious faith. In his great work of theological philosophy, *Fear and Trembling* (1843), Søren Kierkegaard claims that, to make the 'leap of faith', we have to 'believe ... the absurd'. Faith exists, for Kierkegaard, 'in virtue ... of the *absurd*, in virtue of the fact that with God all things are possible'. Yet perhaps mundane reality also, on occasion, demands a belief in the absurd, a 'leap of faith' in reverse. On the one hand, religious faith *may* ask you to believe in things as absurd as resurrection or dinosaurs drowning in the Great Flood; on the other, so-called reality, as depicted in a memoir like this one, might ask you to believe in an evangelical R.E. teacher who was also a Tyrannosaur of Sin, a Bullyosaurus Rex.

Memoir-reality and real-life bullying share this in common: that their extremes often seem absurd, almost impossible to credit. To believe in a memoir can demand a big leap of faith, as can believing in the testimony of a victim of bullying. Indeed, sometimes it's the same leap, given how many memoirs are about bullying or abusive relationships of one kind or another.

A lot of people, I think, struggle to make the leap in any direction – whether that's towards, say, memoir-reality, bullying-reality, or religious faith – and get stuck in the middle. Perhaps the limbo in the middle *is* fiction, or at least 'realist' fiction, which can seem reassuringly rationalistic, anodyne compared with the absurd alternatives.[2]

Someone who was never stuck in the middle, despite suggesting that I turn Mr Nerritt into a novel, was Carrot Hair. Arch-atheist-realist-and-trickster as a teenager, he was born again in his early twenties, exchanging one form of the absurd (Stoke reality) for another (drowning dinosaurs). He went on to bully himself dreadfully.

---

[2] I talk a little more about the tension between certain assumptions of realist fiction, on the one hand, and the absurdities of bullying, on the other, in Chapter 7, 'Politics'.

6

History

There is, on the whole, nothing on earth intended for innocent people so horrible as a school. To begin with, it is a prison. But it is in
some respects more cruel than a prison.... In a prison they may torture your body; but they do not torture your brains.

George Bernard Shaw, *A Treatise on Parents and Children*

Of course, Shaw is wrong. Modern prisons torture your brains
too, maybe to a greater extent, in fact, than they torture your
body. That's certainly what Michel Foucault suggests, in his (in)
famous book *Discipline and Punish* (1975). He argues that, from
the eighteenth century onwards, the penal systems of Western
Europe moved away from torturing the body to controlling the
mind – from physical to psychological forms of punishment. 'The
expiation that once rained down upon the body', claims Foucault,
'[is] replaced by a punishment that acts in depth on the heart, the
thoughts, the will, the inclinations.'

It does so through incarceration and surveillance. In place
of older modes of confrontation and spectacle, where bodies
were publicly beaten, maimed, even dismembered, modern
penal systems substitute a more inward form of punishment,
where convicts are imprisoned, isolated, and watched. The ideal
model of this latter system, according to Foucault, is the notorious 'Panopticon', designed in the late eighteenth century by
the founder of Utilitarianism, Jeremy Bentham. At its simplest,
Bentham's Panopticon is a prison in which all the cells are arranged
around a central watchtower. The person in the watchtower can
see into every single cell, and this induces in the inmates 'a state

of conscious and permanent visibility that assures the automatic functioning of power.' Conscious of being watched, inmates are 'caught up in a power situation of which they are themselves the bearers'. In other words, they internalise the Panopticon's power structures, and impose those structures on themselves. Because they feel permanently visible, they become their own jailers, their own (psychological) torturers.

Which means, ultimately, that they don't need anyone else to perform those roles. It's one of the distinctive features of Bentham's Panopticon that, although the inmates are visible from the watchtower, they themselves can't return the gaze, can't see into the watchtower; it's set up as a kind of one-way mirror, so there might be no one in there. There might be no one watching. The Panopticon is a machine that sustains power relations through a sleight of hand, without any individual having to be in overall control. As Foucault suggests,

a real subjection is born ... from a fictitious relation. It is not necessary to use force to constrain the convict to good behaviour, the madman to calm, the worker to work.... He who is subjected to a field of visibility, and who knows it, assumes responsibility for the constraints of power; ... he inscribes in himself the power relation to which he simultaneously plays both roles.

This self-inscribed power relation is not only that of jailer and convict. It might also be that of manager and worker, doctor and 'mad person', teacher and pupil. According to Foucault, the Panopticon is not only the model of an ideal prison: it is factory, asylum, school. It is the blueprint for all modern institutions and, for that matter, bourgeois society at large. It encapsulates how modern, Western society functions on a grand scale, through technologies of surveillance, through the internalisation of power relations, through self-policing. For much of the time, citizens of a panoptic society don't need a police constable or teacher beating them with a stick, because they (mentally) beat themselves. As educationalist Paulo Freire puts it, 'the oppressed' in modern society 'are at one and the same time themselves and the oppressor whose consciousness they have internalised.' Self-oppression, self-coercion, self-discipline: these can be the most efficient of all forms of bullying.

The move from real sticks wielded by others to internalised self-oppression is gradual, an on-going process. It started in the eighteenth century, but the project is still incomplete, particularly in prisons. The hellish treatment of detainees at Guantanamo Bay detention camp, for instance, shows that physical torture remains a fundamental part of prison discipline, under certain circumstances.

In many Western schools, by contrast, it would seem that the panoptic ideal is close to being realised, given that physical forms of punishment have all but vanished from the teacher-pupil relationship. This happened in most French schools more than 100 years ago, but corporal punishment persisted on this side of the Channel – as 'The English Vice' – for much longer. In the end, the European Court of Human Rights did for it, ruling that corporal punishment couldn't be administered without parental consent. Subsequently, in 1986, the British Parliament banned it in state schools for good.

I was there, in school, at that watershed moment. I witnessed the change from a system based on caning to a system based on surveillance, one that attempted to act 'on the heart, the thoughts, the will, the inclinations.' The change was both gradual and sudden. On the one hand, it was happening throughout my childhood, as teachers used corporal punishment less and less, substituting other modes of discipline for it; on the other, 1986 was a transformative moment, and my school was never the same gothically terrifying place again.

I was overjoyed by the cane's demise, as Mr Bulging Suit's power seemed to melt away before my eyes. It was like the climactic scene of *The Wizard of Oz*, and someone had thrown a bucket of water over him: *I'm melting, melting!* – until all that was left was an empty suit and gown. Not that he was, by any means, really as bad as The Wicked Witch of the West. He just seemed so to me – a trembling, effeminate, 4'8 lion with bows – at the time.

Following the death of The Wicked Witch in *The Wizard of Oz*, everyone rejoices at her demise, even her own slaves, the Winkies and Winged Monkeys. For many years, I thought that was the end of the movie, because that moment also usually coincided with my immovable bedtime. 'It's over now, Jonathan,' my mother would say, 'so you can go to sleep.' But of course, it's not *really* the end of the movie. Dorothy still has to confront the Wizard, get home to Kansas. The movie is full of false endings, as is, to an even greater extent, the original novel by L. Frank Baum.

I wonder now if 1986 was also a kind of false ending. After all, the cane was still legal in many private schools in England until 1998, in Scotland until 2000, in Northern Ireland until 2003; and much as I rejoiced, and still do, at the end of corporal punishment in schools, I can see that other forms of psychological punishment, other kinds of domination, have come to fill the cane-shaped gap. As I've pointed out in previous chapters, psychological and physical forms of domination are never mutually exclusive: even where one seems absent, it's really still lurking there, as an implication or threat or ghost. Bentham's Panopticon may operate without physical beatings, but, by definition, incarceration and timetables affect the body in other ways.

Foucault saw all this back in 1975. He wouldn't have shared my joy at the demise of corporal punishment – especially given what, by all accounts, he enjoyed doing in his spare time. No doubt for dedicated sadomasochists, the shift to more psychological forms of domination is not necessarily to be celebrated. And Foucault also understands that there is a sadomasochism of the mind, of the soul, as well as the body.

In *Discipline and Punish,* he is characteristically ambivalent about whether or not the transition from a predominantly physical punishment to mental discipline is a matter of 'improvement'. 'For a long time', he claims, this shift

has been regarded in an overall way as a quantitative phenomenon: less cruelty, less pain, more kindness, more respect, more 'humanity'.... Is there a diminution of intensity? Perhaps. There is certainly a change of objective ... not to punish less, but to punish better; to punish with an attenuated severity perhaps, but in order to punish with more universality and necessity; to ... punish more deeply.

According to Foucault, psychological forms of punishment are 'better' primarily because they are more effective, more all-encompassing. Rather than straightforwardly representing an improvement in humanitarian terms, they are subtler, cleverer, 'deeper'.

If I can't agree with Foucault entirely, if I still believe that corporal punishment was wrong, its abolition a major humanitarian improvement, I can appreciate the force of his argument. I can understand that mental forms of control can be terrible on their own terms, sometimes worse than the short-sharp-shock of caning or another boy's fist. Even in my own limited experience, I know Foucault has got a point. After all, my darkest experience of bullying as an adult was not overtly physical at all, but psychological; and some of the most harrowing experiences of my schooling had little to do with explicit physical violence.

These experiences might seem trivial in hindsight. Yet adults often underestimate the anxieties and horrors of children, peremptorily chucked into an alien world. They fail to understand how terrifying this brand-new world must be for children, and instead go on to heap more terror on top. Call me a woolly liberal (I'm happy if you do), but I can't help feeling that inducing a constant state of terror in a school kid, whether with canes or more subtle forms of psychological torment, is not the best way of encouraging a positive engagement with education. Some kids respond to such terror defensively, some offensively – and then adults punish them for that response, forgetting what it was like to be a scared child.

Adulthood can be a form of emotional amnesia: all too often, adults forget or repress their own childhood terrors, and hence can't comprehend how anxious most schoolchildren are, whether they show it or not. That's one reason why novels, like those of Dickens and Dahl, and poems, like those of Adrian Mitchell and Les Murray, are so important: they remember the intensity of childhood for us. In George Eliot's words, they attempt to 'recall [the] ... early bitterness [of childhood], and ... the strangely perspectiveless conception of life, that gave the bitterness its intensity'. Through such 'revived consciousness', they teach adult readers not to 'pooh-pooh the griefs of ... children'.

By contrast, memoirs, and particularly British memoirs, do sometimes 'pooh-pooh' childhood griefs and anxieties. This is due to the way they're narrated, which usually involves an older narrator looking back on a younger self. All too easily, such a mode of narration can seem condescending, the older self patronising their own younger self, retrospectively superimposing a humorous lens on experiences that were far from funny at the time. No doubt this present memoir is guilty of that, too, at times: of trying to make light of things that were harrowing when I was young, of trying to distance childhood trauma, of adding a pinch of adult salt to immersiveness, of asking: *Why on Earth did that upset me so much back then? There wasn't even a cane or fist involved, mere words and looks. It all seems so trivial, laughable in retrospect. I was such a Cowardly Lion.*

It's January 1983, and the Cowardly Lion (that is, myself) is in Mrs Marshalsea's form. Corporal punishment is still legal, but she doesn't need it in her class. She has other methods, including a kind of 'kangaroo court' that she convenes when a kid's apparently done something unconscionable.

This morning, the court is not yet in session. Instead, we're learning about Henry VIII and his six wives. Mrs Marshalsea's droning on about Henry's first divorce, while I'm sneaking a glance at the girl I half-fancy, Lisa. She sits at the same table as me, and has a cute snub nose.

Unfortunately, arch-nemesis Lee Hardwick also sits nearby, and has noticed my covert glance. He leans over, pokes me in the ribs: 'You fancy her, don't you?' he whispers.

'Who?'

'Lisa. You fancy her. I can tell.'

'I don't.'

'Yes, you do. Admit it.' He pokes me again. 'Admit it. Admit-it-admit-it-admit-it-admit-it.' Poke, poke, poke.

'Ouch, that hurts,' I say.

Mrs Marshalsea glances over and frowns: 'Stop talking, Jonathan. You're such a chatterbox. Stop distracting Lee.'

Lee beams at Mrs Marshalsea, as if to say how much he's enjoying learning about Catherine of Aragon's misery, and the foundation of the Church of England. 'Yeah, stop distracting me, *Taylor*,' he hisses, out of the corner of his mouth.

A few minutes later, he's poking me again: 'You fancy her, don't you? Don't you?'

'No,' I say, staring down at the table, praying that Lisa can't hear him, 'I don't.' My traitorous face belies my words, by turning a burning red.

'You're blushing, like. So you *do* fancy her. You do-do-do-do-do.'

I decide to stay quiet, let it pass, ignore him. That's what my mum says works best when it comes to bullies.

Lee carries on prodding me, hissing, 'You do fancy her,' over and over for a couple of minutes. Then there's quiet, and I wonder if he's stopped, if my mum's right. But no, he's regrouping, changing tack.

'You know,' he whispers, leaning closer, 'that her little sister's in hospital?'

'Yes,' I say, and instantly regret responding.

He grins. 'Well, you do know it's all, like, *your* fault?'

'Eh?'

'Yeah. Her sister saw you one day at Christmas, near their house. So she cycled off dead quick to tell Lisa: "Oh, God, it's that ugly git following you round again." But she went too fast and got knocked over by a car. *Splat.*'

I'm almost crying: 'It's not true!'

'It is, and now she's in a coma, and got scarlet fever, and is going to die or summit. All because of you.'

'I don't believe you!' Yet part of me does: during the Christmas holidays, I had cycled round a couple of times – or maybe, erm, a few more – to stare at the front of Lisa's house, peddling off furiously if anyone opened the door to get the milk or go out. So perhaps I had scared her sister with my ugly face, caused a terrible accident. Perhaps Lee is right. The oracle of bullies, he seems to know everything.

(In retrospect, I can see it was a lucky guess on his part: he couldn't really have known about my regular visits to Lisa's house. But he had a knack of sticking a needle in or near the truth, whether that truth concerned ballet, testicles, or an infantile stalking habit. There were misses too, when he tried sticking the pin in the wrong place, but his hit rate was high enough for the misses to be overlooked).

On this occasion, it's a palpable hit, and I shout: 'Shut up!' and shove him away. 'It's not true!'

The whole class, including Lisa and Mrs Marshalsea, stares at me.

'Jonathan,' says Mrs M., 'that's enough. You've not listened to anything I've said, have you?'

'No, Miss, I mean, yes, Miss.'

'Alright, then, tell me which of Henry's wives were beheaded?'

'I don't know, Miss.'

'Which of his six wives did he actually love?'

'It wasn't me, Miss...'

'I know it wasn't you, silly boy. It was Jane Seymour.'

'I mean, it was Lee – he was...'

'That's enough, Jonathan. Don't bring Lee into this. You clearly weren't listening. You're always day-dreaming or chattering. Well, you can go and dream and chatter to yourself outside the classroom. Stand in the corridor until you've learned your lesson.'

Quite how I'll learn a lesson on my own in the corridor escapes me. 'But Mrs Marshalsea, I...'

'No buts. Go. Now.'

I get up and slink out of the classroom. The corridor outside is cold – the classroom's a mobile hut, and the front doors don't shut properly.

A few shivery minutes later, the door to the classroom opens. I think it must be Mrs Marshalsea, come to ask me back in. But it's not: it's Lee Hardwick. He doesn't so much as glance in my direction, just breezes past me, humming a tune, on the way to the toilets in the main building. A minute later – I now wonder whether he needed the toilet at all, if it were a pretext – he swans back in, stops in front of me. 'Hey, you okay?' he asks, as if in apology for what happened earlier.

'Yes,' I say. 'Kind of.'

'Must be annoying,' he says.

'I'm cold.'

'Never mind. It's happened to me loads. She'll ask you in dead soon.' He winks at me, knowingly. 'In fact, I bet it'll be sooner than you think.'

At which, he steps back into the classroom, closes the door behind him, and calmly informs Mrs Marshalsea that I've just called her a wicked old bag: 'I'm really sorry, Mrs Marshalsea. I can't believe what Jonathan said about you. Can't believe my ears, like. I don't want to repeat it. But if you *really* insist...'

From outside, I have no idea what he's telling her. All I can hear are muffled voices. Then the door bangs open, and a furious face appears in front of me. A claw shoots out, and drags me inside.

Mrs Marshalsea points to a spot next to her desk – the dreaded spot I've seen her use for previous kangaroo courts, involving other kids. 'Stand there,' she barks, 'and don't move an inch.'

I'm shaking. I don't have a clue what's going on. Everyone's staring at me, happy it's not their turn on the kangaroo spot.

Mrs Marshalsea comes in close, her nose almost touching mine. Her eyes are everywhere. 'I want you to stand there and think about what you said.'

'I don't understand.'

'Oh yes, you do.'

I'm panicking, babbling: 'I only said ... I only said ... I didn't know which one of Henry's wives was beheaded.'

'That's not it. You know full well what you said.' I feel Mrs M.'s spit on my cheek.

'*Please*, Miss, I don't know what I've done.' I wonder for a moment if it's something about Lisa – about fancying her, about causing her sister's accident – and I want to melt into the classroom floor, until there's only a pair of shoes and a sweatshirt left. Maybe Mrs Marshalsea is going to reveal my crush to the whole class, tell everyone I fancy Lisa, and nearly killed her sister. I feel like I'm burning up, *melting, melting*. 'Please, Mrs Marshalsea, *please*. I don't understand.'

'You do. You know what you said. And so does everyone else, now.'

I stare down at my shoes, the one place Mrs Marshalsea's eyes are not. If only I could tap them together, whisper *There's no place like home*, and disappear. But I can't. Home is a long, long way away, and I'm stuck in Mrs M.'s classroom, on this spot, fixed in place.

Mrs M. moves behind me, puts her hand on the back of my head, tilts it upwards: 'Look,' she says, 'everybody's watching you.'

In front of me are thirty kids staring at me from all angles. The classroom is a monster of eyes, Argus Panoptes squashed into a school hut. 'They're all disgusted. *Disgusted.* Everyone knows what you said.'

Everyone except me. 'I don't...'

'You do,' she snaps. 'Say sorry. To me. To everyone.'

I'm terrified, but also exasperated: 'I can't say sorry for something if I don't know what it is!'

'But you *do* know. You said it to Lee and he told me.' I shake my head. 'Admit it.'

'Admit what?'

She steps back around in front of me, points a finger at my face. 'You said' – she pauses dramatically – 'you said that I was a *wicked old bag*.'

She grinds out the phrase between her teeth, making it sound like it's the most obscene profanity ever invoked by a child from Stoke-on-Trent. There's a collective intake of breath. My mouth drops open. 'I wouldn't ever...'

She shakes her head, repeating one of the adjectives *sotto voce*: 'I mean, old! Old! *Old!*'

I look at her furious face, the hair electrified by fury, and almost wish I had said it. But only almost.

'I didn't say it. Please, Miss.'

'You did. I know you did. You've never liked me.'

(This isn't true – I loved Mrs Marshalsea, even after this incident. That, I realise now, was part of the problem: I had no resistance. I loved her, so I was willing to believe her over myself. Hostage to a kind of teacher-pupil Stockholm Syndrome, it wouldn't have crossed my mind to criticise her, or her methods of interrogation, back then. Love, as others have pointed out, can be an oppressor's most powerful weapon.)

'You called me a *wicked old bag*, didn't you? DIDN'T YOU?'

I shake my head, tears stinging the corners of my eyes.

'Don't cry. *You've* got nothing to cry about. It's *me* who should be crying, being called dreadful names by ungrateful boys.' She addresses the class: 'You only have to think of poor Catherine of Aragon or Anne Boleyn to see how badly women are treated by vindictive boys.' She takes a deep breath, prods me in the chest, rather like Lee prodded me earlier. 'And you, you're Henry VIII. You. You called me an old bag, didn't you?'

'No.'

'Didn't you?'

'No.'

'Didn't you?'

The cross-examination goes on and on, round and round. The other kids stare at me from their desks, bored, upset. I glance at Lisa: her eyes are narrowed on me, as if I'm a very long way away. I glance at Lee: his face is blank, innocent. He shakes his head slightly: 'Tut, tut.' No one else moves. The lesson's ground to a halt. There seems to be nothing left in the world to learn. Nothing except my guilt: everything's narrowed towards that point, towards the moment in which I finally confess, and answer Mrs Marshalsea's ever-repeating question correctly: 'Yes, I did call you a *wicked old bag*.'

We haven't reached that point yet. 'You called me a wicked old bag, didn't you?'

'No.'

'If you won't admit it, Jonathan, I'm going to have to call your parents. I know them, they'll be horrified. I'll also inform Mr Scuttle' – that's the headmaster – 'and I'll tell you something for nothing: he'll sort you out, once and for all. With his pump.'

'But, Miss, I didn't say anything.'

My legs ache from standing stock still on the same spot. My head aches from the repeated questions, the multitudinous eyes swimming in front of me. I want to go home. *There's no place like home.*

'Yes, you did.'

'No, I didn't.'

'Yes, you did.'

'No.'

'Yes.'

'No.'

Yes-no-yes-no-yes-no: a quarter of an hour goes by, spooned out in monosyllables, until I cry and stamp a foot: 'NoIdidn'tdidn'tdidn'tdidn't!'

'HOW DARE YOU!' roars Mrs Marshalsea, her full fury unleashed. 'Not only do you say ghastly things about me, now you yell at me too!' She takes a step away, curls her lip, looks me up and down with disgust – as though now she's Henry VIII, and I'm a disgraced wife.

'Right,' she says, 'I've had enough of this, Jonathan. The class has had enough. I want you to stand there and close your eyes.'

I don't understand, and frown up at her.

'Don't pull faces like that at me, young man. You're going to close your eyes and stand there in silence, knowing we're all watching you. Knowing we're waiting for you to admit what you said.'

My legs are shaking. 'But, Miss...'

'Do it now. Close your eyes.' She turns to the class. 'I want all of you to stare in silence at Jonathan.'

Lisa puts up her hand. 'How long do we have to do it for?' she asks. 'It'll be lunchtime soon, Miss.'

'As long as it takes. Everybody stare at him.'

'Eurgh,' mutters Leo, 'what an ugly mug.'

'Shush, Lee,' says Mrs Marshalsea. 'Jonathan, close your eyes. *Now.*'

I close my eyes. There's silence and darkness. I feel everyone's eyes on me, willing me to get the inevitable over with, in time for lunch. I am shut in the Panopticon, my face a one-way mirror. 'Visibility is a trap,' says Foucault, and I've fallen into it – down, down, to a dark place where 'No' seems little different to 'Yes.'

The tears are running down my face. I hear Mrs Marshalsea's voice in the darkness. It's more gentle, sympathetic now: 'You can tell me, Jonathan. Just let it out. It'll be okay, I promise. All you need to do is tell the truth, then everyone can go to lunch, and we can draw a line under this dreadful morning.'

She squeezes my arm. Her sympathy is the final straw, and I sob: 'Yes, I did. I did. I did say it. I did, and it was horrible, and I'm horrible, and I'm sorry. *So sorry.*'

I open my eyes. Through the tears, I see her turn to the class: 'You see,' she declares, triumphantly. 'The truth always comes out in the end. There are no lies in my classroom.'

'I'm so sorry.' I'm crying, and I can't stop. 'I'm horrid, and I'm very, very sorry.'

'I forgive you,' says Mrs Marshalsea.

The bell goes for lunch. She dismisses the other kids, who file out, grumbling, annoyed that I've wasted their morning: *Why didn't he just admit it in the first place? What a stupid cry-baby. All that fuss over nothing. Sooo boring.*

Lee Hardwick's one of the last to leave. He brushes past me: 'Never mind, mate. No hard feelings. Sorry I had to tell Miss.'

He says this loud enough for Mrs Marshalsea to overhear. 'Oh, no, Lee,' she says, 'you did exactly the right thing. You mustn't blame yourself.' She gives him a house-point. 'Always tell the truth, and you'll be rewarded.'

'I will, Miss,' he says, beaming.

Soon, the class is empty, apart from Mrs Marshalsea and myself. She brings me a chair – finally – to perch on. My legs almost give way as I sink down onto it. She squats in front of me, leaning in close again. 'You can stop crying now, Jonathan. I won't punish you' (as if she hasn't already).

I'm still sobbing, mumbling, 'I'msorrysorrysorry' over and over.

She reaches out, and grips my shoulders. Her teeth are bared: 'But one more thing, Jonathan.'

'What, Miss? Anything, Miss.'

'I don't want you going round telling people about this. No one outside this classroom. I don't want you telling your mum and dad. This is between us, *understand*?'

I nod. Sniffle. I'm scared, and I'm not sure why.

'You'll embarrass yourself if you tell anyone,' she says. 'We're going to draw a line under it, and never mention it again. It'll be like it never happened.' She pauses, narrows her eyes: 'So we're agreed – we keep it between us, yes?'

'Yes, Mrs Marshalsea.'

'Good.' She backs off, stands up. 'You can go to lunch now.'

'I'm sorry, Mrs Marshalsea,' I say to her back. 'I'm sorry,' I say, as I get up from the chair. 'I'm sorry,' I say from the doorway. 'I promise I won't tell anybody about it. I'm sorry, sorry, so sorry.'

And somewhere that little boy is still in a trap, still saying *I'm sorry*, and still not telling anyone about what happened, to this day.

Perhaps there's a locked-away part of many of us stuck somewhere in a classroom, a playground, a school corridor, wide-eyed, silent, unable to leave. School, as Australian poet Les Murray puts it, is a place 'where humans can't leave and mustn't complain' and where 'some will emerge who enjoy giving pain.'

Although that little boy didn't complain, didn't tell anyone about what had happened in Mrs Marshalsea's class, there was a TV drama, a few years later, which spoke for him – a drama that made the hairs on the back of his neck stand up, with chilling *déjà vu*. Like a dream, it seemed to be replaying his own experience, albeit in a displaced form: the TV's kangaroo court was set in a 1940s classroom in the Forest of Dean, rather than 1980s Stoke.

The drama in question was *The Singing Detective* by Dennis Potter. In Episode 4, the hospitalised Philip E. Marlow mentally flashes back to school, decades before. Traumatised by a dysfunctional home life, the child Marlow has sneaked back into his classroom, at the end of the school day, to defecate on the teacher's desk. Next morning, the teacher discovers the 'disgusting thing', and goes on the rampage. She's performed by the unforgettably terrifying Janet Henfrey, whose staring eyes fill the screen, seem to loom out of it, implicating not only the schoolchildren, but the TV audience too:

One of you, *one* nasty dirty wicked little boy – for I cannot believe it was one of the girls, no, not for a moment! – One of *you boys* waited until the end of school, waited, then sneaked back in and did this horrible – horrible – filthy – disgusting thing! Right in the middle of this table. My table! And I will tell you this. I will tell you here and now, he won't get away with it, whoever it is! I'll make sure of that! Ab-so-lute-ly sure!

The teacher makes 'ab-so-lute-ly sure' the culprit doesn't get away with it by recourse to various interrogatory strategies, all of which are forms of surveillance. Her eyes are her chosen weapons, and she knows as well as Foucault that 'visibility is a trap'. She 'stares fiercely all around the class', she 'pinions' individual boys 'with a long stare', and the children's 'faces find it difficult to take the fierce, searching, threatening nature of an adult gaze'. She then disempowers the children still further, by making them shut *their* eyes – so they can't even try and return her gaze – and leads them in a prayer. The prayer is itself all about surveillance:

We are going to ask Almighty God Himself ... to point His Holy Finger. Almighty God will tell us who did this wicked deed.... O Lord God look down on us now in Thy Awful Majesty and search out our hearts, look into our heads, seize hold of our innermost thoughts.... *You* can see. *You* know.... You are looking down now upon one boy, one particular boy, one boy in this room.... You are entering the bones. You are peering into the space between the bones.... *Who? Who? Which one? Who is it?*

The teacher's prayer strikes her pupils with a 'mortal terror', which is unsurprising, given that she invokes a divine gaze so invasive it can get inside the spaces between their bones.

Of course, this invasive gaze is really her own, and she watches the children closely during the prayer: 'Her eyes are fiercely studying every one of the boys' faces in turn as they submit to her dreadful prayer, looking at every small tick or twitch for any signs of stress.' Eventually, she picks out Marlow, who is exhibiting 'evident stress', and who starts to cry. She makes him come out to the front of the class, and stand on a spot next to the desk. Then she compels him to stare at the shit on the table, until he either confesses or tells her who did it: 'You will have to stand here for the rest of the day, absolutely still, not moving a muscle, looking at *that thing* on the table, until you decide to be sensible.' During the ensuing lesson, she continually 'darts Philip a sharp look, ... to keep up pressure on him'. The other kids are staring at him, too, their 'eyes ... upon him when they think they are not under the direct gaze of the old woman [the teacher]'.

Both the classroom and the episode as a whole are full of sharp looks, interconnecting networks of gazes – gazes that disempower, subdue, threaten. The child Marlow is bottom of the pile, forced to gaze at his own excrement, while kids, and teacher, and God stare at him; the adult, paranoid Marlow gives his wife 'black looks' and 'mysterious glances'; Marlow's fantasy version of himself, the 'singing detective', sings in a dance hall while 'alertly surveying everything', all too aware that somewhere, out of sight, are two 'mysterious men' who are watching him, waiting for a chance to shoot him; later, Marlow the 'private *eye*' (my italics) watches a girl called Amanda leaving a nightclub, and shouts '*Achtung!*' at her from the shadows. She is seen, he is unseen, so he has power over her, and she runs away, terrified. To be seen without seeing back – because the watcher is hidden, or you've got your eyes closed, or are looking elsewhere, such as at a shit on the table – is disempowering, sometimes violently so. There are violent threats lurking behind all of these one-way gazes: the threat of caning, the threat of divine retribution, the threat of murder, the threat of rape.

None of these threats are actually realised on screen during the episode. They remain off-stage, existing only as absent presences within the narrative. Yet the episode is no less terrifying for that, maybe because, for all the appeals to external threats, the real violence inheres in the gaze itself. Like the Eye of Sauron in *The Lord of the Rings*, the gaze – of the school, the law, desire – is sufficient to terrorise those singled out by it. It inflicts a psychological pain that can be more insidious, more long-lasting than physical pain.

Potter's schoolteacher is aware of this. Even while threatening Marlow with physical violence, her emphasis is not (only) on caning itself, but on the whole school watching Marlow being caned: 'In just over ten minutes' time all of you in Standard Three will join up in the Big Room with Standard One, Standard Two and Standard Four to see a caning that not one of you will ever forget!' Long before the cane was banned, Potter's schoolteacher already understands the kind of violence that will supersede it: the violence of being watched, of being singled out, of public humiliation.

By the traumatic climax of the episode, the young Philip Marlow has learned the violent power of his own gaze. He has learned to stare back. Driven to desperation, he frames another boy as the culprit – a boy called Mark Binney, who cocked a snook at him earlier – and hence diverts blame away from himself. In this regard, the young Marlow seems to embody a version of both myself *and* Lee Hardwick. Like me, he is subjected to surveillance and interrogation, a classroom kangaroo court; like Lee, he gets someone else in trouble for something they haven't done.

Watching the episode as a teenager, I came to a better understanding, without being able to put it into words, of my own nemesis's behaviour. Philip Marlow's only means of escaping the teacher's disciplinary gaze is to divert it to someone else. That is, the victim's only escape route is to substitute someone else in their place, transferring the blame downwards, to whichever scapegoat's at the bottom of the pile. School, it seems, turns Survival of the Fittest into Surveillance of the Unfittest. At my school, Lee and his sidekicks were frequently in trouble with teachers, who kept them under close scrutiny, even when they weren't doing anything naughty. By placing me in the spotlight for once, they managed to get a morning off.

The school's disciplinary gaze, conveyed through teachers' eyes, always needs someone to single out, as a focal point, a scapegoat, a pariah. It doesn't matter, really, whether that someone is innocent or guilty, because the aim is not to find out the truth. The aim is to set up that someone as an example, to focus everyone's gaze on that one person, so they're not looking at one another, or the teachers, or the school as a whole; the aim is to disempower everyone watching by suggesting that: 'Yes, we have singled out this person this time, who may or may not have called the teacher an old bag, or shat on her desk – but next time, soon, it might easily be *you* who is at the centre of all these gazes. For now, be glad it isn't.' No doubt Foucault might argue that many systems in modern society work in an analogous way – not least, national politics.

In this context, the threat posed by the teacher's gaze in *The Singing Detective* is not only levelled at the child who's the focus of it, but also, by implication, the whole class. All the pupils are being threatened through a conduit, an exemplar, and that is why they are all terrified. As the schoolteacher says, none of them 'will ever forget' the caning they're going to witness in the Big Room, precisely because they too are being caned by proxy.[1] By watching it happen, all the school kids are, in effect, subjected to a collective violence.

The same applies to other Big Rooms and kangaroo courts too, whether the violence on display is predominantly physical,

---

[1]For another type of oppressive relationship that works through a conduit or foil, see the discussion on Mr Nerritt and the Rev. Chadband in Chapter 5, 'R.E.'.

psychological, verbal, or ocular. In any kangaroo court, it's really everyone who is on show-trial, everyone who is being watched, everyone who is both judge and accused, disciplinarian and victim, bully and scapegoat, punisher and punishee. This is Classroom of the Spectacle, as Guy Debord might have called it. Despite Foucault's claims, older forms of punishment-as-public-spectacle haven't entirely disappeared. They've just been sublimated, transformed, universalised.

*

We are all guilty of everything: since becoming a teacher myself, I've occasionally been implicated in the spectacle, my gaze on a terrified victim in the kangaroo-dock. In the pessimistic words of my first and best line manager: 'Stay in education long enough and you'll end up doing all the things you once hated. You become what you most detest.'

For example: twenty years after my run-in with Mrs Marshalsea, I'm in a university plagiarism hearing – a.k.a. a kangaroo court set up to pass judgement on students accused of cheating. I'm co-chairing the hearing with another lecturer, a Dr Burgos. He's working himself up into a spluttering rage, like some over-grown public schoolboy who's found out that the other team cheated at sport ('It's just not cricket!'). I've heard his spiel before, so I'm casting my mind elsewhere – idly wondering whether that plagiarist extraordinaire, T. S. Eliot, should be tried next for *The Wasteland*.

By the time I refocus on what Burgos is saying, I realise with a jolt that he's got even more carried away than usual. He's now threatening the tearful undergraduate with the police. If she doesn't confess to plagiarising her first university essay, he says, he's going to call them: 'It's robbery!' he declares, 'and I think you'll find the authorities take robbery very seriously.' He gets as far as striding over to my office telephone, reaching to pick up the receiver.

Only then do I belatedly intervene, to try and restore calm: 'I'd rather you didn't...' Eventually, I send the near-hysterical student away with a caution. I'm trembling too, almost as bewildered by what's happened as she is.

Afterwards – feeling guilty that I've been party to bullying an eighteen-year-old who only moved away from home a few weeks ago – I tell Dr Burgos that I'm appalled by his tactics. I tell him the police don't give a fig about the Harvard Referencing System, and would probably have him arrested, rather than the student, for wasting their time.

In response, he snort-laughs at me, as if it's all been no more than schoolboy high-jinks. Being a humourless state-school prig, I've missed the joke. 'Don't be ridiculous. I'm not *really* going to phone them up, am I? It's a bluff. But it scares the living daylights out of the freshers. That girl, she'll never cheat again. It works.'

And I think now: yes, it worked, precisely because he never got to the point of speaking to the police. If he had, the whole effect would have dissolved into farce. It'd rank up there with people who dial 999 to complain that the pizza delivery guy stole their pepperoni. The threat of phoning the police, then, had to remain a threat for it to be successful. So really the disciplinary violence consisted of the threat itself, rather than what was threatened. The moment the threat was realised, it would have lost its disciplinary force, disappearing in a puff of smoke. Dr Burgos's form of discipline was an illusion, a conjuring trick, a sleight-of-hand – what controversial poet and educator Kate Clanchy calls 'the terrifying confidence trick that is classroom discipline.'

There are a lot of con tricks in education – tricks that rely on threats of shadowy higher authorities, which lurk out of sight. These terrifying overlords reinforce the on-stage hierarchy, but rarely turn up themselves. They are the Wizards of Oz of the classroom, the Godots of education. For Burgos, these Godot-Wizards were the law, the police; for Potter's schoolteacher, they include God Himself, as well as his worldly stand-in, the headmaster – who might publicly cane you in the 'Big Room', a kind of off-stage hell.

In some cases, the threats can be realised if necessary: in *The Singing Detective*, the implication is that one child, probably Mark Binney, will end up being thrashed after the episode's end. Corporal punishment is still legal, so the physical threat to the child is real. Yet it's significant that the older Philip Marlow recalls the kangaroo classroom, not the punishment afterwards. As I've said, threats can seem more real, more psychologically painful than that which is threatened. Threats stretch out violence – they have a longevity that immediate physical violence does not. Once caned, the pupil knows the worst, and to know the worst is no longer to be terrorised. That's why it's a commonplace that horror films are scarier when you don't get to see the monster. As a kid, I was far more terrified of the monster-that-was-the-cane than were boys like Danny Beaker, who were regularly beaten.

Since the cane was banned, discipline in educational settings has become even more of a confidence trick, often depending on vague threats of surveillance, humiliations, detentions, exclusions, referrals, and so on. The teacher acts as a kind of middle-person who might refer you to others above them (heads of department, headteachers, youth workers, parents, police, etc.), who might, in turn, refer you to others above them (social workers, local education authorities, magistrates, God, etc.). The on-stage teacher must *seem* to have a personal hotline to these higher authorities – a hotline that can be metaphorical or spiritual (as in a schoolteacher's prayer for divine retribution) or literal (as in a lecturer's phone call to the police).

Still, the person who *really* has a hotline to these higher authorities, the person who *really* dials 999 or allows God to burrow into the spaces between their bones, is not the teacher or lecturer at all. It's the student. It's the student who, in their own head, realises the end-point of the teacher's threat. It doesn't matter that it's not happening in external reality, that Dr Burgos would never literally call the police, because it's happening in the victim's mind, brought to life in the imagination. Subjected to someone else's gaze, unable to return it, the student can only look inward, doing to him- or herself what the other is doing.[2] Eyes closed in prayer, Potter's school kids look within themselves, torturing themselves with their teacher's punitive imagery. As Foucault suggests, 'He who is subjected to a field of visibility, and who knows it, assumes responsibility for the constraints of power; ... he inscribes in himself the power relation to which he simultaneously plays both roles.' The victim plays both punisher and punishee, disciplinarian and disciplinary subject, sadist and masochist.

In the most radical sense, then, you don't actually need a schoolteacher – or police force, or magistrate, or God. You can perform figures of authority within yourself, making their punishments more terrifying than reality. Monsters from the Id are far more powerful than those outside us, because they are bounded only by the imagination. They can be far more cruel too, given what Freud calls the 'mysterious masochistic trends of the ego.' It's all too easy to be cruel to yourself.

No one understands this better than the older Philip Marlow. Confined to his hospital bed, he's also confined to his imagination, and most of what happens in *The Singing Detective* is happening in his head: the hallucinations, the memories, the fictional crime narrative. It's one of the most introspective TV dramas ever made. He's locked in an internalised spiral of self-flagellation, his psyche's 'masochistic trends' off the leash.

This is punishment-as-solipsism: cursed with guilt, he torments himself by replaying scenes from his childhood over and over; and on top of memories of the past are super-added

---

[2] To echo (plagiarise?) Hegel's language. See 'Philosophy: An Interlude', in Chapter 4, 'Practical: The Cane and the Fist.'

paranoid fantasies about the present.[3] He tortures himself about his wife, imagining she's conspiring against him with a lover. In his head, he scripts their clandestine affair, to the extent that, at one point, the characters start speaking in punctuation marks and stage directions: 'I have this awful dash he stops himself comma and all but shudders full stop.'

Marlow scripts his own punishment, at the hands of his wife, her fictional co-conspirator, the schoolteacher, and others. The flat in which his wife and lover meet is an imaginary stage set, and his childhood classroom has long since disappeared, but he conjures these places into being, trapping his imagination within them. Part of him will always be the boy in the classroom, reliving a kangaroo court. For while physical punishment must ultimately end – even if that ending is death, even if your torturer is Caligula – psychological punishment can go on forever. As one character in Rachel Eliza Griffiths's novel *Promise* (2023) suggests, '[A] mind-whupping outlasts an ass-whupping any day of the week. A mind-whupping doesn't stop hurting.'

Griffiths's character may be speaking from a very different context to the British education system, but the sentiment still applies. Put it this way: an 'ass-whupping' from the cane is a definite end-point, a thwacking full-stop: 'Right, you horrible boy, you've learned your lesson, go back to your seat now, and don't do that again.' By contrast, never-realised threats, psychological punishments which play on the punishee's imagination, might have no audible or tangible full-stops, offer no absolution, no expiation. They can keep going round and round the punishee's head *ad infinitum*, in what Freud famously calls the psyche's 'compulsion to repeat' – its masochistic urge to repeat traumatic events. *The mind is its own place, and in itself / Can make a Heav'n of Hell, a Hell of Heav'n.*

---

[3]On punishment-as-solipsism, see also Chapter 5, 'R.E.'.

In this sense, modern consciousness doesn't need other places. It doesn't need actual prisons, schools, let alone heavens or hells, outside itself. Marlow's childhood classroom might well be dust. It doesn't matter. A system based on internalising power, on carrying around the school or prison inside yourself, only needs real places as starting-points, and they can erase themselves afterwards. Their physical walls can dissolve, turn to chalk-dust, because now those walls are inside you, everywhere and nowhere, for ever and ever. You are your own Panopticon.

Indeed, this self-erasure on the part of the panoptic institution is part of its magical power. It's much harder to fight something that's intangible, that's everywhere and nowhere. You can deface, punch, chip away at physical walls; but once those walls are internalised, all you can do is deface, punch, or chip away at yourself. All that's left to rail against, to attack, is a ghost, a figment, the spaces between your own bones.

Nor does this kind of self-bullying ever have to end. At the end of a prison sentence or your schooldays, you can walk out of a physical building, but you can't walk out of yourself. There is no exit from the internalised Panopticon. Self-incarceration is a life sentence.

Marlow certainly seems imprisoned inside his own panoptic self, to the exclusion of all else. His old schoolteacher is presumably long since dead, and Mark Binney has been committed to an asylum – convinced, in retrospect, that he really did shit on the teacher's desk. Similarly, by telling me not to mention the kangaroo court to anyone, Mrs Marshalsea turned the key on my own mental solitary confinement. She erased the incident from the external world ('It'll be like it never happened'), locking it into my head, and my head alone. In there, it ran amok, round and round in circles, cut off from external reference points. Perhaps, I thought, I was guilty after all, perhaps I really did call her that name ... or perhaps, if I didn't actually say it, I was guilty of other terrible things anyway, so I deserved what happened ... or perhaps the whole morning was in my imagination ... or perhaps...

It's an old con trick used by adults on children, to lock them into their own imaginations, preventing recourse to a world beyond themselves. I've known the con trick to be used by everyone from the relatively benign Mrs Marshalsea, all the way to the other end of a long spectrum, and by serial abusers: 'Don't think of mentioning what happened to anyone else. If you do, they'll be very angry with you.' I told my twins it was a fair rule of thumb that if an adult says something like that to you, you should do the exact opposite. I wish I'd done the opposite, back in the time of Mrs Marshalsea.

At the end of the school year, Mrs Marshalsea went even further in erasing what had happened in her classroom, effectively wiping evidence of the school year from the face of the Earth. Once it's done its job, the Panopticon – the school, the prison, the university – immolates itself.[4] Or, to put this more prosaically, on the last morning before the summer holidays, Mrs Marshalsea made us destroy the work we'd done that year.

First, she circled the class, placing in front of each of us a pile of our notebooks from the year. Then she told us to straighten our piles into neat towers. Then she told us to tear everything up, destroy it.

'Are you sure, Mrs Marshalsea?' asked Lisa, frowning.

'I'm sure,' Mrs Marshalsea answered.

'Are you *really really* sure, Miss?'

There was a pause, an odd silence in the classroom. Mrs Marshalsea sighed, and was strangely honest with us for a

---

[4]On the self-erasure of the Panopticon, see the note on Zygmunt Bauman in Chapter 9, 'Extra-Curricular: Thanks, Notes, Contexts'.

moment: 'Look, I don't want your mums and dads flicking through what you've done, criticising it. I've got enough to deal with. So please, children, yes, tear up your books.'

And we did: no one objected or complained. We set to work, human shredders, tearing into tiny pieces every scrap of work we'd done that year. We even compared how tiny our tiniest shreds were: 'I tore that page into thirty pieces!' 'Well, I tore this one into forty!'

We were enjoying ourselves – the carnivalesque destruction, the joy of being told to destroy something so carefully constructed. We ripped pictures from walls, tore pages into patterns, paired up to pull apart exercise books like Christmas crackers, threw paper over one another like snow. Snowflakes of Maths sums, spellings, show-and-tells, Tudor histories mingled in a blizzard of un-learning – as if we'd been taught this stuff only to mix it all up, obliterate it, at the end.

Once the snow had settled, though, we gazed on the wreckage spread out across the classroom and went quiet, our faces red, ashamed. Some of us suppressed tears. Mrs Marshalsea stalked round with bin-liners, and we scooped knowledge into them by the handful. 'Don't leave any scraps behind,' she said.

That afternoon, once the mess had been cleared up, the classroom felt empty, desolate – as though the whole year, with its joys, its Lisa-crushes, its Hardwick-bullying, its lessons on Henry VIII's wives, its kangaroo courts, had never happened. Except in our heads.

7

Politics

After Tiberius came Caligula.

attrib. Gaius Suetonius Tranquillus, *The Twelve Caesars*

Actually, Suetonius never (quite) said that. It's a fake quotation, like ones you find on internet memes, albeit not as uplifting. I made it up and used it, though, as a kind of hyperbolic shorthand, to sum up what happened towards the end of my first teaching job: *after Prof. Tiberius came Prof. Caligula*, so-called.

You see, I had one manager who was continually away on international conferences or dubious business trips, just as Emperor Tiberius absented himself to Capri during his disastrous reign. He was always about to sort things out, make things better – but then would be called away at the last minute on some 'important, high-level' matter, leaving everything in the hands of brutal deputies, academic Sejanuses. As his reign ground to a halt, a successor emerged from the dangerous vacuum he'd created: 'Prof. Caligula'.

It was always my intention, towards the end of this book, to write about Prof. Caligula, and what happened to me when she was my boss – to tell the story of the most sustained, vicious bullying I have experienced, the dark night of my victimised soul. It was a terrible time, and I thought that writing about it, years later, might exorcise some professorial ghosts. I wanted to be honest about what happened, at least from my point of view. I wanted to show how, with all due respect to Adrian Mitchell, 'The Killing Grounds' of work can be even worse than those of school. I wanted to give a full blow-by-psychological-blow account of my then-manager's behaviour, and how it affected me, how it chipped away at my consciousness over months, years.

I wanted to write about all this. But now I've got to this point, I've kind of gone off the idea. For a number of reasons.

First, it is notoriously difficult to put certain kinds of experiences into words: the closer an experience comes to trauma, the harder it is to translate it into language. As many people have pointed out, trauma is the unsayable, a black hole opening up in language, the irruption of the unspeakable into consciousness.

It certainly feels like a struggle to explain my experience of adult bullying to other people, except in the most general terms; although whether or not it qualifies as trauma in other ways, I don't know. Maybe, maybe not – or maybe one of the common problems for victims is that they find it well-nigh impossible to measure how serious their own experience is. They find it impossible to gain a perspective on it, even long after the event.

That lack of perspective might have another effect on the language used, when attempting to capture such an experience. It might mean that the language is infected with *ressentiment*, distorted by a desire for belated revenge. That's the second reason I don't want to describe the ins and outs of my own experience: I can't help feeling that such a description would be rather unedifying. Of course, I'm furious about what happened. Of course, it still hurts, years later. But I never wanted this book to be an act of vengeance on school or workplace bullies.

Having said that, I am all too aware that revenge on the past, however sublimated or displaced, is a feature of most, if not all, memoirs. That brings me to the third, uglier reason for not describing my experiences with Prof. Caligula in detail – a reason that no doubt constitutes a contorted, paradoxical form of revenge: the revenge of omission. To write about Prof. Caligula might plump up her vanity, her sense of self-importance: *Oh gosh, you're still thinking of me and what I did after so many years? How flattering: I must have won, ultimately, if you're still under my shadow.* To which I'd like to respond, *à la* Carly Simon: *You're so egocentric, no doubt you expected this chapter to be about you*. Well, it bloody well isn't.

Rather, it's about what I learned from my experience of workplace bullying. That's far more interesting and useful (I hope) than a catalogue of academic woes.

And therein lies the fourth reason for not writing a detailed account of what happened: it's just not interesting, really. Or it isn't to anyone but myself and those who were there at the time, those who suffered collateral damage. So much workplace bullying is immensely and grindingly dull – a day-in-day-out process of psychological erosion, of bureaucratic tides coming in and out.

The dullness can actually form part of the bullying. In any bureaucracy, the person who has the most patience, who's willing to devote most attention to the tiny details others miss, who's able to sustain petty schemes over long periods, is going to come out on top. It's a matter of Survival of the Most Officious. But that sort of pertinacity – the sort of dogged, unending persistence shared by academics, lawyers, and cockroaches – doesn't necessarily make for a good story. Whereas physical bullying gives an audience something to visualise, some kind of external drama, psychological bullying can be slow-burn, a matter of numbers on a spreadsheet, ambiguous, passive-aggressive messages via email, threats and anxieties in the head, administrative mines laid one year that the victim inadvertently steps on (preferably in public) two or three years later. It's part of what makes psychological bullying, as opposed to someone punching someone else in the face, so hard to pin down, identify, tackle. Primarily inward-looking, there's not much to point to that's tangible, no obvious spectacle to gawp at. It certainly doesn't make for a mainstream Hollywood blockbuster: *Taylor versus the Professor, now in 3D. Where Paper Cuts Get Personal.*

Okay, so there were moments of external drama between myself and Prof. Caligula; we did have our set-piece rows, our corridor slanging matches, our slammed doors, our moments of unmasked hatred; there were tears, tantrums, tribunals, hearings; after I left, the matter did end up in the hands of solicitors, with claims of defamation versus counter-claims of harassment, constructive dismissal. Yet by and large these were isolated moments. For the most part, the bullying was insidious, underground, and too complexly boring – everything connected to everything else, a matter of details within details, spiralling causes and effects, a kind of bureaucratic fractal – to recount in full. Sometimes, halfway through explaining a particular incident to a friend in the pub, I'd find myself trailing off, bored by the intricacy of my own office horror story.

When people talk about 'office politics', they often preface the phrase with a word such as 'just' or 'only': 'It's *just* office politics', they say, *just* a matter of boring memos, gossip, people stabbing each other in the back with paper daggers. The dismissal implied by that modifier 'just' is connected with a very English suspicion of the word 'politics' in general. 'It's *just politics*', merely a lot of silly people in Westminster or Brussels squabbling about red-tape, vying for a place on the greasy pole. It's *just* a trivial game, something which BBC correspondents report on with a knowing grin, something the English – and I do mean *English*, not Scottish, let alone Northern Irish – wave away.

Dickens recognised this. In *Our Mutual Friend* (1865), there's a character called Podsnap, who 'put[s] behind him' any uncomfortable political truths he doesn't want to confront. You can witness Podsnappery in English homes or cafés every day: 'We don't talk about politics at the dinner table, thank you very much.' 'Look, it's *just* politics. Let's talk about something more interesting instead.' As if '*just* politics' really can be put behind you; as if politics doesn't determine every aspect of our lives; as if politics doesn't cause poverty, starvation, imprisonment, war, genocide.

If *office* politics doesn't usually operate on such a macro-scale, it can still cause anxiety, depression, personality change, family break-up, PTSD (Post-Traumatic Stress Disorder), PTED (Post-Traumatic Embitterment Disorder), and, in extreme cases, suicide – what anti-bullying campaigner Tim Field termed 'bullycide'. Clearly, these effects are not a matter of *just* or *only* to the individuals concerned. They certainly weren't, or aren't, to me.

And the effects can last a long time. It's well-nigh impossible to do the Podsnap thing, and put them behind you. They come back to haunt you. Some years after leaving my first workplace, I was semi-drunk at a party, and a friend suggested to me that I might be suffering from PTSD. I spat out my drink, snort-laughed. At the time, it seemed absurd that something so apparently insignificant as my experience of workplace bullying – as opposed, say, to war, torture, or abuse – might cause PTSD. Even now, I still think I was right to snort-laugh as an immediate response. And yet – without sounding too self-indulgent, and without going too far down the road of casual self-diagnosis (a road that leads nowhere or everywhere) – I do wonder if my initial reaction wasn't covering up something that I didn't want to admit.

After all, as I said in Chapter 4, the subjective experience of cruelty isn't relativistic to the psyche that's affected. Consciously, objectively, I might snort-laugh at my friend's suggestion. But who knows what's going on unconsciously? The unconscious doesn't stand back, rub its chin thoughtfully, and admit: 'Well, yes, I know it was bad, but it wasn't a thousandth as bad as what happens to many people on a daily basis.' The unconscious isn't objective or rational like that, and experiences that might seem trivial in a wider sense can have serious psychological consequences for the individual concerned. No doubt this is the central message of literary portrayals of bullying: that subjective experience, however insignificant on a macro-political plane, matters.

Most sociologists and psychologists of bullying would agree. Experts such as Field make a point of emphasising how serious workplace bullying can be for the individuals involved. In his book *Bully in Sight* (1996), he writes of 'the horrific yet largely unrecognised psychological injuries sustained by the victim', and he suggests that, however apparently 'trivial' one incident in a workplace might seem, the repetition of such incidents over time can be hugely damaging: 'No matter how trivial, over a period of time, the incidents show a different, but consistent pattern of behaviour.... This pattern is one of the key defining features of bullying.' In this sense, bullying is cumulative. Incidents that, initially, are 'just' office politics can, if replicated enough times, morph into a painful pattern, a managerial water torture – *drip-drip-drip* – no longer 'just' or 'only' anything.

Two other words in our language that almost encode their own *just* or *only* are *academia* and the adjective *academic*. 'It's *academic*' is another Podsnappish way of batting something away, by suggesting it's only of abstract interest, not practical value – merely a matter of university types chattering to one another in their ivory towers. Anyone with experience of the modern university – and that means tens of millions of people in the UK alone – knows this is no longer the case. What is *just academic* has been swallowed whole by the leviathan of neo-liberal capitalism, and is no longer separate from the so-called 'real world'. If only it were.

Still, there is a trace of truth in the modifier 'just' when used in connection with words like *academia*, *politics*, and *office*. Although these spheres seem very real to those directly involved, the frenzied activity therein can appear alien, bizarre, full of sound and fury signifying nothing, to external observers like BBC correspondents or Podsnaps. Labyrinthine bureaucracy can seem trivially pointless when viewed from above, the activity of lab rats in a maze. From within the maze, by contrast, the perspective is terrifyingly different; and you never know, there might be a minotaur-rat lurking somewhere, round a bend, lying in wait.

Describing that experience from within, conveying the twists and turns of bureaucratic terror, is notoriously difficult. Dickens, Kafka, Shirley Jackson, even Ricky Gervais manage it at times.

Writing from a more theoretical, but no less emotive, perspective in *Bully in Sight*, Field attempts to capture the micro-politics of workplace bullying in long lists of characteristics, anecdotes, and representative narratives.

For the most part, though, stories about work-life shy away from the maddening minutiae of admin, the purgatory of paper-work, the low-level terrorism of day-to-day management. This is one reason why I'm generally suspicious of campus novels: they often substitute sensational (and interchangeable) stories of murders, affairs, parties, drugs, for the everyday banality of evil, the red-tape nightmares populated by committees, senior management committees, very senior management committees, unofficial-behind-closed-door-gossip-committees, disciplinary hearings, secret disciplinary hearings, committees for secret disciplinary hearings, spreadsheets, regulations, spreadsheets of regulations, regulations for spreadsheets, research audits, teaching audits, audits of audits, league tables, learning objectives, module specifications, pro-gramme specifications, person specifications, student feedback, fabricated student feedback, complaints, drummed-up complaints, spreadsheets of complaints, audits of spreadsheets of drummed-up complaints, committees for audits of spreadsheets of drummed-up complaints ... and, above all, emails, emails, emails, hundreds of them, thousands of them – emails full of urgent or unnecessary or impossible jobs; emails telling you off for not doing urgent or unnecessary or impossible jobs; emails undermining you in front of others; emails undermining minor successes; emails highlighting minor failures; emails damning with faint or ambivalent praise (*you might read this message as covert criticism, but that's your interpre-tation, not mine*); emails sent on Monday mornings, to upset you at the start of the week; emails sent on Friday afternoons, to threaten you with disciplinary action, so you dwell on them all weekend – emails, emails, emails incessantly scything to and fro above you, like a razor-sharp pendulum, looming closer and closer...

*

In the tale by Edgar Allan Poe which famously depicts such a torture device (a scything pendulum, that is, not email), the reader hardly glimpses the torturers themselves. For all but the opening of the story, the Holy Inquisitors remain off-stage, operating the torture machinery from afar. This is what technology of many kinds – from inquisitorial pendulums to institutional email to Twitter – facilitates: for torture to be inflicted remotely, for the torturers to remain invisible. In this regard, so-called 'cyberbullying' and 'trolling' have a long pre-history, all the way back to a caveperson realising that he or she could poke the neighbour, in the next cave along, with an extra-long stick.

The beauty of the extra-long stick (real or cyber) is that it can be disowned: *It wasn't me, guv'nor. I didn't do nothing. Perhaps it wasn't anyone. Perhaps it was the victim themselves crying 'Wolf!'* Remote bullying can efface itself, sticks can be dropped, Twitter accounts anonymised – to the extent that the victims themselves come to be suspected of paranoia: *There's no one there, it's all in your head, stop imagining things, stop poking yourself with that stick.* At worst, the people expressing such concerns on-stage turn out to be the very same torturers who are invisibly operating the technology behind scenes: *What a shame, you need help, don't worry, we'll take care of you. Very, very good care.*

That's because one of the paradoxical signs of bullying, in my limited experience, is kindness. Yes, I know how odd that sounds; but to care for someone, to take them under your wing, is to exercise a dangerous power. Jimmy Savile was a kind philanthropist, a man of charity. As he knew only too well, to be kind to someone can be a form of manipulation – of their feelings and actions – because it imposes a debt of gratitude upon them. It also has the added benefit of muddying the waters when it comes to complaints, tribunals, solicitors. The bully can point to moments of kindness (carefully recorded, of course) that seem to undermine the complainant's claims: *But look how nice I was on this occasion and that occasion.*

This sort of weaponised kindness can be deployed remotely, too. One of the times I came closest to losing my mind, under the shadow of Prof. Caligula's wings, was when a mature student told me, as if spontaneously, that my boss cared for me, that she was concerned about my mental well-being, that she really liked me, and wished I liked her back. I went away thinking: *Oh, perhaps I've been unfair to Caligula. Perhaps I was wrong all along. Perhaps it's all been in my head.*

Rationally speaking, I knew it wasn't. There'd been too many rows, both online and in person, for me to have imagined everything. But the cognitive dissonance introduced by the student's words, and by other strange moments of kindness from Prof. Caligula ('I can help you with that', 'I so enjoy working with you, Jonathan', 'We're such a friendly team here, aren't we?'), induced a terrible vertigo, made my head spin. Looking back on it now, I believe – rightly or wrongly – that the student in question was primed, and the strange nuggets of kindness among the bullying were mines, deliberately laid.

This was non-linear warfare, kindness as sadism, where part of the strategy is to playfully gaslight your enemy. Author Rachel Vail calls this 'subtle bullying', an incongruous type of bullying 'that comes with compliments and praise, ... appreciation [and] ... kind words', along with 'manipulation [and] ... abuse'. As I've said, incongruity can be one of the bully's most powerful weapons, driving the victim round the bend: *It's her, no it's me, no it's her, but she's being kind, no she's not she's being ghastly, but she says she's being reasonable, perhaps it's my problem...*[1]

It reminds me of Lee Hardwick reasonably suggesting, 'We can be friends' and 'Let's shake on it', seconds before attacking me, pinning me down.

And it also reminds me of another non-linear bully I knew, in a different workplace. He mercilessly harassed a friend of mine to the verge of breakdown – and then expressed concern over the

---

[1]On bullying as incongruity, see also Chapter 1, 'P.E.' and Chapter 5, 'R.E.'

latter's mental state, suggesting he consult his union. 'I think you need professional help,' said the bully, 'if you feel you're being bullied. I know myself it can be an awful thing.' In other words, the bully suggested that his own victim get help for being bullied.

I was bewildered when I heard this, and couldn't work out if it was a brilliant double bluff on the part of the bully, or a sign of a startling lack of self-awareness. As I said in an earlier chapter, bullying usually effaces itself, and that can include self-effacement – effacing itself to itself, so to speak.[2] This is 'unconscious bullying', where, as teacher and lecturer Chris Lee writes, 'the action [feels] ... like bullying to the victim yet a notion of considered intent was not present.... Not all forms of bullying are a consequence of a deliberate attempt to hurt.' Still, there are many different kinds of deliberateness, some of which arise from a lack of self-knowledge.

At the time of my first grown-up job, I too was short on self-knowledge and workplace-knowledge. I was immature, a strange mixture of the laid-back and hot-headed, and, above all, naïve. With the possible exception of Lee Hardwick, I hadn't come across non-linear or 'subtle' bullying before, and was driven almost crazy by it. Generally speaking, the bullying at school, such as it was, was more straightforward (*punch-ouch-punch-ouch-stop-it-or-I'll-tell-the-teacher-okay-tell-the-teacher-this-punch-ouch*). By and large, the bullies in my life hitherto had been big, lumbering beasts, who weren't interested in developing long-term game-plans or strategies. Some of them wouldn't have known what a strategy was if it had punched them in the face.[3] Of those who did, even Lee

---

[2]See Chapter 2, 'Playtime: Games of Soldiers'.

[3]My experience in this respect may well be due to gender, at least in part. It's commonplace wisdom that male bullying in schools is more straightforwardly physical than female bullying, which is generally seen as more psychological and verbal. In reality, of course, the differences are more complex, ambiguous, nuanced. See the short note on this subject in Chapter 9, 'Extra-Curricular: Thanks, Notes, Contexts'.

Hardwick only schemed for the short term: *How can I get the spot-light off me this morning? – I know, let's get that ballet-poof Taylor in trouble.*

Prof. Caligula, by contrast, seemed to plan years ahead, laying bureaucratic mines that could blow up in your face on the Last Day of Judgement. It took me almost as long to overcome my callow bewilderment, to comprehend what was happening. Vail says something similar about her own experience of subtle bullying:

It certainly never occurred to me that I was being bullied. I thought I was happy, or should be.... But I wasn't happy. I was a wreck. I was being manipulated with kind words, bullied in such a subtle way the only bruises were invisible even to me.

This is the false consciousness of psychological bullying: that victims are often unaware (or are deliberately kept unaware) they are being bullied, sometimes until long afterwards. As Tim Field says,

In bullying, it may be months, perhaps a year or more, before you begin to realise that the difficulty you are experiencing with a particular individual, or group of individuals, goes beyond what can reasonably be expected in your place of work.

'Not recognising what is happening', according to Field, is one of the 'main reasons that people put up with bullying for so long'. Indeed, sometimes recognition comes even later, long after the bullying has gone away.

Clearly, the 'Post-' in Post-Traumatic Stress Disorder (or Post-Traumatic Embitterment Disorder) is significant in this regard. Stress can emerge months, years after the trauma originated, as can conscious recognition of what has happened (or, for that matter, what is still happening) The emergence of such recognition is what Field calls the 'moment of enlightenment': *Oh God, I understand now what's behind it all, who's behind it all.*

This is why books, like the ones I talk about in this memoir, can be so important: they help bring the moment of enlightenment forward. They help us recognise what happened, what is happening, what might happen. They help us understand abuses of power, before, during, and after the event. They strip away the false consciousness of bullying and show us how things really are. Reading *Nicholas Nickleby* and *Kestrel for a Knave* opened my eyes.

When my eyes started opening back in my first job, I cried for a night or two, and decided I had to leave ... leave the job I'd always wanted ... leave the job I otherwise loved ... leave the job I'd got a few days before my dad died. The last time I saw him, I'd told him about it, and I like to think that maybe he'd smiled, maybe he'd thought his son wasn't such a wastrel after all.

Six or so years after his death, I eventually secured a new post elsewhere, and sent Prof. Caligula my resignation letter. She seemed upset, and contested it. 'She's very sorry to see you go,' another primed student confided on my leaving day. I gurgle-laughed in my coffee – not because what the student had said was ludicrous, but quite the opposite. The student was right: Prof. Caligula didn't want me to leave. The aim was never to get rid of me. She was enjoying herself too much, and had too many on-going schemes, for it all to come to a premature end. In that sense, she really did like me being there, as 'part of her team'. I was a valued colleague, whose face she wanted under her boot forever, and ever, and ever.

Just as the bullying had no intended end-point, nor did it really have a starting-point, an origin, a first cause. This is not unusual. One of the pioneers of bullying research, Nordic psychologist Dan Olweus, claims that 'much bullying seems to occur without apparent provocation on the part of the person being targeted'. Similarly, Claudia Frey and Siegfried Hoppe-Graff define school bullying as 'dominant aggression which occurs when an unprovoked child taunts, intimidates, coerces, makes fun of or assaults another child without a clear external goal for this behaviour'. Bullying often has no (clear) provocation and no goal. Undoubtedly, bullying can arise from all sorts of things, all kinds of 'otherness', in terms of ethnicity, physicality, neurodiversity, sexuality, gender, age, social class, and so forth. But that's not the same as individual provocation. The victim isn't 'provoking' the bully by being different. It's not their *fault*, after all.

And, in some cases, otherness is more pretext than cause. It may seem like the cause, it may even be cited by both bully and victim as the cause; but lurking underneath there may be something deeper, emptier. In Shakespeare's *Othello*, Iago provides various competing explanations for his behaviour, most of which portray him as the victim, but none of them quite convince. Ultimately, he seems to be tormenting his commander, well, because he's tormenting his commander. Beneath the pretexts lurks another, unconscious drive: power play, one-upmanship, sadism.

This is bullying for bullying's sake, bullying 'because it [is] ... fun', as Olweus puts it. It's what author Sarah Moore Fitzgerald describes as the 'unmitigated, brutal ... [and] gratuitous' form of bullying that 'can withstand no explanation'. She gives the example of Josiah Bounderby, the 'Bully of humility' in Dickens's *Hard Times*, 'who invents a fake difficult childhood in order to justify his own selfish treatment of his workers'. As with Iago's pseudo-explanations, Bounderby's fake victimhood is a pretence, and his is really a circular kind of bullying without first cause and without end. Rather than being victims, Bounderby and Iago are rulers of their Killing Grounds – rulers from whom, as Adrian Mitchell suggests, 'those who get it get it and get it / For any damn thing at all'.

The very pointlessness and aimlessness of this kind of bullying can be a horror in itself. For a start, it can drive a victim into a never-ending cycle of self-doubt and self-interrogation, whereby they try and hunt for the cause within themselves: *What is it about me that's made this happen? What am I doing wrong? What can I change to stop it?*

There's no winning here, whether you stay locked in this cycle of questions, or leap beyond it. The latter can be even more harrowing than the former. I wonder now if the most traumatic moment in my first job – my 'moment of enlightenment' to use Field's phrase – was the morning when it dawned on me that the questions I was flagellating myself with were unanswerable, that there were no answers or reasons or aims, that the bullying I was experiencing existed in a causeless vacuum.

The moment of enlightenment was brought about by a letter I'd hand-written to my boss, offering a truce. The letter drove her into paroxysms of unconcealed rage. For a few minutes, her mask slipped: *A truce?!* she yelled down the corridor. *How could there be a truce when there was no war to begin with? How could there be a truce when nothing whatsoever was wrong, when everything was normal, when any problems were in my imagination and my imagination alone?* Or, as I translated her words at the time: *How could there be a truce when stamping on Jonathan over and over again was so enjoyable?* I realised then there was nothing I could do or say that would stop her, pacify her, because – as is all too often the case – the sadistic pleasure of tormenting someone less powerful overrode every other consideration. Before that morning, I'd been aware on a theoretical level that the urge to hurt others could be a strong motivator in people's lives; but I hadn't necessarily come face-to-face with gratuitous sadism in real life, or not much, anyway. No doubt I'd been pretty lucky in that respect.

In many ways, gratuitous sadism is the hardest form of bullying to deal with, because there's nothing there to understand, no underlying cause to fight. Certainly, back in my first job, most people couldn't, or wouldn't, comprehend the causelessness of what was happening. Even among those who admitted that Prof. Caligula was a bit of a bully, many tried to rationalise her behaviour, in terms of cause and effect. Their responses echoed the kinds of questions I'd been asking myself: *Oh, I know she can be a bitch sometimes, Jonathan, but can't you stop doing whatever it is you're doing that's egging her on? Can't you stop encouraging her? She's not* that *bad, surely. You're rocking the boat with all of us in it.*

'Don't rock the boat' is the refrain of what's known in systems theory as 'homeostasis': the idea that organisations crave stability, quiescence, predictability. Systems resist boat-rocking wherever possible in the name of the *status quo.* Challenging a manager is boat-rocking; accusing her of bullying is boat-rocking; accusing her of a concerted campaign of senseless sadistic harassment is tipping the boat right over. After all, to question someone's authority in any hierarchical system is implicitly also to question the system itself, which is responsible for raising that person up according to its own criteria. So the system is bound to resist – first by trying to calm the whistle-blowing boat-rocker, then by tying them to the mast, gagging them, and finally, if necessary, by chucking them overboard.

Dealing with the boat-rocker (otherwise known as 'victim-blaming') is the most efficient way to re-establish homeostasis – much quicker and easier than tackling deeper problems, such as a gaping hole in the hull, or an on-board officer gone rogue. *Pipe down*, says homeostasis, *keep quiet, let sleeping dogs lie, don't upset the apple cart, live and let live, just try and get along, she can't be that bad, can she, really?* Even my union rep at the time, the guy who was meant to be on my side (but turned out to have an eye on a senior management role), echoed that refrain: 'Calm down, we had a good chat, she's not that bad once you get to know her.'

To me, she was *that bad.* But who knows if I'm right? There's probably no absolute right or wrong when it comes to bullying. It's one of the obvious problems faced by organisations trying to deal with it: subjectivity. Bullying, harassment, sadism, sociopathy, narcissism, psychopathy, and so on are all in the eye of the beholder. One person's managerial 'best practice' is another person's bullying; one person's joke is another person's abuse: *It was just horsing around, can't you take a joke, don't you have a sense of humour, if you work here, you'll have to get used to it, it's how we rub along, it's so trivial, you're making a mountain out of a molehill, etc.* As Field puts it, 'the bully, when challenged on any individual incident, is likely to play on the trivial nature of an interaction.... The bully can make it appear to the world that you are making a fuss over nothing.'

Who do you believe in a case like this – the joker or the joke's butt, the fuss-maker or the downplayer-of-fuss? Who do you side with – the accused, or the accuser? And who are 'you' – a bystander, a disciple, a judge, a more senior manager? Such third parties bring their own personal criteria and interpretations to bear. They merely triangulate the subjectivity of the situation, even when they are official adjudicators, representatives of the organisation. I've witnessed, at different times, occasions when those in all three positions – accuser, accused, adjudicator – have been wrong: occasions when the accuser has cried 'Wolf!' for political reasons; occasions when the accused was misguided or downright lying; occasions when adjudicators were hidebound by their institution, which could not bring itself to admit culpability, for legal or reputational reasons (i.e. due to systemic homeostasis). Truth, in this triangle of warped subjectivity, is relativistic at best.

The subjective relativism at play is so pronounced that bullies themselves can come to believe they're the victims, they're the ones who are really hard done by. Sometimes this perception is a delusion, sometimes a falsification (as with Bounderby), and sometimes it's actually true, insofar as one person's bully might be another person's victim, in what is known as the 'bully-victim-bully cycle'. As Benjamin Spock writes, 'Paradoxically, violent individuals almost always think of themselves as victims – victims of the government, of other bullies, of prejudice – and believe that their violent acts are therefore … justified. In this way, the … cycle of violence is perpetuated.'

An individual who's bullied, who feels victimised, goes on to bully someone else, and so on, and so forth – bigs hitting middles hitting babies, to use Bertrand Russell's formulation. As bullying expert Ken Rigby suggests, 'in situations in which there is a constant struggle for ascendancy, … [a] "pecking order"', it's often the case that 'some individuals are both bullies and victims, that is they sometimes bully others and are sometimes victimised by others.'

Such a pecking order of bullies is hard to untangle. Who do you blame for the bullying: the middles? The bigs? Those above the bigs? God? In the end, it's usually easiest to blame the babies for being victims, for inciting violence: *Can't you stop doing whatever it is you're doing that's egging them on?* It's easiest to blame people at the bottom of the pecking order. If truth is relativistic at best, at worst it is determined by institutional hierarchy. In a closed system, power can be its own self-determining truth, which means that those at the bottom of a hierarchy are necessarily in the wrong.

This is especially the case when they're outnumbered, as they usually are, by those ranged against them. Top-dog bullies act as strange attractors to people around them, who readily join in with the bullying, relieved it's not their turn to be victims. These joiners-in are what is known in popular psychology as 'flying monkeys', after the Wicked Witch's acolytes in *The Wizard of Oz*; that is, sidekicks who do the bidding of the alpha bully, conveying his or her messages, carrying out his or her schemes as proxies.

While the alpha bullies and winged monkeys gang up together, their victims are deliberately isolated – divided and conquered. In the words of Paulo Freire, 'it is necessary to divide the people in order to preserve the *status quo* and (thereby) the power of the dominators'. This division makes it difficult for the victims to be heard, especially in a large organisation where numbers count more than individuals. If, as is common, the gang of 'dominators' – along with their informal allies, the non-committal bystanders – outnumber the divided victims, their versions of truth will easily outweigh those of the latter. Hence, as Freire says, individuals who speak out against the dominators will be dismissed as 'marginals [and] rowdies', guilty of 'demonic action', of merely 'being destructive'. A whistler-blower or boat-rocker has no friends.

This process is sometimes known as 'mobbing', whereby dominators band together in a workplace to ostracise a particular individual, or a small group of fellow employees. In its most extreme form of scapegoating, whole organisations can turn *Lord of the Flies*, coming down on an individual like a tonne of psychological bricks, chasing them into the sea.

Such mobbing is clearly an organisational manifestation of the 'tyranny of the majority'.[4] I mean, why would anyone believe one victim's story over that of the overwhelming majority? Why would one person's truth weigh any more than a feather in the face of near-unanimous opposition? *Are you claiming that you're right, while all your eminent senior colleagues are wrong?* All I can say in response is that truth about bullying is not straightforwardly democratic, not a simple matter of numbers one way or the other – especially when a principal aim of bullying is to isolate the victim.

In my case, my own truth gained more traction after I'd left the job. Once I was gone, the alliances drawn up by Prof. Caligula disintegrated, and the 'eminent colleagues' (a.k.a. flying monkeys) all started fighting one another – to the extent that, a few years later, one of her former allies bought me a coffee and cake, and confessed, rather sheepishly: 'Sorry, I was wrong. I thought it was you causing the trouble. She told me you were lazy and difficult, and I believed her. But as soon as you left, the gloves came off.' The episode illustrates what many sociologists have claimed – namely, that bullying, victimisation, and ritual scapegoating serve to

---

[4]See also Chapter 2, 'Playtime: Games of Soldiers'.

consolidate alliances, friendship groups, whole societies. Without a scapegoat, communities disintegrate.

Ultimately, all any scapegoat can provide is their own truth, their individual testimony. As for my truth, you can take it or leave it as you wish. A scapegoat gets used to being disbelieved, and you're free to disbelieve me, as many people did at the time. You're also free not to read this book, or stop here.

In an earlier book, my memoir *Take Me Home*, I wrote about my father's experience of working with a difficult colleague at high school. Rightly or wrongly, my father blamed that colleague for his nervous breakdown and early retirement. He felt he was harassed out of his headmastership by the colleague, and his various allies in the local education authority (L.E.A.) and local council. That was my father's perspective on the matter. In writing about it, two decades later, I contacted the colleague in question, and asked him for his (very different) perspective. He wrote me a letter which I included in *Take Me Home*.

I can't do that here. I can't contact my ex-boss, and ask her for her perspective on what happened. No doubt she has one, which is the near-diametric opposite to mine; and no doubt there were all sorts of conscious and unconscious impulses behind her behaviour, rooted in her past. But I can't ask her about any of that. If I approached her now, even from this distance, it would be an incitement to further hostility, recriminations. So I can only give my perspective on what happened between me and her, and what I say may or may not be 'objectively' true. Who knows?

What is true, at least according to psychologists such as Robert D. Hare, author of the controversial 'Psychopathy Checklist', is that sociopaths, psychopaths, and narcissists are out there, living, working among us, often in plain sight, succeeding in diverse fields other than serial killing or neo-Nazism. They are, for the most part, invisible, unidentified, wearing convincing masks, disguises, suits and ties.

Liberal thinking finds it hard to recognise extreme psychology, based as it is, quite rightly, on empathy, understanding, compassion. The same goes for that outgrowth of liberal thinking, realist fiction, where the emphasis is usually on what E. M. Forster called 'round characters' – that is, characters who have an interior life, whose behaviour and psychology are complex, conflicted. 'Flat characters' – characters who are straightforwardly good or evil, generous or selfish, rational or psychopathic, whose behaviour is entirely predictable – belong to melodrama, tabloid journalism, Dickensian Gothic. The realist novel struggles to contain them, because they undermine modern, liberal notions of what people are *really* like, inside and out.

The modern, supposedly liberal university also struggles to contain them – except perhaps by promoting them. In my experience, it certainly finds it very difficult to recognise, or deal with them. Years before I came on the scene, Prof. Caligula had already notched up a long record of complaints and tribunals, claims and counter-claims, even newspaper exposés about her behaviour. There was already a long trail of human wreckage in her wake. But somehow none of this ever stuck, the university never quite managed to act. The hearers at my internal tribunal read through the paperwork, asked the right questions, nodded sympathetically – and then dismissed the case. Prof. Caligula, they said, was definitely not bullying anyone, merely exercising discipline over her staff, and she and I should sit down, work out our differences in a grown-up fashion. It never crossed their minds that she wouldn't want to work out our differences, that she enjoyed our differences too much.

It never crossed their minds, I think, because she was only doing to me, in a distilled form, what the university all too often does to everyone. For the hearers, her behaviour was a matter of *discipline* not *bullying*.

Educational institutions try their best to differentiate these two things. Discipline is the legitimate exercise of authority, bullying is illegitimate, abusive, *verboten*. The problem is that the line between them can easily seem hazy, even arbitrary. As Ken Rigby writes, 'defining where appropriate discipline ends and bullying begins is fraught with difficulties.' It's a question of *definition*, of how to pin down and delimit the concept of 'bullying' in particular. No one seems quite sure what bullying is. A great many books and essays get mired in trying to define it, as if falling at the first hurdle.

Organisations frequently do the same, declaring: 'Well, yes, but it depends what you *mean* by bullying.' That was the initial response to my own complaint; and it was also the response, years later, from our twins' school, when they were (in my opinion) being bullied by a couple of classmates. For all their bullying policies, organisations are reluctant to commit to such a loaded, and legally fraught, term: 'There has certainly been some friction, yes, but we wouldn't yet call it *bullying*, as such.' In my initial written complaint to the university, I wasn't even allowed to use the word 'bullying', only 'harassment', since it was seen as a less emotive, less loaded, less personal term (all of which assumptions are pretty debatable, to say the least).

So when and how should we use the word *bullying*? What do we mean when we use the word? Any tentative definition has the difficult job of delimiting a word that is used in vastly different contexts – from the macro (countries 'bullying' each other, for instance) to the micro (school playgrounds), from the murderous (school shootings, gang warfare) to five-year-olds calling each other names. Christine Pratt, founder of The National Bullying Helpline, tells me that the service receives calls from a myriad of cases, involving everything from gentle teasing to name-calling to playground scraps to domestic abuse to blackmail to stabbings to international trafficking. How on Earth can a word mean all these things at once? How is it possible that a word might embrace them all, without seeming nebulous, without becoming a meaningless abstraction or metaphor? What do these very different scenarios have in common?

Understandably, most definitions of the word rely on abstractions so they can encompass as many scenarios as possible. Olweus, for example, suggests that bullying might be defined as 'intentional, repeated negative (unpleasant or hurtful) behaviour by one or more persons directed against a person who has difficulty defending himself or herself ... in an interpersonal relationship characterised by an actual or perceived imbalance of power or strength.'

The problem with this definition is that, with a few minor tweaks, it could just as easily be a definition of educational discipline. Discipline, like bullying, might also consist of 'intentional, repeated, negative ... behaviour ... directed against a person who has difficulty defending himself or herself'; and discipline necessarily takes place 'in an interpersonal relationship characterised by an ... imbalance of power.'

The Department of Education's 2017 definition of bullying, which is clearly informed by Olweus's terms, might similarly be misread as a definition of discipline – or it might be if you substitute the more neutral word 'controls' for 'hurts':

Bullying is behaviour by an individual or group, repeated over time, that intentionally hurts another individual or group either physically or emotionally.... Teachers and schools have to make their own judgements about each specific case.... Many experts say that bullying involves an imbalance of power between the perpetrator and the victim.

There is a striking admission of subjectivity embedded in this definition ('teachers and schools have to make their own judgements about each specific case'), as though the definition is throwing up its hands, admitting defeat: *I give up, you decide, or someone decide, please, what the difference is between discipline and bullying.*

But what if the people deciding – the teachers, the school leaders, the university managers – are as confused by the difference between discipline and bullying as the definitions on which they rely? And what if the people deciding are themselves bullies? Olweus and the Department of Education admit that there's usually an 'imbalance of power' between perpetrator and victim, and this means that the perpetrator might have greater power over how bullying is defined. Bullying, as I hope I've shown, is often predicated on a linguistic hierarchy – on who wields greater command of particular kinds of language.[5] And this linguistic hierarchy might involve the very word 'bullying': *No, of course we're not bullying you, don't be silly, we're just horsing around.* Or: *No, of course we're not bullying you, we're concerned about you.* Or: *No, of course this isn't bullying, it's just a matter of exercising our legitimate authority. We're higher up the chain of command than you, and we say that this is discipline, not bullying.*

I've talked about how school bullying functions as part of a chain or continuum – in Russell's terms, 'bigs hitting middles hitting babies' – and how that continuum can be extended to include 'big-bigs', such as, in the past, teachers with canes. The latter were ostensibly part of the school's disciplinary system, but the only thing differentiating the means of discipline from that of bullying was a stick. In a system based top-to-bottom on physical violence, 'legitimate' discipline is in danger of collapsing into 'illegitimate' bullying.

Just such a collapse takes place in that *ur*-text of bullying, Thomas Hughes's *Tom Brown's School Days* (1857). In Tom Brown's early days at Rugby, he's horrendously bullied by a psychopathic fifth-former called Flashman and his winged monkeys. He's beaten, violently 'tossed' in a sheet, and 'roasted' on an open fire.

---

[5]See also Chapter 2, 'Playtime: Games of Soldiers', and Chapter 3, 'Sex Ed'.

The novel is usually seen as an indictment of boarding-school violence and the 'fagging' system. Yet its social criticism is actually quite limited. It does not criticise flogging: floggings are well-nigh omnipresent in the school, and even the novel's real-life hero, headmaster Dr Arnold, is seen to give a boy 'a good box on the ear' at one point. Nor does it criticise 'legitimate' violence between boys, asking of its readers: 'What would life be without fighting? From the cradle to the grave, fighting, rightly understood, is the business, the real, highest, honestest business of every son of man.' So, apparently, is fagging, at least until adulthood: the novel by no means suggests that the fagging system, which causes Tom so much pain, should be disbanded or curtailed. In fact, the whole public school system is shown to depend on older boys teaching and disciplining younger ones (bigs hitting middles hitting babies), in lieu of employing more masters.[6]

Tom Brown's School Days does not really critique or challenge this strict hierarchical system. It merely criticises certain individuals within it. The novel portrays the behaviour of bullies like Flashman as an aberration, which might be cured 'by getting the fellows to respect themselves and one another'. Presumably, by fighting.

The logic of the whole novel depends on the reader recognising the subtle differences between forms of violence. Boy-on-boy fighting is okay; thrashing by teachers and the headmaster is okay; thrashing by sixth-formers is okay; brutal, mass-games of rugby are okay; even 'tossing' may or may not be okay (the text seems equivocal about this). Yet somehow Flashman's behaviour is not. It's 'cowardly', 'ungentlemanly' bullying that goes too far. Flashman's violence is wrong insofar as it is immoderate, near-murderous, and its cowardly aim is extortion, while Dr Arnold's violence is *relatively* mild and has an avowedly 'moral

---

[6]This kind of hierarchised bullying still seems ingrained in the very structure of many boarding schools, albeit in a different form.

intention': it's delivered in the name of learning, betterment, Latin Grammar. *That'll teach 'em.*

It seems to me that these are precisely the kinds of hair-splitting distinctions that most educational establishments rely on, in order to distinguish bullying from what they consider to be legitimate violence (physical or psychological) – in order, that is, to separate the Flashmans from the Dr Arnolds. The distinctions are particularly fine in systems where the principal means of discipline is more or less the same as the techniques used by bullies. This creates a closed disciplinary circle, in which the bullies are punished in the same way that they bullied others: boys at Dr Arnold's Rugby are thrashed for thrashing others; kids in post-corporal disciplinary systems are verbally and psychologically punished in ways that (often) bear a striking resemblance to the original verbal and psychological bullying; and in workplaces, the bureaucratic system used to deal with bullying is generally the same as the one weaponised by bullies to victimise their colleagues. I was repeatedly threatened with disciplinary action by my bully, to which my only recourse was to appeal to the same disciplinary system that was being used against me.

In this way, disciplinary systems reflect, even enable the bullying they're meant to deal with. This is institutionalised bullying. As psychologist Peter Smith puts it, given that 'a disciplinary measure is intended to harm someone who finds it difficult to defend themselves, ... the school' – or, indeed, workplace – 'might be modelling the kind of bullying behaviour that they are supposedly trying to stop'. Therapist and sociologist Ellen Walser deLara goes further, and suggests that

bullying and hazing flourish in organisations where they are inadvertently enabled, tacitly permitted, or worse, openly sanctioned by the behaviour of adults. Parents know that children are great imitators.... Children watch their teachers and other school personnel, and this contributes to their growing moral compass. Yet research informs us that 45% of teachers have admitted to bullying children.... When this happens, bullying is a systemic problem.... While adults admonish children to stop bullying each other, there is an adult moral code witnessed in their behaviour that allows for – and promotes – bullying and revenge.

deLara is appealing here to what's known as the 'ecological model' of bullying. On this model, bullying is understood not as an anomaly, an aberration, but as part and parcel of a wider system. Most immediately, bullying grows out of the organisational ecology in which it flourishes (the school or workplace). There are various factors in this respect which, to a lesser or greater extent, might contribute to its prevalence. In a workplace, Iain Coyne suggests that such factors might include

an organisational climate with little encouragement for personal development, ... when the working climate is strained and competitive, ... when organisational changes occur under authoritarian leadership, ... and when the working conditions and social climate are perceived to be poor.... An organisational environment [can be] conducive to bullying, which is tolerant of such behaviour and in which individuals are socialised into this way of thinking.... Poor leadership (especially autocratic leadership and poor management) is one of the most cited reasons by employees for workplace bullying.... Petty tyrannical leadership promotes obedience, de-individualisation of employees, non-contingent punishment and a forcing style of conflict resolution.... This may create a climate of fear where individuals are bullied but feel unable to complain or criticise.

Such a 'climate of fear' helps foster an ecology where 'bullying behaviours [are] ... normalised'.

The climate can reach beyond the organisation itself. The ecological model of bullying understands the phenomenon as an outgrowth of a whole social network – a network that might include family, friends, and, on a wider scale, government policy, the media, neo-liberal capitalism, and so on. At its most extended, the ecological model implicates everyone, our whole society, in bullying: *I guess we are all guilty of everything*. Individual instances of bullying are a symptom of interconnected local, organisational, and national forces; bullies arise from, and are shaped by, their micro- and macro-environments.

The psychology of the nation is reflected in the psychology of the classroom: Flashman is as much Rugby and, in a wider sense, Victorian Britain, as Dr Arnold. And as for Bullivant, Raynor, Wackford Squeers, Dennis Potter's Old Woman, Lee Hardwick, Mr Yorwin, Mr Bulging Suit, Mr Chandler, Danny Beaker, Mrs Marshalsea, Mr Nerritt, Prof. Caligula, all of them are, to a lesser or greater extent, embodiments, living allegories of different socio-educational ecologies. Their particular educational ecology might, ultimately, disown them – as happens with Flashman and Mr Chandler – but, by and large, they are only doing what they've been encouraged to do; they are only mirroring, and in some cases magnifying, aspects of their own disciplinary systems. Flashman is only doing to Tom Brown what other prefects do, and what the masters do. His bullying is another person's legitimate discipline.

In this context, bullying and discipline are two sides of the same debased coin. Bullies and disciplinarians, dominators and managers, Flashmans and Dr Arnolds, are easily confounded – are maybe, at some level, the same thing. Whether consciously or unconsciously, the bully seems to be the ideal manager in many organisations and ecologies. Organisations, educational and otherwise, secretly want bullies (*Shhh…*). After all, in the seventeenth century, the word 'bully' was used in a positive sense to mean 'an admirable fellow', and it still bears traces of this etymology in phrases like '*bully for you*'...

So really the bully is admirable, the bully is a leader, the bully is an embodiment of masculinity, someone to look up to, someone who has achieved something great ('bully for them'). The bully is a British bull-dog, bull-mastiff, bull-terrier, pit-bull, a top-dog, a Churchill or John Bull eating bully-beef. The bully is a baller who believes in the team spirit, a bully-boy footballer or rugger-bugger who'd never do ballet. The bully is more charging bull than herd-able cow, more brazen bull than bull-shitter, a bullock with big bollocks, brimful of bullish machismo, for whom every potential victim is a red rag, and who will charge them, gore them ('*Olé!*'). The bully is both bull and bull-fighter at the same time, both bucking bronco and Rodeo bull-rider, both Bullivant and Bull-ging Suit. The bully is someone who occupies the bully-pulpit, whose commands are as infallible as papal bulls, someone who wields a bull-whip over others, bully-ragging them, cowing them, bull-headedly bulldozing and outbullying any opposition, like an ebullient bull in a china shop ('*Olé!*'). The bully is someone who ruthlessly meets, even gores, targets, who hits the bull's-eye like a bullet, but who is bullet-proof themselves. The bully is someone of whom an organisation might be proud, a golden bull, a bull's head, a candidate for the Bullingdon Club, a figure of desire, precious as bullion, a sacrificial bull, a prize bull ('*Olé!*').

And not just a prize bull, but a prize pig as well, a bull-pig or top boar in the boardroom, a 'fat porker' like George Orwell's Squealer or Napoleon in *Animal Farm*, demanding 'Discipline, comrades, iron discipline!' Pigs, bulls, top-dogs, Napoleons, Flashmans, Dr Arnolds: all are 'voices ... shouting in anger, ... all alike'. We might look between them, between disciplinarians and bullies, Raynors and Bullivants, Squeers and Squealers – as it were 'from pig to man, and from man to pig, and from pig to man again' – but it is often 'impossible to say which [is]   which'.

And that is a tragedy.

8

In the Sick Bay: Medicine

The bullying propensities of human nature ... are about the most unchangeable thing that this fickle world possesses.

The Times, 1862

Four years after leaving my first teaching job – four years of relative contentment in a new workplace – things started going wrong again. Colleagues I liked started having breakdowns, vanishing. There were cuts, and threats, and redundancies everywhere. This time, it wasn't my line manager. It was someone right at the top.

The initial reign of terror reached its horrifying culmination with a *diktat* to the effect that all staff and students were to put on fake wigs, dress up as Bonnie Tyler, and gather in the university square. *I kid ye not*: the senior manager in question wanted to break the world record for the number of people simultaneously lip-synching to the song 'Holding Out for a Hero'. He didn't come close, and I was one of the people who let him down by not participating.

This wasn't out of a misplaced sense of dignity (something I certainly don't suffer from), but due to my suspicion of so-called 'organised fun'. I can't help thinking it's all too often a disguised manifestation of bullying – of groupthink-sadomasochism. As such, it brings to mind Dmitri Shostakovich's famous (and perhaps apocryphal) description of the finale of his Fifth Symphony: 'It's as if someone were beating you with a stick and saying, "Your business is rejoicing", and you rise, shakily, and go marching off muttering, "Our business is rejoicing, our business is rejoicing".'

My refusal to rejoice in the lip-synching-wig-wearing spectacle marked my card thereafter, and I resigned from the university two or so years later, leaving it to Prof. Bonnie Tyler. It felt like history had repeated itself – to paraphrase Karl Marx, 'the first time as tragedy, the second time as farce'.

But farce can be as painful as tragedy, and afterwards I had what I suppose was a bit of a nervous breakdown. I was prescribed anti-depressants, and cried for a long time. I felt trapped in a repetition compulsion, an unbreakable cycle. I thought that bullying was everywhere, inexorable, inescapable, ingrained in our institutions, and perhaps ingrained in me, too – 'the most unchangeable thing that this fickle world possesses'. It's a common feeling.

Now, some years later, I don't think this is necessarily true, or it doesn't have to be. Bullying can be avoided or dealt with, at least to some extent. Yet I can't for certain tell you how to do this. This memoir isn't a self-help book, and I can't provide a universal panacea. As Ken Rigby writes,

Bullying certainly is a complex problem to which there is no effective simple answer. It is true that peddlers of simple solutions do abound.... At best these are quarter truths; at worst, do more harm than good.... It may be comforting to think that there is just one simple answer to a problem and that other answers are wrong, irrelevant and even to be disparaged. Yet in this area ... it is unwise to think of exclusive solutions.

It is certainly unwise to do so in memoirs. Memoirs don't, and shouldn't, in my opinion, provide unambiguous, comforting solutions. Memoirs aren't straightforward doses of medicine. They can't cure problems outright. This is especially the case when it comes to bullying, where most medicines are at best ambivalent, what philosophers call the '*pharmakon*': cure and poison at the same time.

According to one of those philosophers, Jacques Derrida, there is a long-standing connection between the *pharmakon* and bullying – or, that is, a primal form of bullying. In his essay 'Plato's Pharmacy' (1968), he traces the close relationship between the *pharmakon* and its polysemic sister-word, *pharmakos*. The latter term denotes both 'wizard, magician, poisoner' (i.e. someone who might use a *pharmakon*), on the one hand, and a type of ritual scapegoating in Ancient Greece, on the other. 'The character of the *pharmakos* has been compared to a scapegoat,' Derrida says, involving as it does the victims' 'expulsion ... out ... of the city ... and ... energetic fustigation ... at critical moments (drought, plague, famine).'

For Derrida, this *pharmakos* was also a *pharmakon*. While the scapegoating ritual was meant to cure the 'drought, plague, famine,' it was also a poison, involving civil self-harm, the violence of citizens on citizens: 'the *pharmakos* represents evil both introjected and projected. Beneficial ... and ... harmful.... Alarming and calming. Sacred and accursed.'

There are some pretty obvious analogies to be made between modern forms of national scapegoating (in the media, politics, etc.) and the ancient ritual of the *pharmakos*. If personal bullying is hardly on the scale of the *pharmakos* – given that, by and large, it doesn't involve thousands of people and ritual sacrifice – it can still echo many of the same elements, in displaced form. Like the *pharmakos*, bullying can involve scapegoating, expulsion, group violence, spectacle. Like the *pharmakos*, it can sometimes encode institution-wide, city-wide, even nation-wide ecologies of violence – as it did in a long-ago classroom, when a little boy was castigated for speaking out against the murder of a fictional Argentinian soldier.[1] And like the *pharmakos*, personal bullying can involve ritual, too: my annual fights with Stu 'The Cabbage'

---

[1] See Chapter 2, 'Playtime: Games of Soldiers.'

Cubbage felt like a ritual, as did my eventual expulsion from my first job.

As miniature *pharmakoi*, such instances of ritualised bullying are also *pharmakons* (or *pharmaka*) for the perpetrators and social ecologies in which they operate. Bullying is simultaneously 'beneficial ... and ... [self-]harmful' to bullies and their environment, a violence 'both introjected and projected.' Likewise, the solutions open to victims are at once cure and poison, 'alarming and calming. Sacred and accursed.' Everyone is drugged with the *pharmakon*, bullies and victims alike. For the sacrificial victims of the original *pharmakos*, escape from their suffering involved the ultimate *pharmakon*: death. For the victims of modern-day bullying – those who are not driven to the extremity of *bullycide* – the available solutions to their suffering may seem many and varied, yet almost all of them are a species of *pharmakon*...

For example:

You can tell the teacher, report the bully to a higher authority... But this depends on their listening, on the higher authority not being implicated in the bullying ... And you're in danger of becoming despised, a *tell-tale-tit* as the old-fashioned appellation goes, and hence being bullied further. In the face of the worst kinds of bullying, telling can be almost as traumatic as not telling – as James Scudamore's recent novel, *English Monsters*, about an abuse-ridden English boarding school, makes frighteningly clear...

Instead of telling, you can try and ignore the bully, do the Christian thing of turning the other cheek. That might work... Or it might not: look how it turned out for Christ on Good Friday...

There are, though, different kinds of cheek-turning, some involuntary: in my first job, my naïvety meant that I didn't even notice, at least at first, the quiet conspiracies, subterfuge, sharpenings of knives. I blundered on, turning my cheek by mistake, saying exactly what I thought, and expecting others to do the same. Naïve honesty can be a powerful, if ambivalent, weapon: as various fairytales and kids' TV shows demonstrate, the one thing cynical manipulators can least cope with is people who aren't cynical manipulators themselves.[2] In my case, my immature inability to comprehend, let alone join in with, the non-linear warfare going on around me wound up my persecutor to the nth degree. 'No one ever drew her out like you did,' someone said afterwards, as if it were a compliment. Drawing her out *almost* got her into trouble ... but not quite, and, threatened like this, she was even more enraged, even more determined on her programme of bullying...

Another thing that can both undermine and wind up a bully is laughter. Laughter can be a more active way of dismissing bullying than cheek-turning. In that sense, it's a shame Christ never used it. Laughter can destroy power, discipline, bullying. 'Laughter is ... the anarchist,' as author Wyndham Lewis once said... But as the anarchist, laughter knows no master. It's slippery, dangerous, a loaded weapon that can blow up in your face. You can laugh at the bully, and they can laugh at you. After all, being laughed at, ridiculed, is one of the most common forms of psychological bullying...

Rather than *at*, you might try laughing *with* the bully. You might try joining in, conforming. You might try and change your attitude,

---

[2]No doubt the Panglossian innocent, who thwarts oppression through blundering naïvety, is a modification of the 'trickster' archetype (see below). Like the trickster figure, he or she has a very long history in folktales, poems, and novels. I think I first became aware of the character in a popular children's TV programme of the 1970s called *Chorlton and the Wheelies*. Throughout the series, the Mancunian dragon Chorlton repeatedly defeats the machinations of the wicked witch Fenella through bumbling good humour. I loved the series as a kid, though I can now see that it's riddled with patriarchal tropes.

your hobbies, your clothes, your body language, your accent, your hair, your make-up, even the size of your breasts or skin colour, in order to fit in. Such things can be the cause of harassment, and changing yourself might help... But, at other times, as I've said, they're not the real cause, merely the pretext. Sometimes, bullying is for bullying's sake, sadism is its own cause and effect, and one pretext is all too easily swapped for another... And anyway, some of us just aren't very good at fitting in...

Nor am I personally very good at adopting another possible strategy – doffing your cap. Collectively speaking, the British working- and middle-classes are inured to deference, and it is one method of coping with authoritarianism of different kinds... But history shows it doesn't always work. For the worst bullies, however much you bow and scrape, it's never enough. In the end, Tiberius did away with Sejanus, Caligula with many of his most servile subjects... And as something that confirms rather than subverts hierarchy, bowing and scraping hardly qualifies as a solution to bullying...

Alternatively, you can *pretend* to doff your cap. You can wear a servile mask, but play the trickster beneath it. Trickery, cunning, dissimulation – these are tactics of survival that persist everywhere, in the face of the most brutal forms of oppression. They work a bit like laughter, but a secret laughter, crypto-laughter, laughter-as-duplicity. Trickster tales, where oppressed characters gain a modicum of power through subterfuge, are one of the earliest and most persis tent forms of storytelling. There are various instances of classroom trickster tales in this book. At best, these stories chart moments of instability, of rebellion, of subversion... At worst, though, the tricks they tell of back-fire, hurting the trickster as well as the oppressor. And sometimes the oppressed are too naïve, as I was when I was younger, to mirror the trickery of the powerful back at them...

One trick anyone can play, I suppose, is to wait for it all to end. Even bullying for bullying's sake has to burn itself out eventually. Classes end. School ends. Jobs end. Then, years later, you can search for your old bully on Facebook, compare your relative successes, mock them: look at you, look at them, look at how little they've achieved, look at what a great success you've been, physically, financially, professionally, socially. According to psychologists of bullying, this kind of *Schadenfreude* is one of the most common forms of revenge... But the problem here is that you're merely recycling bullying, inverting it. Now, years later, you're the bully, and they're the butt of your ridicule, whether they're aware of it or not...

Perhaps it's better, if you can, to fight back at the time, like Bullivant, Nicholas Nickleby... But clearly this solution depends on relative strength. And confrontational violence (physical or psychological) can result in collateral damage: Smike still dies in Dickens's novel, despite Nicholas's intervention on his behalf...

You can take the confrontational violence to its logical conclusion, and shoot the bullies. You can even press the red button, try and blow up the whole system that brought them into being, as the rebels do in the movie *If...*. But there are a number of well-documented drawbacks to murder, bloody revolution, apocalypse...

Instead, you can turn away from confrontation and leave. You can vacate The Killing Grounds of school or work. You can go to a different school, a different workplace, enact the 'scape' in 'scapegoat'... But, of course, (e)scaping isn't always possible – and, even when it is, it doesn't treat the original poison. As Derrida says, the act of leaving, 'escape', '*exodus*', 'of going ... astray', that takes 'one [away] ... from one's general, natural, habitual paths, ... out of [one's] proper place', this too is a '*pharmakon*'. It might be a partial and temporary medicine for the victim, but not for the bully. Nor does it cure the trauma, but merely cauterises it, consigns it to the past. Sometimes you've internalised the bullying so much that, as Jeanette Winterson puts it, 'the demons ... travel with you'...

You might go on to write about those demons, in a journal or, say, a memoir... But for Derrida, 'writing is [also] a *pharmakon*', both 'the remedy and the poison'. Maybe that's especially the case for autobiographical writing. Such writing, Derrida suggests, 'cures only the symptom', not the illness (the behaviour, the trauma) underlying it...

So perhaps, I think, there is no answer to bullying that is not a *pharmakon*...

But then I think of Billy Casper in *A Kestrel for a Knave*, explaining falconry to a rapt audience of otherwise rowdy kids and bullies.

And I think of Danny in *Danny the Champion of the World*, the evening after he's been caned, enjoying a midnight feast with his father, talking into the early hours about poaching.

And I think of an afternoon in March 1984 – a time when the bullying from Lee Hardwick and his sidekicks was at its most intense...

That morning, the situation with Lee had bubbled over in the classroom. After being whispered at a hundred times about my lack of British patriotism, defective testicles, and similarity thereof to Adolf Hitler, I lost my temper, stood up, and threw a chair at Lee. He threw one back, accused *me* of bullying *him*.

I guess we are all guilty of everything.

I don't remember what our teacher Mrs Dee did in response to the exchange of flying chairs. But it certainly wasn't caning us, sending us to the headmaster, interrogating us in a kangaroo court, or calling the police. The (Deeian) answer is never *more* discipline, *more* physical or psychological violence. The (Deeian) answer is the opposite of the headmaster's in *A Kestrel for a Knave*. Instead of maintaining the bully-disciplinary cycle like Mr Gryce or Mr Bulging Suit or a thousand others, the (Deeian) answer is to short-circuit it, at least temporarily. It is possible. It can be done, if only by someone who is individualistic enough to resist a whole ecology of power; someone who refuses to be ventriloquised by the system bearing down on them; someone who understands that violence, discipline, and bullying are not entirely deterministic – that the bullying cycle can be broken – that it can even work in reverse. Sometimes, contrary to commonplace British wisdom, *less* discipline can mean *less* misbehaviour; *less* violence can equal *less* violence. Sometimes, not punishing, not disciplining, not bullying can actually be a sign of strength, rather than weakness...

And now, a couple of hours after not being punished, Mrs Dee's disciplineless classroom is peaceful, an aquarium of serene activity.

I'm at my desk, writing a story about an effeminate alien with antennae, who visits Earth to make friends, instead of blowing it up. Somewhere near me, the beautiful Lisa is writing a story about her sister re-learning to walk. At the next table, Lee is painting an angry picture with broad brushstrokes *à la* German Expressionism. One of the sidekicks is adoringly pencil-crayoning a romanticised picture of Lee, sneaking a look at his profile now and then.

Everyone in the room is doing something different: timestables, reading, in one corner, silent dancing. Later, most of us will be changing into sparkly costumes, boarding a coach, and going to somewhere near Crewe, where Mrs Dee's dance troupe – of which I'm an inept minor member – is performing 'Day Trip to Bangor' in a competition.

Despite what happened this morning, I'm happy. I'm enjoying writing a story and looking forward to Crewe.

I look round, and everyone else seems content too. The classroom is complicatedly harmonious, a tranquil fugue of intertwining activities, individuals doing their thing.

This is what it feels to be outside The Wall, on a day trip away from the Panopticon.

The bullying from Lee and his ilk will no doubt resume at some point. But here, now, is a Deeian moment that is its opposite, its *anti*-dote, a moment that has nothing to do with canes, fists, machismo, power, mobbing, Games of Soldiers, *pharmakos*, or *pharmakon*. It won't last forever. But what the moment tells me, above all, is nor does bullying.

9

Extra-Curricular: Thanks, Notes, Contexts

First and foremost, I want to thank everyone reading this book for understanding that some of the names, incidents, and details have been modified, for various compelling reasons.

Second, I want to thank the many wonderful educators I have known, all of whom, in their very different ways, were antidotes to conventional institutional discipline. They include Denise De Wet, Andrew Dix, Alison Gurney, Clare Hanson, Ken Lowe, Mrs Newman, Mr Ollier, Geoff Perry, Mike Whittaker, and many others. Thank you to my wonderful classmates and friends, including 'Bob', 'Steed', 'Pi', and 'Carrot Hair'. Thank you to Marina Pickles, who supported me during my worst period of workplace bullying. I remain forever grateful.

Thank you to Jenn Ashworth, Francis Bowdery, Will Buckingham, Mandy Jarvis, Simon King, Blake Morrison, Hannah Stevens, Louisa Treger, Andy West, and Helen Wood.

Thank you to Nick Everett, Corinne Fowler, Harry Whitehead, friends and colleagues at the University of Leicester.

Thank you to Christine Pratt, founder of the National Bullying Helpline, for sharing her insight and expertise in this area.

A special thank you to my one-time supervisor, long-time mentor, and friend John Schad, who, after all these years, is still teaching me how to write. This book is what it is because of him.

Thank you to all the brilliant editors and reviewers at Goldsmiths Press.

Thank you and love to my family, with whom I shared many of these experiences: Christopher, Robin, Karen, Helen, and, of course, Miranda, Rosalind, and Maria. Thank you, above all, to the two best 'teachers' (in the widest sense) I have known: my mother and father. Amongst much else, they inculcated in me a healthy scepticism of hierarchy.

And thank you to all the 'bullies' out there, which perhaps means every one of us. *I guess we are all guilty of everything.* We are all bullies, all victims. Often, we are our own bully and victim at the same time.

The book's epigraph is from: Charles Dickens, *American Notes for General Circulation* and *Pictures from Italy*, ed. F. S. Schwarzbach and Leonée Ormond (London: J. M. Dent, [1842] 1997), p. 231. What follows is a list of works cited in each chapter, as well as further reading on many of the subjects raised. Thanks to all the authors, living and dead.

Chapter 1, 'P.E.'

The epigraph is from Thomas Hughes, *Tom Brown's Schooldays*, ed. Andrew Sanders (Oxford: Oxford University Press, [1857] 2008), p. 355.

Other texts cited in the chapter include (in order of appearance): Muriel Spark, *The Prime of Miss Jean Brodie* (London: Penguin, [1961] 2000), in particular pp. 78, 83, 112; G. W. F. Hegel, 'Master and Slave Dialectic', in *Phenomenology of Spirit*, trans. A. V. Miller (Oxford: Oxford University Press, 1977), pp. 111-19; T. S. Eliot, 'Tradition and the Individual Talent', in *Strong Words: Modern Poets on Modern Poetry*, ed. W. N. Herbert and Matthew Hollis (Tarset: Bloodaxe, 2000), pp. 31-8, 32; Carsten Bagge Lausten, '*Dispositifs* of Bullying', in *School Bullying: New Theories in Context*, ed. Robin May Schott and Dorte Marie Søndergaard (Cambridge: Cambridge University Press, 2014), pp. 97-126, 121;

Mocol Ostow, 'A List: Twenty-Eight Things I've Been Made Fun of For', in *Dear Bully: 70 Authors Tell Their Stories*, ed. Megan Kelley Hall and Carrie Jones (New York: HarperTeen, 2011), pp. 83–4; Barry Hines, *Kestrel for a Knave* (London: Penguin, 1969) where the famous football lesson and its aftermath take place, pp. 85–108; William S. Burroughs, *My Education: A Book of Dreams* (Harmondsworth: Viking, 1995), p. 188.

The idea that Hegel's individualistic model of the 'master-slave' relationship is complicated when the masters band together has been pointed out by various critics and theorists. For instance, psychoanalyst Jacques Lacan writes of 'the Hegelian dialectic ... [that] an accusation of inadequacy, which has often been laid against it [concerns] ... the question of what bound the society of masters together' (*Écrits: A Selection*, trans. Alan Sheridan [London: Tavistock, 1977], p. 308). Incidentally, the PhD I undertook ended up as a book, which, in a strange and distant way, shares certain themes in common with this memoir: Jonathan Taylor, *Mastery and Slavery in Victorian Writing* (Basingstoke: Palgrave-Macmillan, 2003).

The well-known Wildean epigram 'all criticism is autobiography' seems to be a shorthand composite of various actual quotations. In *The Picture of Dorian Gray*, Wilde writes that: 'the highest, as the lowest, form of criticism is a mode of autobiography' (see *The Complete Works of Oscar Wilde* [London: Collins, 1966], pp. 17–167, 17). Similarly, in the essay 'The Critic as Artist', one of the characters remarks that 'the highest criticism ... is the only civilised form of autobiography' (see *The Soul of Man under Socialism and Selected Critical Prose*, ed. Linda Dowling [London: Penguin, 2001], pp. 213–79, 237).

For an introduction to some of the 'whys' of bullying, in terms of gender, ethnic, and physical differences, a good starting-point is Chapter 8, 'The Contribution of Differences', in Ken Rigby, *New Perspectives on Bullying* (London: Jessica Kingsley, 2002), pp. 171–94.

On '*ressentiment*', see Friedrich Nietzsche, *On the Genealogy of Morals*, trans. Douglas Smith (Oxford: Oxford University Press, 1996), for example, pp. 23-9.

A note on terminology: I generally prefer to use the term 'victim' throughout this book to signify the target of bullying. I'm aware that the term is contested among educational theorists, for various understandable reasons. It is, though, still in general popular usage, and is used in most literary portrayals of bullying. It also captures the oppressive nature of bullying, in a way that alternative, more neutral terms do not. Its etymology is significant: the word can be traced back to the late fifteenth century, when it signified an animal or human religious sacrifice (from the Latin *victima*). In this sense, the term 'victim' bears traces of the kind of ritual scapegoating and sacrifice (*pharmakos*) which, as I point out later, underlies modern bullying as its cultural unconscious.

Chapter 2, 'Playtime: Games of Soldiers'

The epigraph is from James Hilton, *Goodbye Mr Chips* (London: Hodder, 1969), p. 19.

Other texts cited in this chapter include (in order of appearance): Jan Needle, *A Game of Soldiers* (London: HarperCollins, 1985), pp. iii-v, 1-44 (the report by the Education Officer for Central Independent Television is cited in the Introduction); William Shakespeare, *Hamlet*, ed. G. R. Hibbard (Oxford: Oxford University Press, 2008), p. 274 (Act 3, Scene 3); C. G. Jung, 'The Psychology of the Unconscious', in *Two Essays on Analytical Psychology*, trans. R. F. C. Hull, in *The Collected Works of C. G. Jung*, 20 vols, ed. Herbert Read et al. (London: Routledge and Kegan Paul, 1953), VII, pp.1-117, 4; Alexis de Tocqueville, *Democracy in America*, ed. Henry Steele Commager, trans. Henry Reeve (London: Oxford University Press, 1946), p. 199; Muriel Spark, *The Prime of Miss Jean Brodie*

(London: Penguin, [1961] 2000), pp. 8, 14, 97, 111; Fleur Jaeggy, *Sweet Days of Discipline*, trans. Tim Parks (Sheffield: And Other Stories, 2018), in particular, pp. 5–6, 53–5, 78–9.

On Harry Potter's scar, see J. K. Rowling, *Harry Potter and the Philosopher's Stone* (London: Bloomsbury, 2014), p. 16.

On the much-debated aspect of 'repetition' in bullying, Dan Olweus's canonical definitions are a useful starting-point. According to Olweus, bullying consists of 'intentional, *repeated* negative (unpleasant or hurtful) behaviour by one or more persons directed against a person who has difficulty defending himself or herself' (Dan A. Olweus, 'Bullying in Schools: Facts and Intervention', *Kriminalistik*, 64:6 (2010), 1–29, 2: my italics). 'A student is being bullied or victimised', claims Olweus, 'when he or she is exposed, *repeatedly and over time*, to negative actions on the part of one or more other students' (Dan Olweus, *Bullying at School: What We Know and What We Can Do* [Oxford: Blackwell, 1993], p. 9: my italics). Since Olweus, most definitions of bullying have included some element of repetition in their criteria. A common acronym now used for bullying in schools is 'STOP: Several Times on Purpose' (see, for example, www.kidscape. org.uk/advice/advice-for-parents-and-carers/talking-about-bullying-with-your-child/ [last accessed 8.7.2023]). Similarly, Isabel Cuadrado-Gordillo writes: 'the criteria that researchers use to classify aggressive behaviour as bullying are *"repetition,"* *"power imbalance,"* and *"intent to hurt"*' – though she goes on to question whether these three criteria, and particularly that of 'repetition', map onto the perception of bullying among teenagers (Isabel Cuadrado-Gordillo, 'Repetition, Power Imbalance, and Intentionality: Do These Criteria Conform to Teenagers' Perception of Bullying? A Role-Based Analysis', *Interpersonal Violence*, 27:10 [2011], 1889–1910). Other critics have similarly challenged or problematised the 'repetition' criterion of bullying, on various grounds. Jaana Juvonen and Sandra Graham, for example, point out that: 'if the definition states that hostile actions are repeated over time, it is difficult to judge what constitutes adequate repetition of action. Furthermore, by defining bullying as repeated, the effects of single incidents are discounted' (Jaana Juvonen and Sandra Graham, 'Research-Based Interventions on Bullying', in *Bullying: Implications for the Classroom*, ed. Cheryl E. Sanders and Gary D. Phye [London: Elsevier, 2004], pp. 229–55, 230). Ken Rigby summarises some of the issues raised by the repetition criterion in *New Perspectives on Bullying* (London: Jessica Kingsley, 2002), pp. 31–2.

On homophobic bullying, see Ian Rivers, *Homophobic Bullying: Research and Theoretical Perspectives* (Oxford: Oxford University Press, 2011). On the etymology of the word 'bullying', see Peter K. Smith, *The Psychology of School Bullying* (Abingdon: Routledge, 2019), p. 9.

On the complex relationship between scapegoating, victimisation, and desire, see René Girard: 'The principle of mimetic desire, its rivalries, and the internal divisions it creates are identical with the equally mimetic principle that unifies society: the scapegoat' (René Girard, *The Scapegoat*, trans. Yvonne Freccero [Baltimore, MD: Johns Hopkins University Press, 1986], p. 187). Many writers have explored the 'internal divisions', the complex and volatile compound of desire and violence, *Eros* and *Thanatos*, implied by different kinds of scapegoating, bullying, and victimisation. In his short article 'The Culture of Hell' (*The Independent Monthly*, 5:7 (1994), 18), for instance, Les Murray strikingly argues that personal bullying might be seen as the mirror image of rape, its inversion. The victims of this 'crime', he claims, are those

whose sexual morale was destroyed early by rejection, by scorn, by childhood trauma, by fashion, by lack or defection of allies, by image…. They are called wallflowers, ugly, wimps, unstylish, drips, nerds, pathetic, fat, frigid, creepy – the epithets go on and on. All are victims of something we haven't developed a word for yet, but which I've called anti-rape or *epar*, which is rape spelled backwards. A better term might be formed by analogy with erogenous: *erocide*. This crime, which appears in no statute book, is definable as the concerted or cumulative sexual destruction of a person.... In schools, it is usually called bullying or harassment, and all children who enter school are tested to see if it works on them. If it does, they will cop it unremittingly, and the psychological scarring may persist lifelong.

Chapter 3, 'Sex Ed'

The epigraph is from the eminently sensible – perhaps impossibly, idealistically sensible – chapter on 'Sex Education', in Bertrand Russell, *On Education* (Abingdon: Routledge, 2010), pp. 132–9. Thanks to the Bertrand Russell Peace Foundation for kindly giving their permission to use this quotation.

Other texts cited in this chapter include (in order of appearance): Charles Dickens, *Great Expectations*, ed. Charlotte Mitchell (London: Penguin, [1861] 2003), where the fight between Pip and Herbert Pocket takes place in Chapter 2, pp. 91–4; William S. Burroughs, *My Education: A Book of Dreams* (Harmondsworth: Viking, 1995), p. 10: italics in original; Michel Foucault, *The History of Sexuality: Vol. 1, An Introduction*, trans. Robert Hurley (Harmondsworth: Penguin, 1990), pp. 29–30; Muriel Spark, *The Prime of Miss Jean Brodie* (London: Penguin, [1961] 2000), pp. 16–17.

The episode in *Dallas* where J. R. causes Pamela Ewing to miscarry is called 'Bar-B-Que', and is the fifth instalment of the first series (1978).

Ken Rigby defines 'personal bullying' as 'bullying ... for which no convenient sociological category – and no accompanying pressure group serving its interests – can be found.' Rightly or wrongly, he believes that 'people in this "non-category" are by far the most numerous', when it comes to bullying (see Ken Rigby, *New Perspectives on Bullying* [London: Jessica Kingsley, 2002], p. 235).

The so-called 'incongruity theory' of humour has a long phil-osophical lineage, which includes Francis Hutcheson, Immanuel Kant, James Beattie, Jean Paul Richter, Arthur Schopenhauer, and Herbert Spencer. In *On Laughter, and Ludicrous Composition* (1764), Beattie claims that

laughter arises from the view of two or more inconsistent, unsuitable, or incongruous parts or circumstances, considered as united in one complex object or assemblage, or as acquiring a sort of mutual relation from the peculiar manner in which the mind takes notice of them.

(See: *Essays: On Poetry and Music as They Affect the Mind; On Laughter, and Ludicrous Composition; On the Usefulness of Classical Learning* (London: E. and C. Dilly and W. Creech, 1779), pp. 297–450, 320.) As another, slightly later critic puts it, 'Ridicule … is precisely that emotion of the will, which, in the first instance, arises upon every perception by the understanding of an incon-gruity' (*Letters of Junius: With Notes and Illustrations; Historical, Political, Biographical, and Critical,* 2 vols, ed. Robert Heron [London: Harrison & Co., 1804], II, p. 278n).

There are many books that explore the dangerous effects of sexual ignorance, and the ways it can be exploited. See, for instance, *The Friday Gospels* (London: Sceptre, 2013) by Jenn Ashworth, where unreliable teenage narrator Jeannie is unable to grasp what has happened to her. The adult reader understands she has been raped, but she does not have the language to vocalise this, to bring it fully to consciousness.

Chapter 4, 'Practical: The Cane and the Fist'

The epigraph to Part I is from Proverbs 13:24 (see *The Holy Bible* [London: HarperCollins, 1957], p. 621). The epigraph to Part II is from Terence Rattigan, *The Browning Version* (London: Nick

Hern Books, [1948] 1994), pp. 6–7. Permission to quote from *The Browning Version* by Terence Rattigan is kindly provided by Alan Brodie Representation (on behalf of the Rattigan Estate) and Nick Hern Books.

Other texts cited in this chapter include (in order of appearance): Bertrand Russell, *Education and the Social Order* (Abingdon: Routledge, [1932] 2010), particularly pp. 18, 65, 167; Friedrich Nietzsche, *On the Genealogy of Morals*, trans. Douglas Smith (Oxford: Oxford University Press, 1996), p. 23; Charles Dickens, *Bleak House*, ed. Nicola Bradbury (London: Penguin, [1852] 2003), p. 23; Max Weber, *On Charisma and Institution Building* (Chicago, IL: Chicago University Press, 1968), p. 48; Helene Guldberg, 'Sorry, But It Can Be GOOD for Children to Be Bullied', *Mail Online*, 27 May 2010, www.dailymail.co.uk/femail/ article-1281630/DR-HELENE-GULDBERG-Sorry-GOOD-children-bullied.html (last accessed 22.12.20); Rosalyn H. Shute and Phillip T. Slee, *School Bullying and Marginalisation: Harmonising Paradigms* (Singapore: Springer, 2022), pp. 35, 132; Ken Rigby, *New Perspectives on Bullying* (London: Jessica Kingsley, 2002), pp. 19, 22; Ellen Walser deLara, *Bullying Scars: The Impact on Adult Life and Relationships* (Oxford: Oxford University Press, 2016), pp. 211–12; 'The Stinker' (1980), dir. Alan Gibson, *Tales of the Unexpected*, Season 3 Episode 7; 'Galloping Foxley' (1979), dir. Claude Whatham, *Tales of the Unexpected*, Season 2 Episode 3; Roald Dahl, 'Galloping Foxley', in *The Complete Short Stories: Volume 1, 1944–1953* (London: Penguin, 2015), pp. 426–45; Adrian Mitchell, 'Back in the Playground Blues', in *Come on Everybody: Poems, 1953–2008* (Tarset: Bloodaxe, 2012), p. 56, quoted in full with the permission of the Estate of Adrian Mitchell, granted by United Agents Ltd; *One Million Years B.C.*, dir. Don Chaffey (Hammer Film Productions and Seven Arts, 1966); George Bernard Shaw, *Misalliance* and *The Fascinating Foundling* (London: Penguin, 1984), pp. 60–1: italics in original; Charles Dickens, *Nicholas Nickleby*, ed. Mark Ford (London: Penguin,

[1838-9] 2003), particularly pp. 104, 108, 156-9; Alan Sillitoe, 'Mr Raynor, the Schoolteacher', in *The Loneliness of the Long Distance Runner* (London: HarperCollins, [1959] 2007), pp. 68-77; Michele Elliot, 'Bullying: Harmless Fun or Murder?', in *Bullying: An International Perspective*, ed. Erling Roland and Elaine Munthe (London: David Fulton, 1989), pp. 105-14; William Golding, *Lord of the Flies* (London: Faber, [1954] 2005); Susan Hill, *I'm the King of the Castle* (London: Penguin, [1970] 1973); J. D. Salinger, *The Catcher in the Rye* (London: Penguin, [1951] 1958), particularly Chapter 22, pp. 176-7; *Dead Poets Society*, dir. Peter Weir (Touchstone Pictures, 1989); G. W. F. Hegel, *Phenomenology of Spirit*, trans. A. V. Miller (Oxford: Oxford University Press, [1807] 1977), pp. 111-19; Jacques Lacan, *Écrits: A Selection*, trans. Alan Sheridan (London: Tavistock, 1977), p. 308; Bertrand Russell, *Unpopular Essays* (Abingdon: Routledge, [1950] 2009), p. 60; Gaius Suetonius Tranquillus, *The Twelve Caesars*, trans. Robert Graves (London: Penguin, 2007), pp. 137, 160-1; Thomas Hardy, *Jude the Obscure*, ed. Dennis Taylor (London: Penguin, [1895] 1998); Barry Hines, *Kestrel for a Knave* (London: Penguin, 1969), pp. 55-7, 119; J. K. Rowling, *Harry Potter and the Philosopher's Stone* (London: Bloomsbury, 2014); *If....*, dir. Lindsay Anderson (Paramount Pictures, 1968); Bertrand Russell, *Autobiography* (London: Routledge, [1951] 1998), p. 389; Roald Dahl, *Danny the Champion of the World* (London: Puffin, [1975] 2016), particularly pp. 17, 112-24: italics in original; Charles Dickens, *American Notes for General Circulation and Pictures From Italy*, ed. F. S. Schwarzbach and Leonée Ormond (London: J. M. Dent, [1842] 1997), p. 231; Philip Larkin, 'This Be the Verse', in *The Complete Poems*, ed. Archie Burnett (London: Faber, 2012), p. 88; Roald Dahl, *Boy* (London: Puffin, 2016), particularly pp. 50-8, 176-80; Benjamin Spock and Steven Parker, *Dr Spock's Baby and Child Care* (New York: Dutton, 1998), pp. 435, 899; Herodas, *The Mimes of Herondas*, trans. M. S. Buck (New York: Private Printing, 1921), available here: http://elfinspell.com/Mimes.html

(last accessed 22.12.20); John Locke, *Some Thoughts Concerning Education* and *Of the Conduct of the Understanding*, ed. Ruth W. Grant and Nathan Tarcov (Indianapolis: Hackett, [1693 and 1706] 1996), pp. 36, 38: italics in original; Pink Floyd, 'Another Brick in the Wall (Part 2)' (1979, single), and 'The Happiest Days of Our Lives', *The Wall* (Harvest/EMI and Columbia/CBS, 1979, album); H. G. Wells, *The War of the Worlds*, ed. Patrick Parrinder (London: Penguin, [1898] 2005), p. 164: my italics.

The dynamic described by Russell (bigs-hitting-middles-hitting-babies) is neatly dramatised in Shirley Jackson's early novel, *The Road Through the Wall* (1948). On the suburban street she describes, 'the youngest children ... were an in-between generation, awed and overruled by the thirteen- and fourteen-year-olds, expecting in their turn a younger generation to bully and educate' (Shirley Jackson, *The Road Through the Wall* [London: Penguin, 2013], p. 21). The novel as a whole seems to me a sophisticated allegory about the complex hierarchies of bullying and scapegoating. It all ends, predictably enough, with murder and suicide.

Freud's views on masochism can be found in his essay, 'The Economic Problem of Masochism' (1924), in *The Ego and the Id and Other Works*, in *The Standard Edition of the Complete Psychological Works of Sigmund Freud*, 24 vols, ed. and trans. James Strachey et al. (London: Hogarth, 1961), XIX, pp. 155–70. See also *Beyond the Pleasure Principle, Group Psychology and Other Works*, in *The Standard Edition of the Complete Psychological Works of Sigmund Freud*, 24 vols, ed. and trans. James Strachey et al. (London: Hogarth, 1955), XVIII, pp.1–64, 55, where Freud writes: 'Masochism, the turning round of the instinct upon the subject's own ego, [is] ... a return to an earlier phase of the instinct's history, a regression.'

On the relation between suicide and bullying, and the 'bully-victim-bully cycle', see deLara, *Bullying Scars*, pp. 103–4, 197, and also Tim Field and Neil Marr, *Bullycide: Death at Playtime* (Didcot: Success Unlimited, 2001).

The origin of the quotation 'My education was only interrupted by my schooling' is discussed by 'Quote Investigator' here: https://quoteinvestigator.com/2010/09/25/schooling-vs-education/ (last accessed 13.11.21). Versions of the epigram can be traced back to the work of the nineteenth-century Canadian author Grant Allen, but a variant of it was also attributed to George Bernard Shaw as early as 1913, in the *Joliet Evening Herald*, 26 February 1913.

Incidentally, as regards Mr Chandler, I wrote a heavily fictionalised account of my encounters with him in my story 'Scablands' (see Jonathan Taylor, *Scablands and Other Stories* [Cromer: Salt, 2023], pp. 158–92). In many ways, that short story was one of the origins of this book.

Chapter 5, 'R.E.'

The epigraph is from Matthew, 23:25 (see *The Holy Bible* [London: HarperCollins, 1957], p. 29).

Other texts cited in this chapter include (in order of appearance): Kathy Acker, *Blood and Guts in High School* (London: Penguin, 2017), p. 68; William Shakespeare, *Hamlet*, ed. G. R. Hibbard (Oxford: Oxford University Press, 2008), p. 281 (Act 3, Scene 4); William S. Burroughs, *My Education: A Book of Dreams* (Harmondsworth: Viking, 1995), p. 188; Fyodor Dostoevsky, *The Brothers Karamazov*, trans. David McDuff (London: Penguin, [1880] 2003), p. 216; John Milton, *Paradise Lost*, ed. John Leonard (London: Penguin, [1667] 2000), p. 9 (Book 1, lines 254–5); *The Exorcist*, dir. William Friedkin (Warner Bros., 1973); Charles Dickens, *Bleak House*, ed. Nicola Bradbury (London: Penguin, [1852] 2003), pp. 410–11, 826; Edmund Gosse, *Father and Son: A Study of Two Temperaments*, ed. Michael Newton (Oxford: Oxford University Press, [1907] 2004); Jeanette Winterson, *Oranges Are Not the Only Fruit* (London: Bloomsbury, [1985] 1993), in particular pp. 18–20, 129, 195, 247–9, 254; Jeanette Winterson, *Why Be Happy When*

You Could Be Normal? (London: Vintage, 2012); Tara Westover, *Educated* (London: Windmill, 2018); Søren Kierkegaard, *Fear and Trembling, The Book on Adler*, trans. Walter Lowrie (New York: Alfred A. Knopf, [1843] 1994), pp. 27, 37–8.

All Biblical allusions in this chapter are to the King James version – see *The Holy Bible* (London: HarperCollins, 1957).

On Katharine Birbalsingh and the row over her Twitter feed, see Barney Davis, 'Headteacher "faces calls for her job" after sparking Original Sin debate on Twitter', *The Standard*, 29 October 2021, www.standard.co.uk/news/uk/katharine-birbalsingh-twitter-original-sin-michaela-community-school-wembley-b963335.html (last accessed 27.4.23).

On the 'reasonableness' of realist fiction versus the 'absurdity' of reality, see J. B. Priestley's wonderful short essay, 'Truth and Fiction', in *Delight* (Manchester: HarperNorth, [1949] 2023), p.174: my italics:

A newspaper has just informed me that there has been a marriage between a bride of seventy and a bridegroom of forty-three; that their romance having begun with a helping of bread-pudding (a speciality of the bride's cuisine), they have had an eight-pound bread-pudding instead of a wedding cake; and that there would be no immediate honeymoon because the bridegroom must return to his work at the Dogs' Home. No doubt we novelists and playwrights are capable of inventing such characters and such situations, but we have allowed ourselves to be *bullied* out of them. We hear a sneering little voice whispering 'Absurd ... overdrawn ... unconvincing ... Dickensian ...' and out they go, these glorious extravagances. But Reality pleases itself and does not give a damn.

Chapter 6, 'History'

The epigraph is from George Bernard Shaw, *A Treatise on Parents and Children*, in *Misalliance* and *The Fascinating Foundling* (London: Penguin, [1910] 1984), pp. 9–112, 25.

Other texts cited in this chapter include (in order of appearance): Michel Foucault, *Discipline and Punish: The Birth of the Prison*, trans. Alan Sheridan (London: Penguin, [1975] 1991), particularly pp. 16, 201–3; Paulo Freire, *Pedagogy of the Oppressed*, trans. Myra Bergman Ramos (London: Penguin, [1968] 2017), p. 22; *The Wizard of Oz*, dir. Victor Fleming (Metro-Goldwyn-Mayer, 1939); L. Frank Baum, *The Wonderful Wizard of Oz* (London: Puffin, [1900] 2019); George Eliot, *The Mill on the Floss*, ed. A. S. Byatt (London: Penguin, [1860] 2003), p. 71; Les Murray, 'Where Humans Can't Leave and Mustn't Complain', in *Collected Poems* (Manchester: Carcanet, 1998), pp. 406–7; Dennis Potter, *The Singing Detective* (London: Faber, 1986), particularly Episode 4, pp. 127–66: italics in original; J. R. R. Tolkien, *The Lord of the Rings* (London: HarperCollins, [1954] 1995), pp. 902, 924; Guy Debord, *Society of the Spectacle* (London: Rebel Press, 1994); T. S. Eliot, *The Wasteland and Other Poems* (London: Faber and Faber, 2002); Kate Clanchy, *Some Kids I Taught and What They Taught Me* (London: Picador, 2020), p. 1; Samuel Beckett, *Waiting for Godot: A Tragicomedy in Two Acts* (London: Faber, 2006); Sigmund Freud, *Beyond the Pleasure Principle, Group Psychology and Other Works*, in *The Standard Edition of the Complete Psychological Works of Sigmund Freud*, 24 vols, ed. and trans. James Strachey et al. (London: Hogarth, 1955), XVIII, pp. 1–64, 14, 20; Rachel Eliza Griffiths, *Promise* (New York: Random House, 2023), p. 146; John Milton, *Paradise Lost*, ed. John Leonard (London: Penguin, [1667] 2000), p. 9 (Book 1, lines 254–5).

On links between Foucault's writings, school discipline, and bullying, see Carsten Bagge Lausten, '*Dispositifs* of Bullying', in *School Bullying: New Theories in Context*, ed. Robin May Schott and Dorte Marie Søndergaard (Cambridge: Cambridge University Press, 2014), pp. 97–126, and Elizabeth Nassem, *The Teacher's Guide to Resolving School Bullying: Evidence-Based Strategies and Pupil-Led Interventions* (London: Jessica Kingsley, 2020). In her essay 'Teachers and Secondary School Bullying: A Postmodern

Discourse Analysis', Alexa Hepburn discusses ways in which Foucault's ideas might be helpful in challenging and reconceptualising common assumptions about bullying (*Discourse & Society*, 8:1 [1997], 27–48).

On the power of the gaze, see Laura Mulvey's famous essay, 'Visual Pleasure and Narrative Cinema', *Screen*, 16:3 (1975), 6–18.

On ways in which narrators in memoir sometimes patronise (bully?) their younger selves, downplaying their own traumas, see James Olney's essay 'The Uses of Comedy and Irony in Autobiographies and Autobiography', *Yeats*, 2 (1984), 195–208. Olney suggests that there is often a 'great emotional and intellectual divide [in] ... autobiography, giving an ironic ... distancing to the past', and this results in a 'kind of ... semi-comic irony, exercised at the expense of a younger self', a 'self-mockery' (197–9). See also Jonathan Taylor, *Laughter, Literature, Violence, 1840–1930* (Basingstoke: Palgrave-Macmillan, 2019), particularly pp. 106–10.

On the self-erasure of the Panopticon, its 'immolation', see the work of sociologist Zygmunt Bauman, particularly *Liquid Modernity* (Cambridge: Polity Press, 2012), p. 11: italics in original. According to Bauman, this self-erasure is part of a historical process. We are living in a 'post-Panoptical' modernity, in which the Panopticon has dissolved, liquefied, such that it is now everywhere and nowhere:

For all practical purposes, power has become truly *extraterritorial*, no longer bound, not even slowed down by the resistance of space (the advent of cellular telephones may well serve as a symbolic 'last blow' delivered to the dependency on space).... This gives the power-holders a truly unprecedented opportunity: the awkward and irritating aspects of the panoptical technique of power may be disposed of.... What mattered in [the] Panopticon was that the people in charge were assumed always to 'be there', nearby, in the controlling tower. What matters in post-Panoptical power-relations is that the people operating the levers of power ... can at any moment escape beyond reach – into sheer inaccessibility. The end of [the] Panopticon augurs *the end of the era of mutual engagement*: between the supervisors and the supervised, capital and labour, leaders and their followers, armies at war. The prime technique of power is now escape, slippage, elision and avoidance, the effective rejection of any territorial confinement.

Presumably, in the educational sphere, liquid modernity's rejection of territorial confinement hasn't (yet) been completed: school buildings generally still exist. But maybe the learning-from-home methods developed during the Covid-19 lockdowns point the way to a post-panoptical education system, where the school Panopticon becomes truly extraterritorial, everywhere and nowhere. As many people have pointed out, the Panopticon is now both portable and personalised, in the form of the mobile phones, tablets, and other gadgets we carry around with us. So is bullying.

Chapter 7, 'Politics'

Texts cited in this chapter include (in order of appearance): Adrian Mitchell, 'Back in the Playground Blues', in *Come on Everybody: Poems, 1953–2008* (Tarset: Bloodaxe, 2012), p. 56; Carly Simon, 'You're So Vain', *No Secrets* (Elektra, 1972); Charles Dickens, *Our Mutual Friend*, ed. Adrian Poole (London: Penguin [1865] 1997), p. 131; Tim Field and Neil Marr, *Bullycide: Death at Playtime* (Didcot: Success Unlimited, 2001); Tim Field, *Bully in Sight: How to Predict, Resist, Challenge and Combat Workplace Bullying. Overcoming the Silence and Denial by Which Abuse Thrives* (Didcot: Success Unlimited, 1996), particularly pp. xxi, 114, 115, 149; Edgar Allan Poe, 'The Pit and the Pendulum', in *Selected Tales*, ed. David Van Leer (Oxford: Oxford University Press, [1842] 2008), pp. 135–48; Rachel Vail, 'Subtle Bullying', in *Dear Bully: 70 Authors Tell Their Stories*, ed. Megan Kelley Hall and Carrie Jones (New York: HarperTeen, 2011), pp. 45–8; Chris Lee, *Preventing Bullying in Schools: A Guide for Teachers and Other Professionals*

(London: Paul Chapman, 2004), p. 20; Dan A. Olweus, 'Bullying in Schools: Facts and Intervention', *Kriminalistik*, 64:6 (2010), 1–29, 2; Claudia Frey and Siegfried Hoppe-Graff, 'Serious and Playful Aggression in Brazilian Girls and Boys', *Sex Roles*, 30 (1994), 249–69, 250; William Shakespeare, *Othello*, ed. Michael Neill (Oxford: Oxford University Press, 2008); Sarah Moore Fitzgerald, 'Bullies in Books Help Us Tackle the Real Life Ones', in *The Guardian*, 4 June 2014, www.theguardian.com/childrens-books-site/2014/jun/04/bullies-in-literature-sarah-moore-fitzgerald (last accessed 9.9.23); Charles Dickens, *Hard Times*, ed. Paul Schlicke (Oxford: Oxford University Press, [1854] 2008), p. 19; Benjamin Spock and Steven Parker, *Dr Spock's Baby and Child Care* (New York: Dutton, 1998), p. 644; Bertrand Russell, *Education and the Social Order* (Abingdon: Routledge, [1932] 2010), p. 18; Ken Rigby, *New Perspectives on Bullying* (London: Jessica Kingsley, 2002), pp. 86, 145; Paulo Freire, *Pedagogy of the Oppressed*, trans. Myra Bergman Ramos (London: Penguin, [1968] 2017), p. 119; William Golding, *Lord of the Flies* (London: Faber, [1954] 2005); Alexis de Tocqueville, *Democracy in America*, ed. Henry Steele Commager, trans. Henry Reeve (London: Oxford University Press, 1946), p. 199; Jonathan Taylor, *Take Me Home: Parkinson's, My Father, Myself* (London: Granta, 2007), pp. 207–26; E. M. Forster, *Aspects of the Novel* (London: Penguin, [1927] 2005), pp. 54–84; Department of Education, 'Preventing and Tackling Bullying: Advice for Headteachers, Staff and Governing Bodies', July 2017, p. 8, https://assets.publishing.service.gov.uk/government/uploads/system/uploads/attachment_data/file/623895/Preventing_and_tackling_bullying_advice.pdf (last accessed 16.7.23); Thomas Hughes, *Tom Brown's Schooldays*, ed. Andrew Sanders (Oxford: Oxford University Press, [1857] 2008), particularly pp. xxxix, 182–6, 282–302; Peter K. Smith, *The Psychology of School Bullying* (Abingdon: Routledge, 2019), p. 85; Ellen Walser deLara, *Bullying Scars: The Impact on Adult Life and Relationships* (Oxford: Oxford University Press, 2016), p. 212; Iain

Coyne, 'Bullying in the Workplace', in *Bullying in Different Contexts*, ed. Claire P. Monks and Iain Coyne (Cambridge: Cambridge University Press, 2011), pp. 157–84; George Orwell, *Animal Farm: A Fairy Story* (London: Penguin, [1945] 2000), pp. 37, 95.

On PTED (Post-Traumatic Embitterment Disorder), see the definition on The National Bullying Helpline's website, www. nationalbullyinghelpline.co.uk/pted.html (last accessed 6.6.23):

PTED is best described as a reaction to negative life-events. Whilst it is often attributed to an injustice or to social rejection, it may also be attributed to a traumatic life-changing experience, … which results in chronic feelings of bitterness and anger.

On cyber-bullying, see Robin M. Kowalski, Susan P. Limber, Patricia W. Agatston, *Cyber Bullying: Bullying in the Digital Age* (Oxford: Blackwell, 2008), and Ian Rivers, Thomas Chesney, and Iain Coyne, 'Cyberbullying', in *Bullying in Different Contexts*, ed. Claire P. Monks and Iain Coyne (Cambridge: Cambridge University Press, 2011), pp. 211–30.

On the vexed question of whether all bullying is intentional or deliberate, see Rigby, *New Perspectives on Bullying*, pp. 27–32, and 49–50. Many common definitions of bullying emphasise intentionality on the part of the bully, whereby they set out with a conscious desire to hurt the victim. Rigby, however, problematises the idea of intentionality, discussing, among other things, 'non-malign bullying' which can arise from a lack of awareness or 'ignorance'.

On the tricky question of gender differences in relation to bullying, a good starting-point is the short summary provided by Smith in *The Psychology of School Bullying*, p. 48. He writes that:

Gender differences are interesting as they may be changing…. Boys are more often the perpetrators of bullying, and this is most marked for physical bullying…. There is less gender difference in terms of verbal bullying … [though] some studies find girls more likely to be perpetrators.

Rigby also writes about the role of gender in *New Perspectives on Bullying*, pp. 172–80, particularly in terms of masculinity and aggressivity. For a more in-depth view of gendered bullying in relation to female students, see Dawn Jennifer's essay, 'Girls and Indirect Aggression', in *Bullying: Experiences and Discourses of Sexuality and Gender*, ed. Ian Rivers and Neil Duncan (London: Routledge, 2013), pp. 45–59.

The term 'flying monkeys' is used in popular psychology to describe a narcissist's entourage; see, for example, Claire Jack, 'Are You a Narcissist's Flying Monkey?', *Psychology Today*, 7 October 2020, www.psychologytoday.com/gb/blog/women-autism-spectrum-disorder/202010/are-you-narcissist-s-flying-monkey (last accessed 1.5.22).

On 'mobbing', see Rigby, *New Perspectives on Bullying*, pp. 43–7.

On the 'Psychopathy Checklist', see Paul Babiak and Robert D. Hare, *Snakes in Suits: When Psychopaths Go to Work* (New York: HarperCollins, 2007), and Jon Ronson, *The Psychopath Test* (London: Picador, 2012).

On the 'bully-victim-bully cycle', homeostasis in disciplinary systems, and institutionalised bullying in schools, see deLara, *Bullying Scars*, pp. 9, 197, 212.

On the 'ecological model' of bullying, see Smith, *The Psychology of School Bullying*, pp. 38–42. Smith also discusses the etymology of the word 'bullying' on p. 9.

Special thanks to Christine Pratt and The National Bullying Helpline (www.nationalbullyinghelpline.co.uk/ [last accessed 16.7.23]), for help with this chapter.

Chapter 8, 'In the Sick Bay: Medicine'

The epigraph from *The Times* is from 6 August 1862, and is quoted in Hyojin Koo, 'A Timeline of the Evolution of School Bullying in Differing Social Contexts', *Asia Pacific Education Review*, 8:1 (2007), 107–16, 109.

Other texts cited in this chapter include (in order of appearance): Bonnie Tyler, 'Holding Out for a Hero', in *Footloose*, dir. Herbert Ross (Paramount Pictures, 1984); Dmitri Shostakovich, *Testimony: The Memoirs of Dmitri Shostakovich as Related to and Edited by Solomon Volkov*, trans. Antonia W. Bouis (London: Hamish Hamilton, 1979), p. 140; Karl Marx, *The Eighteenth Brumaire of Louis Bonaparte*, in *Selected Writings*, ed. David McLellan (Oxford: Oxford University Press, [1852] 1977), pp. 300–25, 300; Ken Rigby, *Bullying in Schools: And What to Do About It* (Camberwell: Acer, 2007), pp. 126–7; James Scudamore, *English Monsters* (London: Jonathan Cape, 2020); *Chorlton and the Wheelies* (1976–8), dir. Chris Taylor; Wyndham Lewis, *The Complete Wild Body*, ed. Bernard Lafourcade (Santa Barbara: Black Sparrow, 1982), p. 151; Charles Dickens, *Nicholas Nickleby*, ed. Mark Ford (London: Penguin, [1838–9] 2003); *If...*, dir. Lindsay Anderson (Paramount Pictures, 1968); Adrian Mitchell, 'Back in the Playground Blues', in *Come on Everybody: Poems, 1953–2008* (Tarset: Bloodaxe, 2012), p. 56; Jeanette Winterson, *Oranges Are Not the Only Fruit* (London: Bloomsbury, [1985] 1993), p. 249; Barry Hines, *Kestrel for a Knave* (London: Penguin, 1969), particularly pp. 63–70; Roald Dahl, *Danny the Champion of the World* (London: Puffin, [1975] 2016), particularly p. 124.

On the *pharmakon*, see Jacques Derrida, 'Plato's Pharmacy', in *Dissemination*, trans. Barbara Johnson (London: Bloomsbury, [1968] 2016), pp. 65–181, particularly pp. 73, 76, 109–10, 129–30. The links between *pharmakon*, *pharmakos*, and scapegoating are developed further by philosopher and anthropologist René Girard; see, for example, *Violence and the Sacred*, trans. Patrick Gregory (London: Continuum, [1972] 2005), pp. 100, 303–312.

On the ambivalence of strategies adopted by victims of bullying, see Ken Rigby, *New Perspectives on Bullying* (London: Jessica Kingsley, 2002), pp. 67–72, and Tim Field, *Bully in Sight: How to Predict, Resist, Challenge and Combat Workplace Bullying: Overcoming the Silence and Denial by Which Abuse Thrives* (Didcot: Success Unlimited, 1996), p. 39.

A useful resource which details various strategies to deal with school bullying is provided by the BBC: 'One in Four Children Are Bullied: What Can Parents Do?', www.bbc.co.uk/bitesize/ articles/z9gqqfr (last accessed 25.5.23). The Anti-Bullying Alliance (https://anti-bullyingalliance.org.uk/ [last accessed 30.6.23]) also provides a great deal of useful information in this respect.

Author Biography

Jonathan Taylor is an author, editor, lecturer and critic. His previous books include the acclaimed memoir *Take Me Home* (Granta, 2007), the novel *Melissa* (Salt, 2015), and the short story collection *Scablands and Other Stories* (Salt, 2023). He teaches Creative Writing at the University of Leicester. Originally from Stoke-on-Trent, he now lives in Leicestershire with his wife, the poet Maria Taylor, and their twin daughters, Miranda and Rosalind.